Selecting and Developing Media for Instruction
THIRD EDITION

Selecting and Developing Media for Instruction

THIRD EDITION

Angus Reynolds & Ronald H. Anderson

 VAN NOSTRAND REINHOLD
New York

Printed in the United States of America.

Van Nostrand Reinhold
115 Fifth Avenue
New York, New York 10003

Chapman and Hall
2-6 Boundary Row
London, SE1 8HN, England

Thomas Nelson Australia
102 Dodds Street
South Melbourne 3205
Victoria, Australia

Nelson Canada
1120 Birchmount Road
Scarborough, Ontario M1K 5G4, Canada

16 15 14 13 12 11 10 9 8 7 6 5 4 3 2 1

Library of Congress Cataloging-in-Publication Data

Reynolds, Angus.
    Selecting and developing media for instruction / Angus Reynolds & Ronald H.
    Anderson.
            p.   cm.
        Rev. ed. of: Selecting and developing media for instruction /
    Ronald H. Anderson, c1983.
        Includes bibliographical references and index.
        ISBN 0-442-00653-5
        1. Education technology.   2. Teaching—Aids and devices.
    I. Anderson, Ronald H.   II. Anderson, Ronald H. Selecting and developing media
    for instruction.   III. Title.
    LB1028.3.A5   1991
    371.3'078—dc20

                                                                91-27704
                                                                    CIP

THIS BOOK IS DEDICATED TO THE MEMORY OF

RONALD H. ANDERSON

AUGUST 29, 1930 — AUGUST 7, 1983

Contents

Foreword

SELECTING MEDIA FOR INSTRUCTION IS THE CRITICAL POINT at which design intelligence and instructional media effectiveness intersect. It is not automatic, nor does it necessarily follow from good training design. Reynolds' and Anderson's book is the only one in the field that specifically treats the issue of selecting media for training at a pragmatic level. It is less theoretical than academic works on the subject. Selling-out through two editions attests to its uniqueness and to its value to practitioners. I am not aware of any other book that would compete with this one for the attention of trainers, course writers/designers, and training managers. Its systematic range of considerations would also be very attractive to graduate courses in Instructional Technology programs that offered an emphasis on placement in corporate training and development.

Characteristics don't make books special, people do. Those who were privileged to have known Ron Anderson, knew that his views emerged from his years of experience in developing training around the world under quite adverse conditions and from the warmth and understanding that was his nature. Ron achieved successes in the face of trying conditions. It gave him deep insights into how things really work "in the trenches." He understood what designers and course writers really need to know to get the job done. When he first wrote *Selecting and Developing Media for Instruction* it emerged as just that type of book: it tells training designers what really works and what they need to know to obtain the desired learning outcomes.

Angus Reynolds is very well qualified to revise this book. He, like Ron Anderson, has had years of experience in the national and international training fields. He draws upon this experience to enrich the current edition. He is well-known internationally for his corporate, consulting, and academic excellence and has authored an important book—*Technology Transfer: A Project Guide for International HRD*—as well as chapters in others on related training and HRD topics. In addition to this, Angus brings an exceptional degree of expertise in computer-based training to this edition. Fortuitously, this was the part of the book that was most in need of revision. His knowledge of the newer learning technologies is at a level of mastery which, I believe, have enabled him to simplify them.

The book is a decision-making tool for trainers, course writers and training managers—its format is a job-aid for media selection. It even has a job-aid for making job-aids! The decision charts provide a thorough and systematic process for the selection of media, but as Anderson reiterated often, they are not rigid formulas. The charts lead one through the selection process and suggest optimum delivery systems but they do not preclude— in fact they suggest—applying situational variables to temper these choices. This was apparent in the revised Second Edition, which included expanded information on learner factors, computer-based and computer-aided learning, and information on "culture" as an instructional variable. The book, as a decision-making aid, proposes that people follow a routine decision path and be willing to consider the human values and social organization of the learners involved and to deviate from the charts when necessary.

The book makes two critical sets of distinctions that are not well-made elsewhere in the literature of the field. It differentiates *instruction* from *information* (the former being material the audience is held accountable for) in a way that clarifies training needs, and it also differentiates between *instructional aids* and *instructional media* (the former being materials used by an instructor, the latter materials used without an instructor). These distinctions can save corporate training departments a lot of time and expense: aids are often designed as though they were to be used alone ("instructor proof") and information is often given the expensive design attention that should be reserved for instruction.

The single most valuable and timeless trait of *Selecting and Developing Media for Instruction* is its pervasive theme of selecting the simplest and least expensive medium that will get the job done. All the decision charts are based on this standard; the authors even advocate such simple and inexpensive instructional materials as pencil sketches and typed text in revisable looseleaf binders, when they will suffice for the training demand. We need a lot more of this "appropriate technology" kind of thinking in our field. The reality of our profession—one that is not often acknowledged in graduate programs—is that most instructional designers and course writers are just that: writers. This book gives instructional writing its important status in the scheme of instructional media. Unfortunately, as pointed out in the major studies of media selection, we in training and instructional technology have tended to be overly enamored of the more complex and expensive media and have earned the reputation of being device-oriented. The final conclusion of the most thorough study of the media selection process in our field, Wilbur Schramm's *Big Media—Little Media* is that we should select the simplest and least expensive instructional medium, or combination of media, that will accomplish the objectives. Reynolds' and Anderson's book provides the most intelligent and cost-effective media selection model that can be advocated. This has always been true, but with the advent of the newer electronic learning devices like computer-based learning and interactive videodisc, the cost has now risen to the point where those who fund training are beginning to demand thorough cost-benefits analyses before investing in high-tech delivery systems. Such analyses are the foundation of *Selecting and Developing Media for Instruction*. Of all the fine features of the book, this is the one I would insist be kept prominent in any future revisions.

The overall structure of the book and its approach to media selection and development is as sound and timely today as when it was first written and it provides welcome and much needed information on new computer-based technologies. The progression of the media sections, from simple to complex, supports the basic theme of the book—using the simplest and least expensive medium suitable. This theme remains dominant throughout. The newer electronic media can do a lot of different things, but they can, when used inappropriately, be elitist and extremely expensive. The book maintains a desirable "neutral" position and not an advocacy statement for high-tech instruction. ∎

John B. Bunch
Head, Instructional Technology Program
University of Virginia
Charlottesville, VA

Preface

W E WANT THIS BOOK TO MEET THE WELL-IDENTIFIED NEED suggested by its title. We wanted to present a book that could be useful to those involved with selecting media: a practical instead of academically oriented or theoretical book. And, surely not one that represents "warmed over" research reports. Our colleagues have been generous in their reviews of previous editions. They tell us that a book based on practical experience with this aspect of developing training is very appealing. The first two editions served that constituency. That concept was still with us in the preparation of the third edition. Reviews of the draft manuscript have helped us refine our aim and remember people "in the trenches." Practical is what this book is about.

Part of the problem is that people who are, or want to be, intimately involved with developing training are often not aware of the complexity involved. Or, it intimidates them. Our challenge was to provide enough background to help you understand the problem. And, we want to supply practical information about how to apply it in real-world situations. In each succeeding edition, this book has refined explanations of the selection and development process.

This edition faced a new and still changing world of technological products and processes important to media developers. We felt the need to provide considerable background about the technology basis of media, and the new and evolving environment in which you will use them. Costs and associated risks are up. Many of our colleagues are just coming to grips with these new technologies. They lack first hand experience with what can be a bewildering array of "computer stuff." We share our experiences here to help you become involved in a painless way.

Cost itself is a relative thin, depending on budget considerations. Industrial and government budgets are often larger and more flexible than those in the public schools or university. Therefore, references to "high cost" or "cheap" must be considered in your own context. We do have one strong prejudice in this regard. We feel no organization has so much money that it should waste it. We prefer to use the methods and media that get the particular job done right—at the least cost possible.

We hope this book becomes an important part of your training development "tool kit." To use this book, read it from start to finish. Then use it whenever needed. We have organized it to serve as a useful reference when you work in an applicable situation.

This book is the product of the help of and encouragement of many people. Naturally, we are indebted to the staff and management of Van Nostrand Reinhold. They provided the opportunity for this book to meet one important part of the needs of those involved in training development. Not insignificantly, they provided the support and encouragement we needed to bring this edition to completion.

We are grateful for the cooperation and specific help of many individuals. Their willingness to share information and make valuable specific suggestions enabled us to present a coherent picture of media selection. Many people have helped over a wide spectrum of ways. This book would be incomplete without special tribute to people whose help, in a specific time or way, has been invaluable.

We thank John Bunch, Hui-Chuan Cheng, Hal Christensen, Ivor Davies, Richard W. Davis, John Eldridge, Ray Fox, Robert Gagné, Harvey Long, Robert Mager, Paul E. Novak, David C. Paquin, Anthony Piazza, George Piskurich, Carlene Reinhart, Cheryl Samuels-Campbell, Peter Schleger, August K. Spector, Tom Sutherland, Kim Stevenson, Robert Von Der Linn, and Katie Weldon.

We also want to tell the world of the tolerance and support of our wives and children: Emiko, Elizabeth, Mari Ellen, and Thomas Reynolds; and the Anderson family—Stel, Pam, Skip, and Mike. ■

Angus Reynolds
Reston, Virginia

June 1991

CHAPTER 1

Introduction

THIS BOOK IS A JOB AID AS WELL AS A REFERENCE GUIDE FOR anyone involved with choosing media or planning the development of media for instructional purposes. It is aimed primarily at the course writers and instructors who do these tasks. It can also be a valuable tool for managers of training departments, students of instruction and media, or supervisors of development programs. ∎

Problems of Media Selection

Selecting the best medium or media for instructional purposes is not an easy job. Anyone who has struggled with the problem can testify to that fact. The process involved in reaching a choice can be both complex and difficult. A combination of interrelated factors makes it so. These questions exemplify the difficulty:

1. To what degree must the training imitate or simulate real working conditions and environments?
2. What medium or media are most practical for packaging, implementing, and updating the program?
3. Is equipment needed to use the medium chosen? If so, is it readily available? Is special equipment justified to implement the course?

4. Will the media fit the learning needs of the students or will it be a distraction? (Factors to consider include, but are not limited to, culture, age, and learning habits.)
5. After training is complete must student achievement be *exactly* as prescribed? If not, to what extent may they diverge?
6. Does the value of the course justify the cost of the medium or media considered? We can measure value by: the degree of behavior change, the number of students trained, or the life of the course.

We must answer these questions and many others during the course development process. These examples show the complexity of the problem. Yet, they also suggest that picking the media best able to assure student learning is an integral part of the entire course planning process. Skillful course developers can evaluate and balance priorities among the many available choices. The courses that they develop not only meet student requirements, but nonetheless respect organizational realities.

Unfortunately, few guidelines are available to help a course developer decide about media. There are no simple, foolproof formulas or reference tables that match any specific medium with any particular course objectives. Validated historical data or research reports about various media used for instruction in widely differing circumstances are sparse. Those available are often contradictory and imprecise.

Other Related Problems

The total cost of using each medium and its accompanying equipment is often difficult to determine. Also, the increased rate of technological advances makes equipment obsolete fast. Literature extolling the virtues of various types of hardware is available, but is often misleading or of little help.

However, we have progressed toward developing a solid basis for media selection as we develop instruction. One term widely used to represent this process is *instructional technology*. The definition below, taken from a 1970 report to the President and the Congress of the United States,[1] is equally true and totally valid twenty years later. It lays a basis for this book:

> In order to reflect present-day reality, the Commission has had to look at the pieces that make up instructional technology: television, films, overhead projectors, computers, and the other items of "hardware" and "software" (to use the convenient jargon that distinguishes machines from programs). In nearly every case, these media have entered education independently, and still operate more in isolation than in combination. . . . Instructional technology goes beyond

---

[1] Commission on Instructional Technology To Improve Learning. *A Report to the President and the Congress of the United States* (Washington, DC: U.S. Government Printing Office, 1970). p. 19.

any particular medium or device. . . . It is a systematic way of designing, carrying out, and evaluating the total process of learning, teaching, and communication, and employing a combination of human and nonhuman resources to bring about more effective instruction.

A study by the American Institutes for Research pointed out there is no clear rationale to explain why we see information presented in a given media. For example, presentation by motion pictures instead of by print, or by textbooks rather than by slides and audio tape. Often, the only apparent reason for a choice is the background of the production talent: Film makers work in their medium. Text writers work in theirs. Competition among media producers, or the availability of a talent, has a strong influence on the training materials produced. The absence of theoretical knowledge and lack of procedural practices upon which to base media selection encourage such practices.

Media selection is complicated further. Course developers tend to consider media choice as an isolated and independent function undertaken at some point well along in the instructional development process. There has been some controversy concerning media selection indicating that the type of media should not be chosen until after the design phase. This is so the instruction is not designed for the media but for meeting educational goals only. According to this theory, the type of media will be a natural fallout of the instructional design phase. In reality this is often impossible due to such factors as including the availability of media, cost justifications, and media design factors. However, at the opposite end of the spectrum training/educational developers must watch out for the following pitfall: "If your only tool is a hammer everything begins to look like a nail." It is inappropriate to think that all instruction fits nicely into one type of media. As a result, it is very important that there is a balance between designing for instructional goals and designing for media characteristics.

Sometimes, this viewpoint has resulted from attempts to make the media selection process mechanical, and as scientific and exact as possible. Although the goal may be worthy, the present reality does not permit scientifically precise decisions. Therefore, instructional technology, as a total system, provides the most practical means to consider the essential elements in course development. And, we can consider each at the proper time.

Necessary Assumptions

Within the instructional process, however, there is continuing need for aids to deciding about media. Developers of training programs want to know what to use, when, and why. This book is offered as a practical handbook in this important activity. It is not the first word on the subject. We could not have written this book without the diligent work of many people. It surely won't be the last word either. It is simply our attempt to set forth a practical method to aid course developers in this process. We ask the user of this book to accept several assumptions upon which we based the content of this book.

- Media selection is an integral part of the total instructional development process. It is NOT a precise science. You must consider media decisions throughout the development process and adjust to meet production and implementation conditions.
- The choice of efficient and effective media for instruction calls for balancing lesson content and purposes with the characteristics of specific media.
- In the real world, compromise may be necessary. In the selection process, developers often make compromises. Often they are unavoidable. Use the procedures suggested here to replace decisions based on whim, convenience, or political expediency by those based upon analysis and program design.

Before we discuss how to use this book, you should know that we designed it for at least four different circumstances:

- For use as a minitext in a formal or informal course for instructional development personnel.
- For use as a self-instruction textbook. It can help a new course developer to become acquainted with various media useful for training and education.
- To serve as a job aid. It can be useful as a reference in day-to-day course development. It can help assure attention to the relevant decisions in selecting and developing media.
- As a reference for managers of course development projects. They can ensure adequate attention to media selection and design activities.

This is not a media production textbook. To treat the production of the many useful media in adequate depth requires many volumes. However, the guidelines supplied here will quickly give you an adequate background. You will be able to work in the practical problem area of media selection and development. The guidelines will also help determine what added knowedge you need that you can get from other sources such as publications, workshops, and association with production personnel.

Soon we will undertake the media selection and development procedures that form the principal content of this book. First, we present an example of the total instructional development process. Though we maintain a tongue-in-cheek spirit in the example, we stress two key points:

1. Always select media in the context of a total instructional development process.
2. *Even before we decide to train* we must be sure that a need for training exists.

The Development Process

The courseware development process most frequently used is the instructional systems development (ISD) or "systems approach."[2] ISD is used because the phased approach, and emphasis on instructional objectives and concept of "mastery" that characterize it, match perfectly with many developers own philosophy of instruction.

The use of the ISD model results in the division of an instructional development project into distinct phases. The phases of a typical model used for training development include:

- analysis
- design
- development
- implementation
- evaluation

Most activities in a particular phase are the same, regardless of the delivery method or media to be used. We will look briefly at each of the phases.

Analysis

During the Analysis Phase, one of the tasks typically carried out is defining the needs and the constraints. Identifying the constraints can point up how the various restrictions can effect possible solutions in a particular case. The availability of funds and the delivery environment are two factors that could affect an HRD project. The basic analysis is of the job performed. During the analysis of the target population, factors such as learners' previously acquired knowledge and skills and present qualifications are identified. Geographic distribution of learners can favor various strategies. This phase also includes the analysis of the job involved and its specific functions. A key possibility of the analysis is determining that instructional activities will not solve the particular performance problem. Another possible outcome is the determination to develop a job aid—rather than training.

Design

Regular chores included in the Design Phase include: specification of learning activities; and assessment, evaluation, and learning transfer systems. Determinations about the media best suited are made at this time. Learning activities may include a full spectrum of methods and media—called the instructional strategy. An internal and external search is conducted for appropriate existing instructional materials, since they are almost always cheaper than developing new instruction.

---

[2]Almost all models of instructional development are based on the landmark Center for Educational Technology (1976) work entitled *Interservice Procedures for Instructional Systems Development* (Contract No: N61339-73-C-0150), Tallahassee, FL: Florida State University.

Development

The Development Phase is unique for any particular project. The activities, and the people involved, depend on the methods and media selected for the learning activities. Formative evaluation activities are conducted to ensure that the instruction works. The formative evaluation is conducted while the course is under development, via individual and small group trials, to try out and revise the course materials. The revisions made at this point make the materials better when they are put into general use. The actual production of the final materials is not begun until the formative evaluation is completed. Formative evaluation is (unfortunately) often omitted from development. This is done at great peril. Implementing untested courses will nearly always result in unpredicted problems in the initial training environment.

Implementation

The nature of the Implementation Phase obviously depends on what training strategy was pursued. All instructional activities are part of this phase, and generally include efforts towards delivery, support, and maintenance. Support may include a course "help" telephone hotline for remote learners. Maintenance includes upkeep of the instructional materials.

Evaluation

Evaluation comes in two parts, formative and summative. The formative evaluation was described as a part of the Development Phase. The summative evaluation is is to measure the effectiveness of the course in solving the problem for which it was created. This phase is conducted as the course is in regular use. The relative ease of revising courseware already in use makes the summative evaluation a powerful technique, rather than an "empty" exercise.

A Case Example of the Instructional Development Process

Suppose our "big boss," John Smith, is tired of seeing wads of wastepaper scattered over the floors in the company offices. He wants it stopped. The desks of employees are all ten feet from the wastebaskets, and he believes leaving a desk to dispose of a wad of paper is a loss of valuable time. The boss calls you in and says, "Train all employees to hit the baskets! I want a training film made right now!" Analysis of the situation suggests that this is not a training problem. Someone should convince the boss that more, properly located waste baskets would save time and money. They will also reduce hazards from sailing wads. The implication is that, during consideration of training needs, you may find solutions for important organizational problems. Unfortunately, *there are many problems you should not solve by instruction.*

The message is: Try to avoid needless training. Search for the problem, identify it, study alternative solutions, such as more waste baskets. Don't train when you can find non-training solutions.[3]

For our purposes, however, let's accept the boss's dictate. You must train the staff to hit wastebaskets. Here is a simplified approach to the instructional development procedure.

Step	Activity
Analyze the task	During this step you need to determine the difference between a good and poor performer. Why is a good performer good? What are the different conditions under which the staff throws paper wads? You note everything the staff must do, and under what conditions. For example: note locations of open windows, deflecting walls, and air ducts, and you list the differences between successful and poor performers. You are also determining possible alternatives to training, such as performance aids, and note data for their design.
Prepare objectives and tests	Here, you determine what the boss has decided is acceptable performance. You prepare a performance test that will prove that the students meet these standards. You also prepare the objectives that describe what they must be able to do, how well, and under what conditions. Your objective may read like this:
	Given ten various sized wads of paper, the students will be able to sink at least eight of ten papers wads in the wastebasket. The wastebasket is 12 inches in diameter, its rim is 20 inches off the floor, and it is placed 10 feet away against a plastered wall.
	Please note that you have already made some decisions regarding media—at least for the testing phase.
Refine and sequence objectives, select media, design and prepare materials	Now you begin breaking the complete objective down into smaller objectives to teach those skills that separated the good throwers from the bad. Your lesson content may need to teach many things. These include how to check for open windows or hot air drafts. The lesson may also teach how to discriminate between the weights of

[3]Robert F. Mager and Peter Pipe. *Analyzing Performance Problems* (Belmont, CA: Fearon Publishers, 1984).

different sizes of paper wads, hold paper wads, and judge distance to the basket and wad entry angle into it. Here again, we must make some media decisions to communicate the lesson content effectively. We must make decisions on how to distribute the material in the most practical manner. What media can best demonstrate, prompt, inform, provide practice, and give feedback to the students? It also must fit the constraints of your budget and facilities.

Test the materials and revise the content and media as necessary

For maximum efficiency, design your lesson content as "lean" as possible to be sure you are not over-teaching. You also prepare a set of pretests for the course and for each lesson unit. This step is critical. It prevents those who can already do some or all the tasks from having to take all the lessons . . . whether they need to or not.

During this step you take your rough lesson and perormance aids and test them with the cheapest materials, most flexible medium, or media available on a small group of *representative* students you have intentionally *under-taught* with the material. You can later add instruction in places where students do not perform to our standard. Remember, you can always find out what you didn't teach, but you will never know what you over-taught.

The same principle holds true for the medium or media used to present the instruction. Too often we assume the lesson needs a more costly and exotic medium than it really needs.

So you revise, and test, and revise again. You continue until the lesson finally works—the students complete the objective, at an acceptable level of performance.

Now you're ready to conduct the training and make the boss happy. During this phase you follow up on the lesson results frequently to make final adjustments. You also worry and pray a lot.

The boss was happy. Simply because you did the training. In order for you to be happy it has to achieve its purpose. If missed baskets meant a loss to the company it would matter greatly whether the training worked. And, if the training was important enough to do, its outcome matters. You follow up to ensure that the learners can actually do what you trained them to do on the job.

You have successfully solved the wastebasket performance problem. Now it is time to explain the process used in this guide to help you in selecting and developing media for instruction.

CHAPTER 2

The Media Selection Process

Sometimes, the phrasing of the training request eliminates the best medium for an instructional program. "We need a videotape on . . ." or "You should make a slide-tape unit for the course on . . ." are statements that replace one problem with another. The statement implies that someone has completed several essential steps in the course development process. The implication is that:
- need for training has been clearly established,
- student population has been analyzed and defined,
- content and objectives have been specified, *and*
- the medium has been selected on the basis of some judgmental decisions.

We would like to believe that this recommendation for a specific medium resulted from careful thought about the most efficient and effective instructional vehicle available. The recommendation is best for production, distribution, and utilization within the organization. Unfortunately, such important considerations are rarely the basis for choice of media at the time of the initial request. Often, the results of such decisions seriously hamper the course developer's or instructor's efforts.

This book represents a contrast to imposed decisions about media at the outset of planning. It presents a logical series of steps for the selection process. We base the procedures for the process upon a series of questions that *relate course objectives and content to alternative media characteristics.*

11

The questions posed reflect a series of media choices. They help you to narrow choices by reasonable decisions. To further narrow your choices, you refer to another set of questions about a particular selected group of media. Conditions such as their compatibility with the backgrounds, age, and culture of the students, local production capabilities, facilities, and budgets are the basis for choice. Lastly, we refine the selection decision by the results of developmental testing. This process guides acceptance, or revision and re-testing, of the medium and materials.

The process is not cumbersome and it is systematic. Practice in its use will make continual reference to the questions less and less necessary. And, there is no reason you should not be adapt the questions to fit your special local conditions. The process is not engraved in stone. It is based, to a degree, on the kinds of decisions we make naturally in our daily lives when we need to communicate with others.

We may choose to telephone, write a letter, or have face-to-face communication with another person. We usually base the choice upon several variables that we analyze almost automatically. We may choose to call someone on the telephone to get instant feedback about how they received our remarks to stress or change our presentation. Or, if we need to have an absolutely clear and verifiable record of what we are saying, we probably write a letter and keep a copy for comparison with the reply. Sometimes, to be sure of accurate communication, we include visuals such as photographs, drawings, and maps. If sound is important to communication, we include audio tapes. If we repeat a message often, we improve its delivery. As we gain experience with the responses of our correspondents or our audience, we use a form of developmental testing. And, should we have a large, geographically dispersed audience, we may choose one of the many forms of teleconferencing methods available today.

The choice of appropriate media for instructional purposes is an extension of this communication skill. It is only more elaborate, and somewhat more complicated, because of the need for specific and measurable results of the instruction. The selection process presented here is structured to insure inclusion of necessary decisions. ∎

Overview of the Selection Process

Please read the overview chart and the explanatory paragraphs on pages 16 and 17. Follow through each path until you feel confident you understand the structure of the process. After you become comfortable with the process and the charts and checklists involved, you will be able to adapt them to fit your own particular situation and working environment.

Step by Step Through the Process

To help you better understand the entire selection process, we will follow a case through the series of charts. A situation calls for the use of *instructional media*. With a situation calling for *instructional aids*, we would use a similar process. In that case, the only difference would be that in Step 4 you would use Charts 2a through 2d. In the sample situation we will use Charts 3a throgh 3d.

As you follow this process, you will recognize that the charts serve as job aids. You may adapt and use them repeatedly as you develop instructional units and courses.

Now, look at Chart 1. Please familiarize yourself with its content before continuing. Note that the first thing you do is to take practical action—you make a decision that starts you well on your way.

Information Or Instruction? —Step 1

Step 1 determines whether the project purpose is *information* or *instruction*.

For practical purposes, we place all communication projects in one of two categories: information or instruction. Information may include such things as entertainment and in-house information organs like bulletins, brochures, and meetings. *Either category* may justify different media because of its different characteristics. Course developers are not normally asked to produce information programs. But, sometimes you may be! For example: Occasionally, we need a generalized presentation to inform management or other persons about a new instructional program. In another situation, you may be tagged to do some form of course overviews or introductions, and there are always those special reports. Because of differences in purposes, the type of message you will present is likely to affect the media choice.

The principal differences between information and instruction programs are these:

Information. The receivers of the information are not responsible for measurable, specific actions or performance. Often, the presentation is general in content, and is to give an overview of ideas or subject matter. Its purpose may be to generate interest, to give background information, or to promote an idea. (If the receivers will take responsible action, the program approaches an instructional purpose.)

Instruction. The receivers of the instruction give demonstrable proof that they have learned. Course writers, instructors, and students are all held responsible for the success of the instructional program. Our purpose is to produce learning leading to measureable results.

Keep in mind there are many informational programs where performance improvement would have vastly improved the return to their sponsors. Typical improvement comes from planning and production through instructional development procedures and inclusion of some means of feedback. In recent years, many "local" productions using video have used some form of these procedures with good results. The discipline involved in establishing a clear sequence of objectives, careful design, and testing can successfully apply to other media as well.

Determining Transmission Method—Step 2

Many designers of instructional development systems would prefer to put this consideration later in the process. But, because of typical practices in business and industrial training, this decision is often strongly directed by institutional practices or policy. In the latter case, does your organization have a training center that has formal courses, a staff of instructors, and a policy of teacher-centered instruction? That is, do instructors lecture, give demonstrations, lead class discussions, and set up student activities with continual and close instructor supervision? If this is the case, then you will be likely to seek *instructional aids.* That is, media designed and produced for use by the instructor in teaching. The overhead projector would be an example of a piece of equipment typically and widely used as an instructional aid. Some other examples are slides, maps, graphs, flip charts, and chalkboards. Instructional aids, then, are media and equipment used to help an instructor to produce learning. But, if your organization provides instructional materials for many students scattered over a wide area and in many locations, you probably would use the second form of resources, *instructional media.*

Instructional media are those media that provide a direct link between the work of the course developer and the student. Usually, with the use of instructional media, the role of an instructor is vastly different from a standup teacher. When using instructional media, the role of the instructor is usually that of a course monitor, administrator, counselor, and supervisor. Students undertake most work by self-direction and by the guidance supplied within the instructional media themselves. Sometimes, the instructor also serves as an evaluator, especially when performance testing is fundamental to the instruction.

There are clear differences in the types of instruction just described. You can readily understand the need for use of the two terms, *instructional aids* and *instructional media.* You must choose the method of instruction early in instructional planning.

We must not overlook combinations of instructional methods, however. You may develop or instruct in courses that use both instructional aids and instructional media. Therefore, you may be using the references from both areas of the charts.

By arbitrarily choosing instructional media, let us examine the next steps. Turn to Chart 3a, Instructional Media, and familiarize yourself with its content before we continue with Step 3.

Determining Lesson Characteristics—Step 3

We assume here that you have worked through the preliminary steps in instructional development. You have analyzed the need for training, determined broad goals for the instruction, and written the instructional objectives with great care. Further, you have picked the ways you will determine that the students have achieved the desired learning.

Each of the chapters that describe media in this book address that medium's suitability for instruction in each of the three domains. They are: cognitive—intellectual, psychomotor—physical or manual, and affective—attitude or opinion. All media are not equally effective in supporting learning in all of the domains. You must determine which domains are involved in your instruction. Recording the learning objectives and domains on a copy of the Media Selection Worksheet shown in Figure 2.1 may be helpful.

Note that, at entry in the chart, you review your lesson objectives and the content you have chosen. You decide whether and to what extent the proposed learning is cognitive. Cognitive learning is knowledge and facts;

rules, principles, discriminations, and others you may identify. If an objective is clearly cognitive learning, you proceed to other questions. Note that psychomotor (skill, physical) learning objectives will direct you to the same first question. It is: Does the lesson involve objects or things unfamiliar to the student? If YES, then you move to Step 4, Chart 3c. Please turn to Chart 3c and familiarize yourself with it before continuing.

As you work your way down through the questions that relate to the needs of your lesson material, you answer questions that relate to your lesson content: Is motion necessary? Sound? Real things? Color? When you reach the bottom of Chart 3c, you have come to Step 4.

Select An Initial Class of Media—Step 4

For Step 4 turn to the Media Classification Table, Figure 2.2. Examine this table until you are familiar with the classes and the types of items in the columns. In this exercise, of course, use the column, "Instructional Media."

Here again, for practical considerations, the media are classified arbitrarily, based principally on their characteristics. Each medium has many characteristics, including special capabilities and limits. These vary according to the quality and type of communication you are expecting of it. Some media are especially capable of presenting information in graphic forms. Others are also able to communicate with graphics, but can add an element of motion. Examples of this include changing colors and guide symbols appearing and disappearing. There are media especially made to provide sound. Some media appear to involve the learner more easily than others. They make possible time and opportunity for active responses and performance demonstrations. Some media are especially economical in presenting verbal information, and some, nonverbal graphic information. Some are especially convenient to produce, change, and revise, or to package and distribute. For a few minutes, study the table and note the media classifications in the left column. For example, read across: "IV. Audio only. Instructional Media/Instructional Aid." Remember we _suggested_ that this is an arbitrary classification. Also, remember that the authors' own experiences and background limit the process with this chart. After you have gone through Chart 3c, you may immediately see another way you can, and probably should, use a medium. You may be right—in your situation. So please look upon this system as an aid for you—a course writer and planner—and not as cast in bronze. If it stimulates your imagination to new alternatives, all this work has been worthwhile. You have simplified the process of deciding what medium to use for an instructional situation—and narrowed your choices.

The remaining section of this book, dealing with various specific media, provides added help.

Analysis of Media Characteristics—Step 5

As each medium is discussed, you will find pages that analyze the instructional capabilities and limitations of the medium. This information will help you reconsider your decision. You should read these pages when you come to the end of Step 5 to help you decide finally upon the particular medium or media to use. You may often find a choice that is simpler to use, or more economical, or within your immediate capability for production. Turn to Chapter 6 and read the material there about printed material, or to pages 111-118 and read about slides. Note how the analysis can help you study your objectives. Later, it can help as you consider the several media recommended for consideration.

Many users of these aids may be working in international instructional situations. The checklists include an important item for such consideration. It should always be necessary to analyze the intended student population's learning habits based on age, expectations, habits, and culture. This analysis is especially critical when working with other cultures. Sometimes you must make compromises to what appears logical to fit the learning needs of the students or trainees. Ways of learning vary greatly among different peoples. But, attentive consideration of these factors during lesson design and media selection can make a course very successful.

As you read the reference pages named above, and as you explore other media, note pertinent considerations basic to picking one or another medium for a particular training responsibility. Now, please turn to the final step, developmental testing, which follows the charts and begins in Chapter 3.

Figure 2.1
Media Selection Worksheet

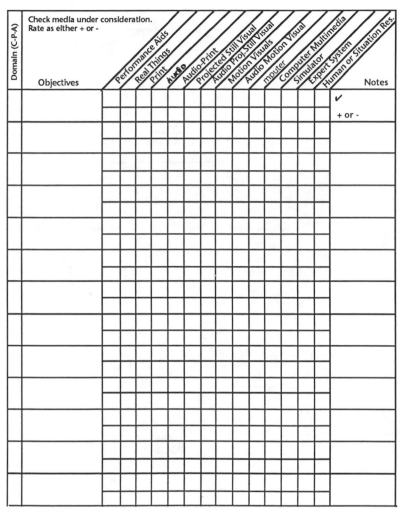

To use this chart:
1. Note your objectives and domain in the spaces at the left of the form.
2. Select the media you are considering with a checkmark.
3. Use the checklist at the end of each chapter to determine strengths,
   weakness, and considerations for each.
4. Note the relative strengths in large space to the right with a plus or minus.
5. Select those appropriate.

Figure 2.2
Overview of the Selection Process

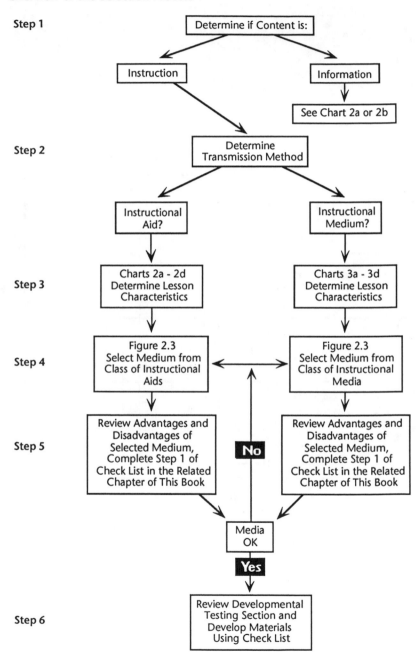

Selection Process

On the opposite page is a flowchart of the entire selection process. With the explanations below, you can walk through the series of six steps, which call for you to work with, at most, three of the charts.

Step 1.
(Chart 1)

You decide whether your message is instruction or information. If you have been assigned a project that clearly has an informational purpose, then refer to Chart 4a or 4b for help.

Step 2.
(Chart 1)

You determine how you will transmit the message. Is it a medium or media to support an instructor to provide either self-paced or group-paced instruction, without an instructor?

Step 3.
(Charts 1, 2a- 2d or 3a- 3d) (Media Selection Worksheet)

Using either Charts 2a through 2d *or* Charts 3a through 3d, you determine the characteristics of your lesson. Further, narrowing your choices of media leads you to pick a specific class of media that is appropriate for your instructional purposes. You determine which domains your instructions includes. Record the instructional objectives and note the domain(s) for your planned instruction on the Media Selection Worksheet, Figure 2.1.

Step 4.
(Chart 2)

You will turn to the Media Classification Table, Figure 2.3, to choose a promising medium from the class indicated— one that you believe suits your student population, local production capacities, facilities, policies, and budget.

Step 5.
(Chapter(s) of This Book)

You refer to your first choice of medium and review the list of unique characteristics of that medium and its advantages and disadvantages for presenting the lesson material in the appropriate chapter of this book.

If the medium still appears appropriate, you then complete the first section of the checklist. This forces you to review and further refine your choice. The questions here relate to students' or trainees' expectations, lesson content, and objectives.

But, if after these refinements of selection you find that the medium no longer seems proper, go back to Step 4. Make another choice from the same list. Again, review the checklist for that medium, and repeat the process until you are satisfied that the medium is appropriate and meets your conditions for instruction.

Step 6.
(Chapter 3)

Having chosen the most feasible medium for your purposes, you then start the last Step—to plan the developmental testing of the medium and your lesson materials.

Figure 2.3 Media Classifications Table

Class	Media	Instructional Media	Instructional Aid
I.	Performance Aids	checklists, flow charts, etc.	—
II.	Physical Objects	actual objects, mock ups, models, or real parts	actual objects, mock ups, models, or real parts
III.	Print (all types of printed matter—including drawings and photos	manuals, job-aids	handouts, easels whiteboards charts, graphs, maps, etc. used by instructor
IV.	Audio (sound only)	audio tape, audio disc, radio (live or recorded "one way" transmissions	telephone ("live person)" radio (used in "two way" dialogue), teleconference
V.	Audio-Print (combinations of Class I a & II)	workbook and audio tape reference materials, used with audio source	teleconferencing, using pre-mailed materials
VI.	Projected Still-Visual	slides and film strips (recorded verbal message)	slides, transparencies, film strips, holograms
VII.	Audio-Projected Still-Visual	sound slide set (audio tape or disc with slides)	teleconferencing, using slides
VIII.	Motion-Visual	silent film (with captions)	silent movie
IX.	Audio-Motion-Visual	motion picture film, prerecorded video	picturephone, video (conference), video (immediate playback)
X.	Computer	CAI	CMI, CSLR
XI.	Computer-Multimedia	computers and various display equipment	—
XII.	Simulator	aircraft or nuclear simulator	—
XIII.	Expert System	electronic performance aid	
XIV.	Human and Situational Resources (teachers, peers, environment)	—	role play, case studies using group members group participation in decision making, field trips

Chart 1

Step 1: Determine if you need to provide Instruction or Information

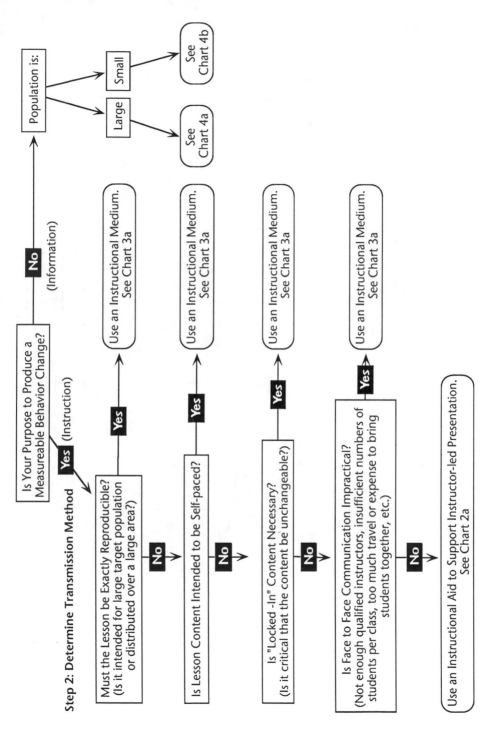

Is Your Purpose to Produce a Measureable Behavior Change?

No (Information)

Population is:

Large → See Chart 4a

Small → See Chart 4b

Yes (Instruction)

Step 2: Determine Transmission Method

Must the Lesson be Exactly Reproducible? (Is it intended for large target population or distributed over a large area?)

Yes → Use an Instructional Medium. See Chart 3a

No →

Is Lesson Content Intended to be Self-paced?

Yes → Use an Instructional Medium. See Chart 3a

No →

Is "Locked -In" Content Necessary? (Is it critical that the content be unchangeable?)

Yes → Use an Instructional Medium. See Chart 3a

No →

Is Face to Face Communication Impractical? (Not enough qualified instructors, insufficient numbers of students per class, too much travel or expense to bring students together, etc.)

Yes → Use an Instructional Medium. See Chart 3a

No → Use an Instructional Aid to Support Instructor-led Presentation. See Chart 2a

Chart 2a
Instructional Aids

Step 3: Determine lesson characteristics
Consider lesson objectives and content—learning is:

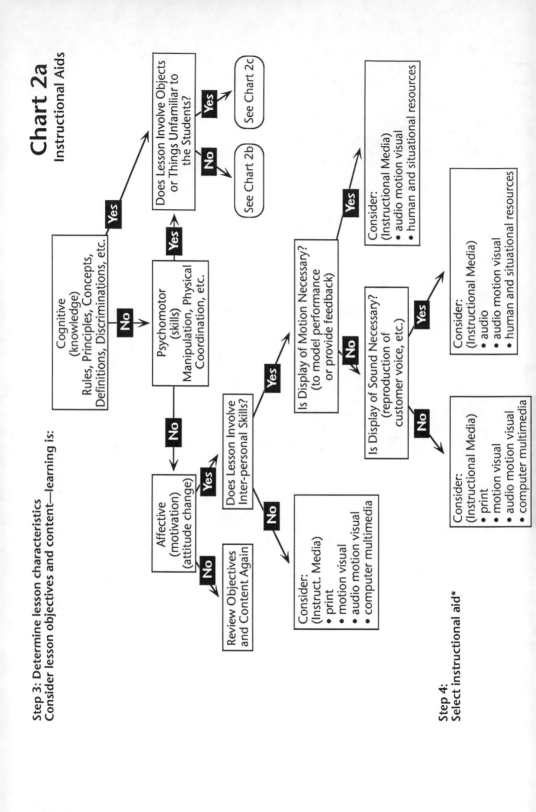

Step 4:
Select instructional aid*

Chart 2b
Instructional Aids

Step 3: Determine lesson characteristics
(continued from Chart 2a)

Lesson Does Not Involve Objects or Things Unfamiliar to Students:

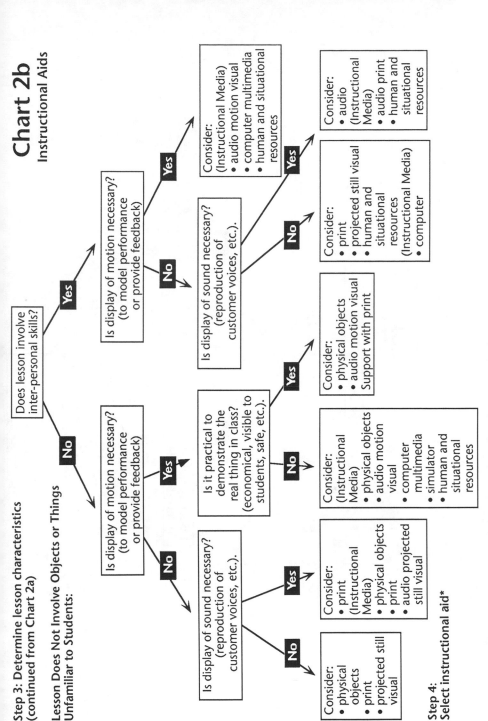

Does lesson involve inter-personal skills?

No

Is display of motion necessary? (to model performance or provide feedback)

No

Is display of sound necessary? (reproduction of customer voices, etc.).

No

Consider:
• physical objects
• print
• projected still visual

Yes

Consider:
• print (Instructional Media)
• physical objects
• print
• audio projected still visual

Yes

Is it practical to demonstrate the real thing in class? (economical, visible to students, safe, etc.).

No

Consider:
• (Instructional Media)
• physical objects
• audio motion visual
• computer multimedia
• simulator
• human and situational resources

Yes

Consider:
• physical objects
• audio motion visual
Support with print

Yes

Is display of motion necessary? (to model performance or provide feedback)

Yes

Consider:
(Instructional Media)
• audio motion visual
• computer multimedia
• human and situational resources

No

Is display of sound necessary? (reproduction of customer voices, etc.).

Yes

Consider:
• audio (Instructional Media)
• audio print
• human and situational resources

No

Consider:
• print
• projected still visual
• human and situational resources
(Instructional Media)
• computer

Step 4:
Select instructional aid*

*Unless identified as instructional media, all selections are from class of instructional aids.

Chart 2c
Instructional Aids

Step 3: Determine lesson characteristics
(continued from Chart 2a)

Lesson Involves Objects or Things Unfamiliar to Students:

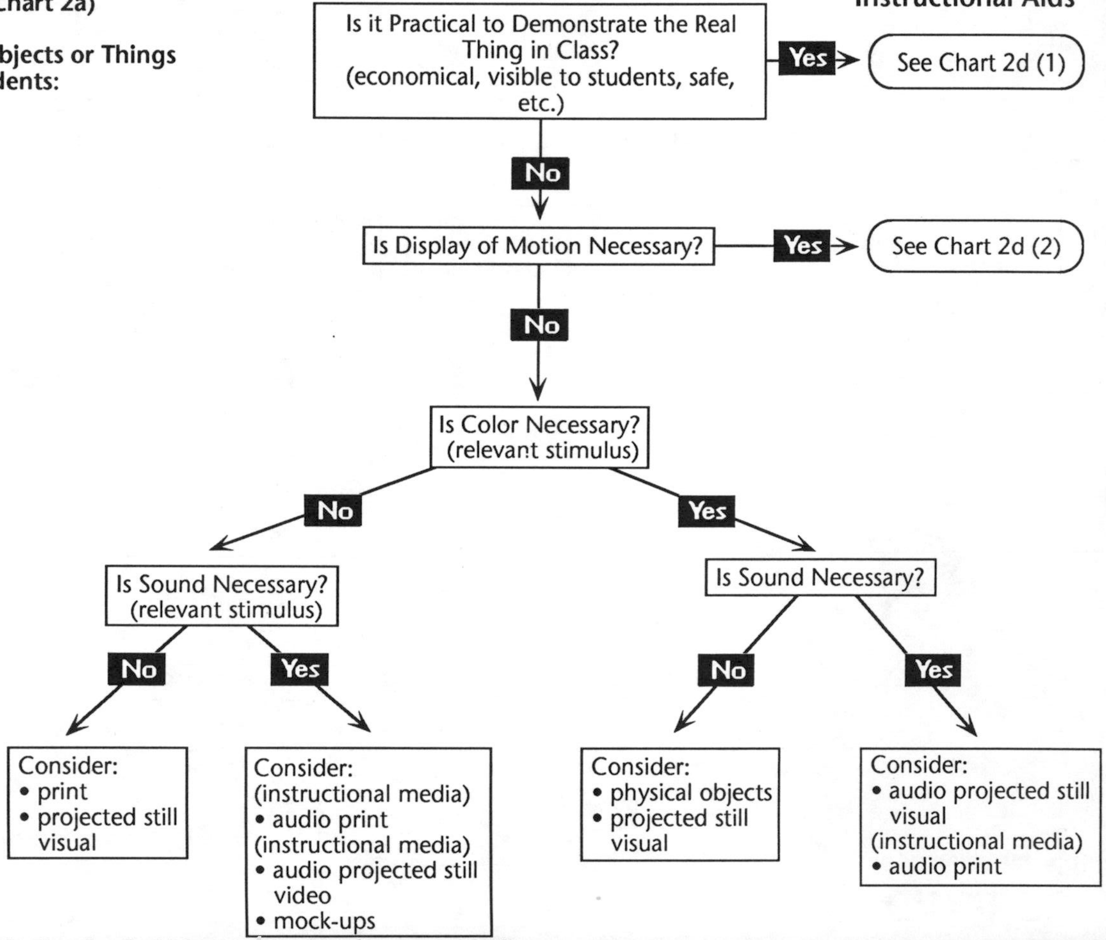

Is it Practical to Demonstrate the Real Thing in Class? (economical, visible to students, safe, etc.)

Yes → See Chart 2d (1)

No →

Is Display of Motion Necessary?

Yes → See Chart 2d (2)

No →

Is Color Necessary? (relevant stimulus)

Yes →

Is Sound Necessary?

Yes →

Consider:
• audio projected still
  visual
  (instructional media)
• audio print

No →

Consider:
• physical objects
• projected still
  visual

No →

Is Sound Necessary? (relevant stimulus)

Yes →

Consider:
• (instructional media)
• audio print
  (instructional media)
• audio projected still
  video
• mock-ups

No →

Consider:
• print
• projected still
  visual

Step 4: Instructional Aid*

Chart 2d
Instructional Aids

Step 3: Determine lesson characteristics
(continued from Chart 2c)

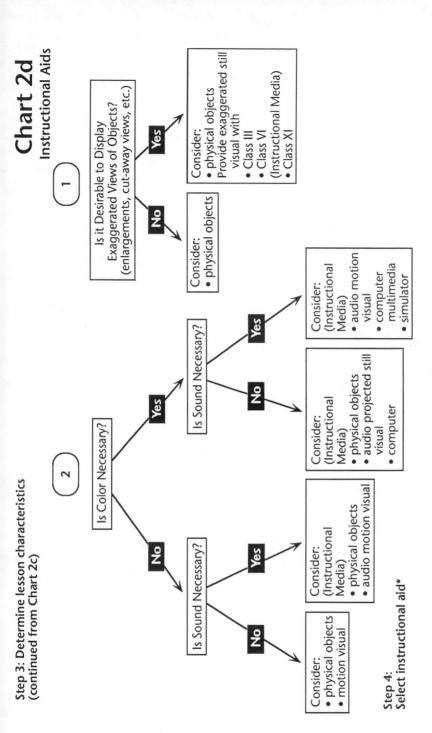

①

Is it Desirable to Display Exaggerated Views of Objects? (enlargements, cut-away views, etc.)

No

Consider:
• physical objects

Yes

Consider:
• physical objects
Provide exaggerated still visual with
  • Class III
  • Class VI
  (Instructional Media)
  • Class XI

②

Is Color Necessary?

No

Is Sound Necessary?

No

Consider:
• physical objects
• motion visual

Yes

Consider:
(Instructional Media)
• physical objects
• audio motion visual

Yes

Is Sound Necessary?

No

Consider:
(Instructional Media)
• physical objects
• audio projected still visual
• computer

Yes

Consider:
(Instructional Media)
• audio motion visual
• computer multimedia
• simulator

Step 4:
Select instructional aid*

*Unless identified as instructional media, all selections are from class of instructional aids.

Chart 3a
Instructional Media

Step 3: Determine Lesson Characteristics

Consider Lesson Objectives and Content. Learning is:

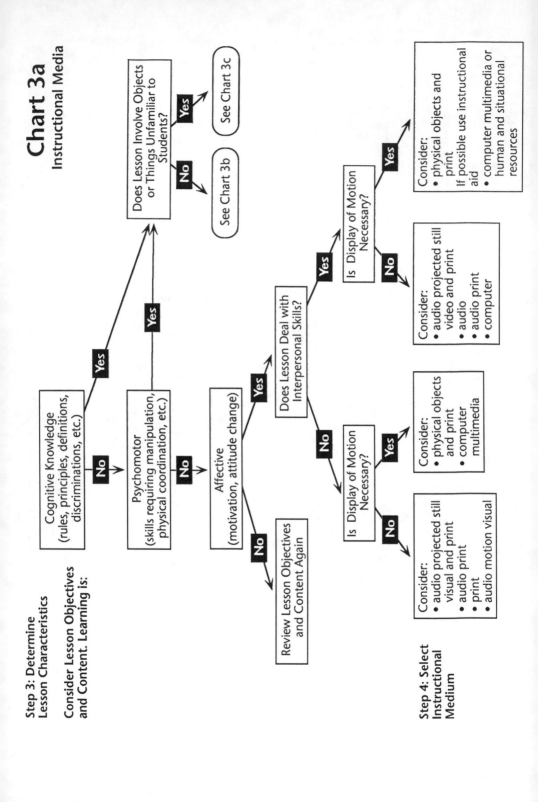

Step 4: Select Instructional Medium

Chart 3b
Instructional Media

Step 3: Determine lesson characteristics
(continued from Chart 3a)

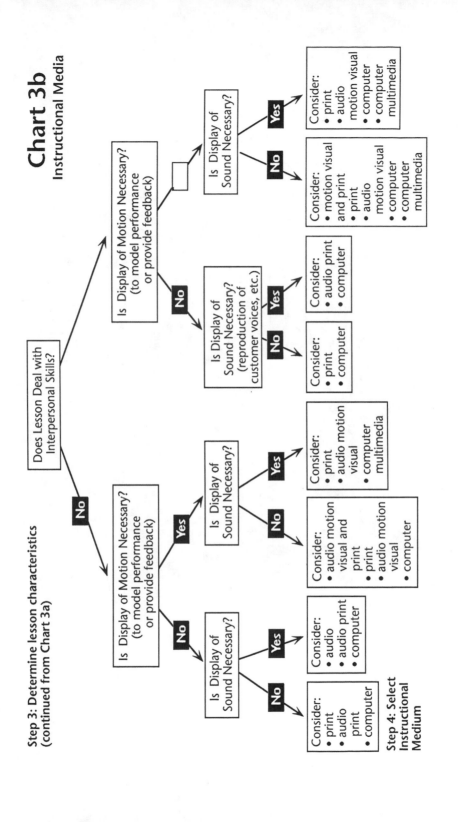

Step 4: Select Instructional Medium

Does Lesson Deal with Interpersonal Skills?

No

No

Is Display of Motion Necessary?
(to model performance or provide feedback)

Yes

No

Is Display of Sound Necessary?

No

Consider:
• print
• audio print
• computer

Yes

Consider:
• audio
• audio print
• computer

Is Display of Sound Necessary?

No

Consider:
• audio motion visual and print
• print
• audio motion visual
• computer

Yes

Consider:
• print
• audio motion visual
• computer multimedia

Is Display of Motion Necessary?
(to model performance or provide feedback)

No

Is Display of Sound Necessary?
(reproduction of customer voices, etc.)

No

Consider:
• print
• computer

Yes

Consider:
• audio print
• computer

Yes

Is Display of Sound Necessary?

No

Consider:
• motion visual and print
• print
• audio
• motion visual
• computer
• computer multimedia

Yes

Consider:
• print
• audio
• motion visual
• computer
• computer multimedia

Chart 3c
Instructional Media

Step 3: Determine lesson characteristics (continued from Chart 1c)

Lesson Involves Objects or Things Unfamiliar to Students:

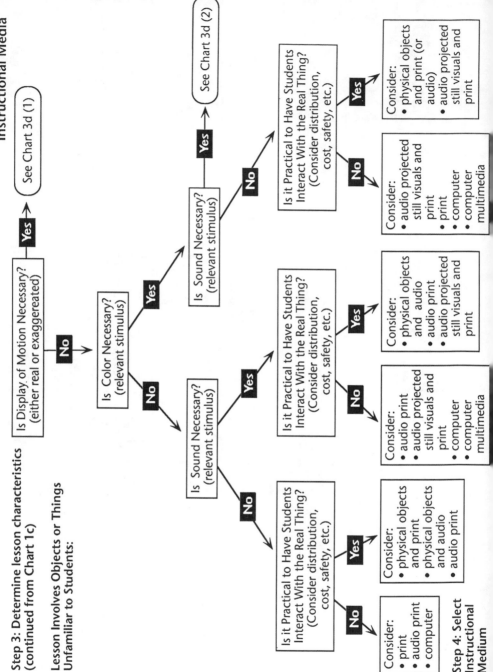

Step 4: Select Instructional Medium

See Chart 3d (1)

See Chart 3d (2)

Is Display of Motion Necessary? (either real or exaggerated) — **Yes** / **No**

Is Color Necessary? (relevant stimulus) — **Yes** / **No**

Is Sound Necessary? (relevant stimulus) — **Yes** / **No**

Is it Practical to Have Students Interact With the Real Thing? (Consider distribution, cost, safety, etc.) — **Yes** / **No**

Consider:
- physical objects and print (or audio)
- audio projected still visuals and print

Consider:
- audio projected still visuals and print
- print
- computer
- computer multimedia

Consider:
- physical objects and audio
- audio print
- audio projected still visuals and print

Consider:
- audio print
- audio projected still visuals and print
- computer
- computer multimedia

Consider:
- physical objects and print
- physical objects and audio
- audio print

Consider:
- print
- audio print
- computer

Chart 3d
Instructional Media

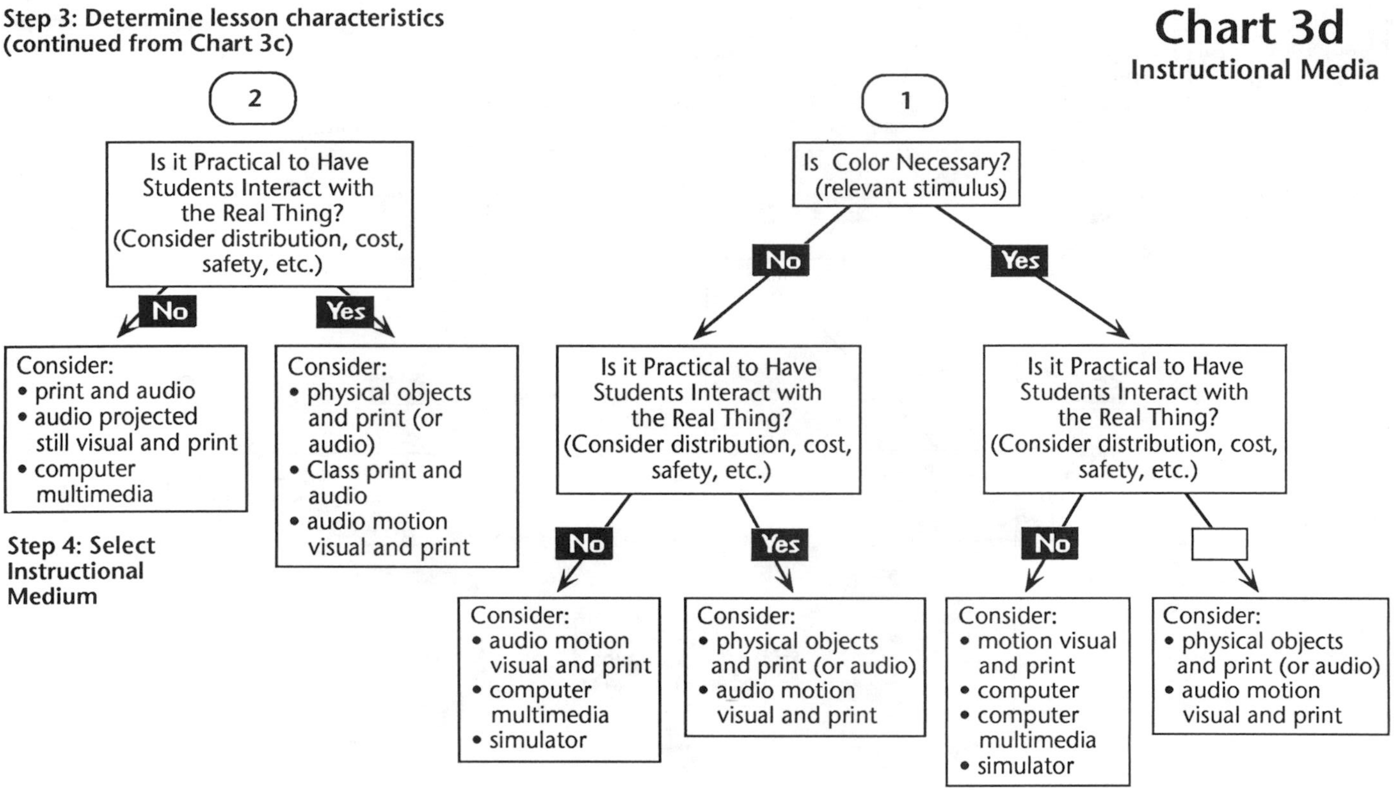

Step 3: Determine lesson characteristics (continued from Chart 3c)

(1)

Is Color Necessary? (relevant stimulus)

Yes →

Is it Practical to Have Students Interact with the Real Thing? (Consider distribution, cost, safety, etc.)

→

Consider:
- physical objects and print (or audio)
- audio motion visual and print

No →

Consider:
- motion visual and print
- computer
- computer multimedia
- simulator

No →

Is it Practical to Have Students Interact with the Real Thing? (Consider distribution, cost, safety, etc.)

Yes →

Consider:
- physical objects and print (or audio)
- audio motion visual and print

No →

Consider:
- audio motion visual and print
- computer multimedia
- simulator

(2)

Is it Practical to Have Students Interact with the Real Thing? (Consider distribution, cost, safety, etc.)

Yes →

Consider:
- physical objects and print (or audio)
- Class print and audio
- audio motion visual and print

No →

Consider:
- print and audio
- audio projected still visual and print
- computer multimedia

Step 4: Select Instructional Medium

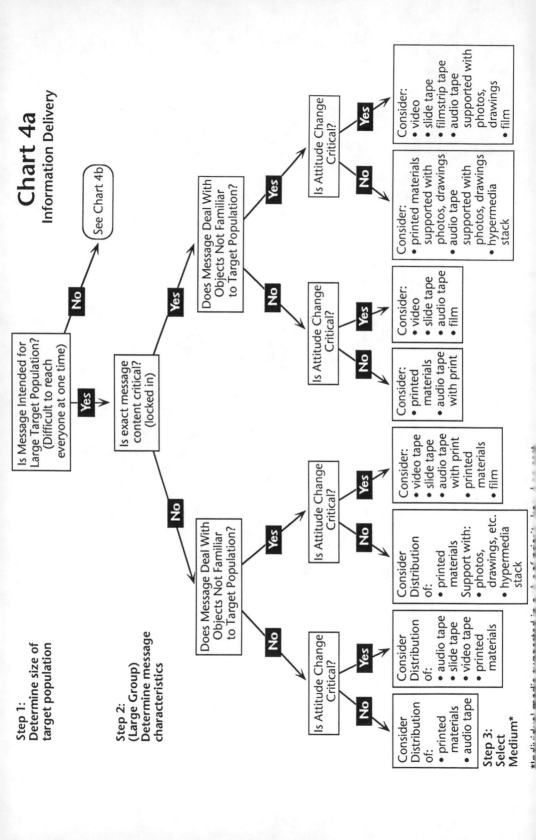

Chart 4a
Information Delivery

Step 1:
Determine size of target population

Is Message Intended for Large Target Population? (Difficult to reach everyone at one time)

No → See Chart 4b

Yes

Step 2:
(Large Group)
Determine message characteristics

Is exact message content critical? (locked in)

No

Yes →

No branch (exact message content not critical)

Does Message Deal With Objects Not Familiar to Target Population?

No → Is Attitude Change Critical?
- **No** → Consider Distribution of:
  - printed materials
  - audio tape
- **Yes** → Consider Distribution of:
  - audio tape
  - slide tape
  - video tape
  - printed materials

Yes → Is Attitude Change Critical?
- **No** → Consider Distribution of:
  - printed materials

  Support with:
  - photos, drawings, etc.
  - hypermedia stack
- **Yes** → Consider:
  - video tape
  - slide tape
  - audio tape with print
  - printed materials
  - film

Yes branch (exact message content critical)

Does Message Deal With Objects Not Familiar to Target Population?

No → Is Attitude Change Critical?
- **No** → Consider:
  - printed materials
  - audio tape with print
- **Yes** → Consider:
  - video
  - slide tape
  - audio tape
  - film

Yes → Is Attitude Change Critical?
- **No** → Consider:
  - printed materials supported with photos, drawings
  - audio tape supported with photos, drawings
  - hypermedia stack
- **Yes** → Consider:
  - video
  - slide tape
  - filmstrip tape
  - audio tape supported with photos, drawings
  - film

Step 3:
Select Medium*

Chart 4b

Informational Delivery

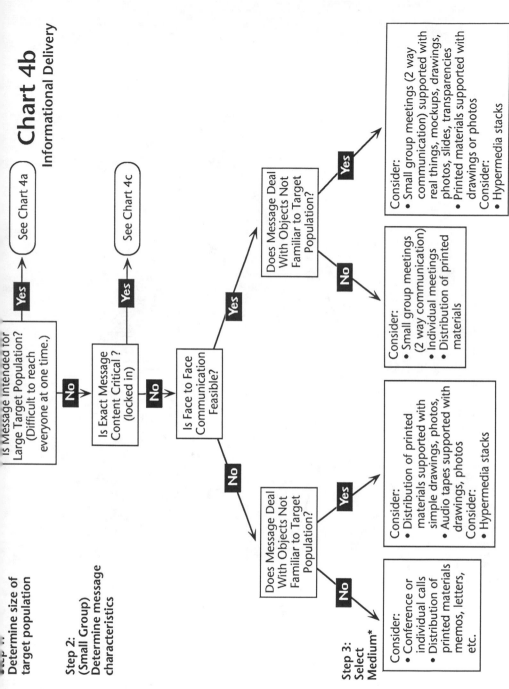

Step 1:
Determine size of target population

Is Message Intended for Large Target Population? (Difficult to reach everyone at one time.)

Yes → See Chart 4a

No

Step 2:
(Small Group)
Determine message characteristics

Is Exact Message Content Critical? (locked in)

Yes → See Chart 4c

No

Is Face to Face Communication Feasible?

Yes

Does Message Deal With Objects Not Familiar to Target Population?

Yes

Consider:
• Small group meetings (2 way communication) supported with real things, mockups, drawings, photos, slides, transparencies
• Printed materials supported with drawings or photos
Consider:
• Hypermedia stacks

No

Consider:
• Small group meetings (2 way communication)
• Individual meetings
• Distribution of printed materials

No

Does Message Deal With Objects Not Familiar to Target Population?

Yes

Consider:
• Distribution of printed materials supported with simple drawings, photos,
• Audio tapes supported with drawings, photos
Consider:
• Hypermedia stacks

No

Step 3:
Select Medium*

Consider:
• Conference or individual calls
• Distribution of printed materials memos, letters, etc.

*Individual media suggested in order of priority based on cost

Chart 4c
Information Delivery

Step 2: Determine message characteristics (Small Group)

(continued from Chart 4b)

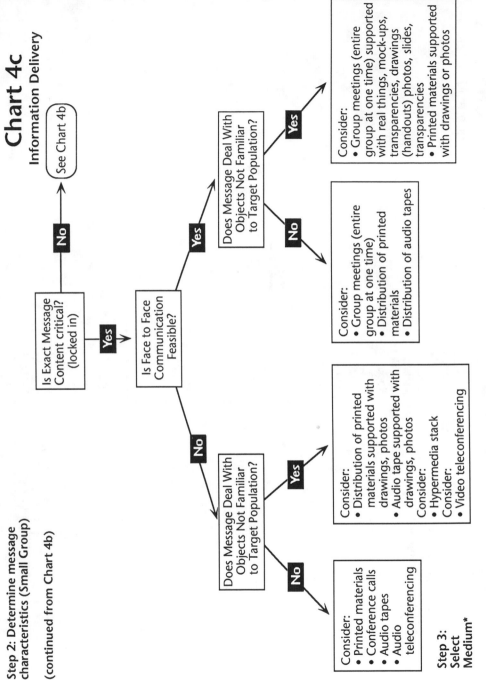

See Chart 4b

Is Exact Message Content critical? (locked in)

No →

Yes ↓

Is Face to Face Communication Feasible?

No ← | → **Yes**

No side:

Does Message Deal With Objects Not Familiar to Target Population?

No | **Yes**

Consider:
• Printed materials
• Conference calls
• Audio tapes
• Audio teleconferencing

Step 3: Select Medium*

Consider:
• Distribution of printed materials supported with drawings, photos
• Audio tape supported with drawings, photos

Consider:
• Hypermedia stack

Consider:
• Video teleconferencing

Yes side:

Does Message Deal With Objects Not Familiar to Target Population?

No | **Yes**

Consider:
• Group meetings (entire group at one time)
• Distribution of printed materials
• Distribution of audio tapes

Consider:
• Group meetings (entire group at one time) supported with real things, mock-ups, transparencies, drawings (handouts) photos, slides, transparencies
• Printed materials supported with drawings or photos

*Individual media suggested in order of priority based on cost

CHAPTER 3

Developmental Testing

THE LAST STEP IN THE PROCESS FOR MEDIA SELECTION described here is the developmental testing of lesson materials. This phase provides an opportunity to test the many decisions and assumptions you have made as you developed the lesson. You will test your objectives and content, and choose the media for the course. Developmental testing allows the developer an opportunity to revise the material according to the findings that result from trial. Your purpose is to be sure you have made the right decisions—that your instruction has produced the desired learning—and you have proof of your success. You also learn where and to what extent your planning might have included *wrong* decisions. Also, you can repair any inadequacies in your course before you send it to the field. In effect, you are checking to see whether your students do as you hoped and predicted they would.

Many leaders in instruction have advocated the use of *lean* lesson materials during developmental testing. They do lean testing by intentionally overestimating student background and skills and therefore, carefully under-teaching the content of the course. Students will show where and to what degree you must increase the teaching you must provide. This process is essential to be sure that your course can bring students to the competence specified in your objectives in the most efficient manner. There are other benefits of developmental testing.

You will often find that you have saved the student's (and the organization's) time, and have reduced the cost of training. Another rewarding byproduct of this phase is elimination of student frustration with studying what they already know.

Lean development applies to the selection and production of media. It is important to overestimate student skills and background in the subject. You consciously plan to produce lesson content in media that give fewest possible visual and audiovisual displays. You also pick the forms you consider to have *least cost and complexity.* You test the effectiveness of each part of the course. This developmental process gives you ample opportunity to revise and increase the media presentations, as justified. You do this *only* when the test results warrant a different, or more complex and costly, approach. A good maxim to follow when testing media and instructional procedures is: If it works, leave it alone! This holds true, not only for the quantity of material presented to students, but for the quality of the display as well.

Therefore, during the early stages of course development it may be a waste of resources to produce completely finished materials of high technical quality. Although, much of the instructional material produced at the start of production development will survive. You will include it in the final product. If you must discard, or heavily revise, materials you are likelier to put aside low cost initial media. And, you can do it with least regret. For practical purposes (both instructional and economic) do not commit yourself to costly media production in the early stages. Keep developmental phases of production flexible, economical, and simple. Base necessary revisions on the results of developmental testing.

In the following material, we suggest some procedures for completing the media selection and development process. You will use them during the developmental testing phase of your instructional program. We outline two tests with hints for conducting the testing. Other refinements in testing procedures will depend upon your growing background in test and evaluation procedures. ■

Hints for Testing Media During Course Development

General

You *may* want someone other than yourself to conduct the testing to gain from their objectivity. However, you must stay sufficiently involved to be sure of proper test administration.

If possible, leave an obvious error in the beginning of the lesson to allow the student to criticize the material and feel more relaxed and comfortable during the testing.

If the test is in performance, put the students at ease by showing confidence in their abilities.

Note carefully where the student appears bored, distracted, or confused and "bogged down." Later, ask about the problems you observed.

Don't rush to the aid of any student when you detect confusion or perplexity. Take notes, and discuss any problems later. Always encourage students to ask questions if they feel the need, and make notes privately of questions asked. Seek clues for revising either test or course.

Experiment to seek the least complex media available to achieve course purposes. For example, use only one medium—audio or visual—to determine achievement of student performance. If students achieve the predetermined standards, you probably don't need a more complicated audio-visual presentation.

In a private, post test session, ask each student—without reference to course material—to recall important parts of the lesson. Be sure their identification of important points matches the intent of the course. Discuss the effectiveness of the media with the students privately. Ask their opinion of the design of materials and how comfortable they felt with the equipment and materials. Edit or revise the course and the media if necessary.

Developmental Test 1

Pick the cheapest, most flexible medium available that *approximates* what you have considered as a final medium for instruction.

Final Product	*Approximation Test Material*
Audio materials	Typed copy of script to be read by student. Cassette copy of script to be narrated by developer.
Printed Materials	Copies of hand-written or rough-typed materials. Hand printed easel sheets or printing on chalk boards. If binders are *necessary*, use reusable loose-leaf binders.
Audio and Printed Materials	Combination of approximations noted above.
Projected Still Visuals (slides, filmstrips transparencies)	Pencil sketches of intended visuals. Simple drawings and typed words on negative slides. Simple drawings and hand-written words on overhead transparencies. Instant photos pasted on sheets or cards.
Audio and Projected Still Visuals	Combination of approximations noted above.
Video (film)	Simple drawings and printed narration on storyboards. Simple visual drawings with audio narrated on cassette by developer.

	Rehearsal video tape using local talent and produced with portable VTR unit. Filmograph—video or film of still pictures—motion simulated by camera or movement of the art or photos.
Computer Screen	Simple drawings and printed narration on storyboards. Paper prints of developmental screens.

Developmental Test 2

After revising the materials, based on the results of Test 1, continue to test using materials produced in closer approximation to the final product.

Final Product	*Approximation Test Material*
Audio Material	A cassette tape incorporating script changes and narrated by the course developer.
Printed Material	Same as Test 1. Typed clean copy of materials incorporating revisions. Use simple line drawings or black and white photographs.
Audio and Printed Materials	Revised copies of approximates noted above.
Projected Still Visuals (slides, filmstrips, transparencies)	Simple drawings on negative slides. Slides shot on location, or on copy stand.
Audio and Projected Still Visuals	Audio tape narrated by course developer, accompanied by slides. (If slides will ultimately be changed automatically by synchronized tape, add an audible cue sound on the tape during narration recordings to indicate slide change.)
Video (film)	Slides and audio tape (narrated by writer). Revised run-through of rehearsal quality, video tape using local talent and portable VTR unit.
Computer Screen	Developmental program, possibly augmented by planned, but not yet developed, screens represented on paper.

Continue to edit and revise the lesson materials until testing shows the wanted student performance. When ready to field test the final product, use the final product or the closest possible approximation. Rules for this final testing method are not clear cut. Every case may be different. These differences depend on:

- the attitudes of the intended students and their supervisors,
- the cost of the media production, and
- the likelihood of revisions.

As indicated earlier, the skill of the individual developer controls any further refinements in testing and selection. They will vary according to:

- the time available for testing,
- the cooperation of students, and
- the ingenuity of the developer.

Again, remember, *if it works, leave it alone*!

CHAPTER 4

Performance Aids

PERFORMANCE AIDS OR JOB AIDS COME IN MANY FORMS. JOB aids are identified during the instructional development process. If a job aid can be used, we may avoid the development of instruction. We must still train the learner—but only to use the job aid. Often, results are more satisfactory than training. They are *always* less costly.

Job aids are commonplace in our daily lives. For example, a repair person beginning the repair of complex equipment might enter the category of the repair required in a computer terminal. As a result, a list of all the parts required for the repair would be printed automatically in the parts department. There, they would be drawn from stock and marked for the particular item of equipment and repairperson. In some industries, a system like the one described could help avoid a disaster. Other examples of job aids include:

- printed materials; checklists, matrix, charts
- computer-based; storage and retrieval for diagrams and schematics, expert systems, and electronic diagnostic procedures reference
- misc; telephone assistance, on-line aids or aids built into job hardware

Computer-based performance aids are quickly becoming popular tools. CD-ROM and videodisc technologies have large storage capabilities and retrieval is quick and easy. These technologies are particularly advantageous in areas that have limited space or require quick retrieval of information, such as submarines. These technologies replace the large number of manuals and other printed materials with a "paperless environment."

Job aids are most appropriate when used for:

39

- new tasks,
- tasks performed infrequently, and
- tasks that require a knowledge base that the user lacks.

Simple but *infrequently* performed tasks, suggest job aids such as:

- indicators as guides to locations,
- directions for making telephone calls, and
- small plastic wheels commonly used for calculating light and heat values, metric conversion, and other simple calculations.

Complex tasks or activities done *infrequently,* demand job aids such as:

- directions for assembling complicated radio, television, or testing equipment.,
- lists of steps with expected results when "troubleshooting" problems in equipment, and
- step-by-step instruction manuals for completing income tax returns, or other computer forms.

Tasks or activities performed *infrequently* involving risk to life health or damage to costly equipment, require job aids such as:

- list of steps to cleanse eyes posted in a lead acid battery shop,
- operating steps listed on fire extinguishers,
- warning notices or operating steps listed on dangerous equipment, and
- procedure manuals for nuclear reactors.

Complicated or long series of steps calling for attention paid to detail because of risk to lives and expensive equipment. Probably the two most common examples of this type of job aid are:

- checklists for airline pilots when preparing for flights, and
- elaborate checklists for astronauts when conducting a space mission.

Despite the many useful applications of job aids, there are a number activities for which they are inappropriate. One example is: as a form of instruction. Two other examples of inappropriate situations are:

1) Tasks or activities requiring *quick response* and speed of completion such as:

- tasks that require frequent and accurate performance when employees enter the job,
- answering customers' or clients' questions about products or services,
- assembly line tasks when one slow employee can affect the production of others, and

- conditioned responses of police and fire professionals faced with emergency or hazardous situations.

2) Use of an otherwise appropriate job aid could have a negative emotional effect on a customer or client who observes the aid being used. For example:

- A well-designed job aid may help a physician to diagnose a patient's symptoms or interpret an X-ray more quickly and thoroughly. This approach, however, is likely to give the patient a feeling of insecurity.
- Technicians needed to repair a large variety of the same product can face difficulties just finding the "combination" to remove the equipment cover. Using a job aid to open the equipment engenders little confidence in the customer.

A performance aid assumes some previous training or education has taken place. Performance aids are not designed to replace the initial training/education of a novice. However, they are effective for replacing follow-up training in some instances. ■

Performance Aids in General

Business and industry is giving increasing attention to the subject of performance or job aids as one viable way to reduce the time and cost of instruction. Managers are learning to consider this alternative as a means to make new employees productive sooner while reducing training costs. Training departments may view the application of job aids to some curriculum merely as a means to control budgets and reduce instructional expense. Students often view job aids as a way to earn salaries sooner and to avoid (sometimes boring) classroom work.

Today, more organizations recognize that training and methods groups have overlapping areas. The responsibility of determining when and how to use job aids is rapidly becoming a part of the training function. How well the training or instructional personnel meet this responsibility depends on the time and effort devoted to:

- isolating the job components and tasks that a job aid can help complete,
- determining the specific information needed from the aid,
- eliminating needless or confusing information in the aid,
- sequencing the steps or procedures in a correct manner, and
- designing the job aid so it is easy and practical to use.

Neither the text nor the checklists in this chapter will try to cover all the possible situations that could involve job aids. There are too many and they are too complex. This is simply an effort to present the most common issues that most developers meet when considering developing job aids. We will also consider their design for use on the job.

This chapter avoids the semantic debates over job aids versus training aids. We take a broader view here. The two concepts are not as neat and separate as "cat" and "dog." In the world of training it is common for training aids, found in the classroom, to be later used on the job. Conversely, many job aids find their way into the classroom to become training aids. Often, a job aid used frequently in the workplace gets "phased out" and later serves as a training aid. Naming the separate characteristics is less useful than determining proper applications and designing better products.

We have also avoided defining the differences between job aids and tools.[1] Ours is a world of rapidly changing technology. Whether tools are an extension of our muscles while job aids are an extension of our minds may soon become irrelevant. When the possibilities of job aids and their functions were unfolding, this was a convenient definition of a then-new concept. Job aids are expanding in acceptance as a normal part of our lives. This debate may soon become an interesting exercise in mental gymnastics.

A criterion for deciding which tasks are appropriate for training and which tasks are appropriate for a job aid. Many factors need to be considered, a difficult process. The following guidelines were adopted from a more extensive list.[2]

Put in Training:

- tasks that are performed frequently on the job,
- tasks performed by a large proportion of the individuals in a given specialty,
- tasks that are not easy to learn on the job,
- tasks that are hard to communicate with words, and
- tasks that do not take an exorbitant amount of money to train.

Put in Job Performance Aids:

- Behavior sequences that are long and complex,
- Tasks that involve readings and tolerances,
- Tasks that are aided by the presence of illustrations,
- Tasks that utilize reference information such as tables, graphs, flowcharts and schematic diagrams,
- Tasks with branching step structure, and
- Tasks that are performed rarely.

Research shows that, if the knowledge of the user is overestimated, there is the likelihood that the aid will not be useful.

---

[1] Expert systems are only electronic job aids. You might want to make the comparison with the descriptions in Chapter 14.

[2] Many relevant criteria are listed in Joyce, et al. *Handbook for Job Performance Aid Developers*. Air Force Human Resources Laboratory, 1973. According to them, the last criterion, not listed, is common sense. If a task seems appropriate for training, develop training. If it seems appropriate for a job aid, develop a job aid. If it seems appropriate for both, put it in both.

Relating Performance Aids to Performance Objectives

Class of Media: Instructional support.

Characteristics: Performance Aids do not teach. They assist the employee to perform the one or more tasks of the job.

Applications to types of learning:

Cognitive objectives. Not applicable.

Psychomotor objectives. Not applicable.

Affective objectives. Not applicable.

Advantages and Disadvantages of Performance Aids

Advantages:

+ Possible to support on-job performance without (costly, long, difficult) training.
+ Less expensive to the organization than training.

Disadvantages:

− Does not teach or instruct.
− May not be directly tied to particular learning objectives.
− User access to the information depends on the user's motivation.

✔✔✔
Checklist of Considerations for Performance Aids

(Consider adapting these checklists to fit the local situation.)

We intend the following checklists, again, as "mind-joggers" for course developers or managers of instruction. These checklists are intended as a job aid for job aids.

A. Determine where job aids will apply to the tasks or activities. A YES answer must apply to at least one of the following questions. If all answers are NO, the task should probably be re-designed, eliminated, or if necessary, trained to recall level.

	Yes	No
Is the task dangerous enough to need a job aid because of safety factors?	❏	○
Will performance errors lead to costly damage of either equipment or property?	❏	○
Is the task very complicated? Should it be entrusted to memory?	❏	○
Is the task only done infrequently? Might a performer forget the steps or procedures?	❏	○
Can less qualified people, with guidance, perform a task normally done on the job from memory?	❏	○
Would having less qualified people do the job negatively affect the productivity of others?	❏	○
Are there frequent changes in details or steps of the task?	❏	○

B. **Consider applying the job aid to the work situations.** All answers should be YES. (Any NO answers indicate it may be practical to re-design the job or train for at least part of the task.)

	Yes	No
Will the use of a job aid reduce the likelihood of error?	❏	○
Will the job aid be practical in the job environment? Will it get in the way or slow up either the performer or other workers?	❏	○
Will the job aid be safe to use within the work situation? (Not interfere with physical activities especially those requiring quick reaction?)	❏	○
Will the working environment support the use of a job aid? (Is space available, enough light, etc.?)	❏	○
Will the performer be able to use the job without disturbing the confidence of others? (If dealing with the public, the performer will not appear inept or incapable.)	❏	○

C. Plan development of the job aid. (All answers should be YES.)

	Yes	No
Have you gotten all information about the prescribed method of performance? (For example: practices, work rules, and published methods.)	❑	○
Have you examined the work environment and noted physical characteristics that may support a job aid. (For example, working surfaces, lighting, cleanliness?)	❑	○
Have you observed the task being done in actual work locations? (If possible you should also try to do the task yourself.)	❑	○
Have you observed and noted how competent performers do the task?	❑	○
If differences exist between prescribed performance and good performance on the job, have you resolved which is the best way to do the task?	❑	○

D. **Design the initial job aid for developmental testing.** (All answers should be YES.)

	Yes	No
Have you developed the job aid test material using the *least* expensive possible medium?	❑	○
Have you considered the physical characteristics of the working location? (Accessibility of job aid, portability, cleanliness of working area, and lighting.)	❑	○
Have you checked to determine that another job aid does not include some procedures in this task?	❑	○
If another job aid includes some steps in this task, have you tried to combine them into one aid?	❑	○
Have you developed your job aid based on the proper sequence of events?	❑	○

E. Developmentally test the job aid. (All answers should be YES.)

	Yes	No
Have you picked new workers (workers who do not already know how to do the task reliably) for testing the job aid?	❏	○
Have you observed their performance without rushing to help them when they faltered?	❏	○
Have you noted where they appeared to have difficulty or made errors?	❏	○
Have you discussed their opinion of the job aid with them? Did you ask about the times they appeared to have problems?	❏	○
Did you, if possible, test the job aid yourself in real working conditions?	❏	○
Is the job aid compatible with the working conditions? (If portable, will it fit into a pocket? If used in a confined working area, does it take up valuable space, etc.)	❏	○
If used with other job aids, does it complement the existing job aids?	❏	○
Have you used terms and phrases on the job aid familiar to the performer?	❏	○

F. Repeat developmental testing until satisfied with the content and the basic design.

G. Produce and distribute the job aid. (All answers should be YES.)

	Yes	No
Have you checked the job aid for completeness and accuracy?	❏	○
Have you considered durability of the job aid when used in the work location? (Will it be resistant to environmental hazards?)	❏	○
Will the job aid be easily legible?	❏	○

Have you avoided using color if unnecessary? (Color materials are expensive and the more colors used the greater the expense.)   ❏   ○

If you must revise the job aid frequently, have you compensated for this factor in the design?   ❏   ○

Have you checked with local production personnel for suggestions on design, production, and distribution?   ❏   ○

CHAPTER 5

Physical Objects–
Real Things

F OR BEST RESULTS FROM TRAINING PROGRAMS, ONE WIDELY recommended suggestion is to have learning happen in a "real" environment. That includes one that approximates actual working conditions as closely as possible. This technique of allowing students to learn tasks in a highly simulated condition shortens overall learning time. It also reduces the need for students to transfer learning from one environment to another.

Either actual objects or highly simulated mockups provide an important stimulus for students to learn tasks that need psychomotor skills. This form of instruction can use all the student's senses. This is particularly true of the tactile sense, when learning calls for the manipulation of, or interaction with, mechanical devices.

The decision to use real things or simulations depend on several working conditions. These include:

- safety of students and others,
- chance of damage to costly equipment,
- noise level of the environment,
- availability of space to conduct instruction, and
- cost of supplying expensive equipment for the training activity.

There are no simple rules for the decision to provide real things or simulations. You must analyze each situation separately. For example, the cost of supplying simulated flight trainers for airline pilots is hefty. Nevertheless, simulators are in wide use when training or providing refresher experiences for many pilots. The cost of simulators is many times less than the cost of using aircraft in actual flight. The hazard reduction may be even more important!

However, there are situations in which the course was not first submitted to developmental testing. This process could have determined whether using actual objects or expensive simulators was cost-justified. The result is expensive, hands-on training equipment. Each case requires analysis, and often experimental trials. The right tool for the right job is a key thought—how would you feel being a passenger with a novice pilot trained only with a sound-slide presentation?

It is not always possible to provide instruction in a real working environment. Sometimes, even the actual objects or devices that students will be using on their jobs are not available. Therefore, often you must make compromises. This is necessary to provide safe, effective, and economical instruction and yet mimic actual working conditions as closely as possible. Below we discuss the three most commonly used training situations for using physical objects. ■

On-the-Job Training. In this situation learners can work with the actual objects of the job within the real work environment. Although this can be a slow process it is particularly useful for learning complicated long processes. One note of caution, you must be cautious that the student doesn't also learn all the instructor's *wrong* habits while learning the job.

Hands-On Training. In this situation students still work with the actual tools, devices, machinery, and materials of the job, but not in the actual working environment. You normally accomplish this by bringing the tools, devices, and materials of the job to the student in a classroom.

Simulation Training. The students must work with mockups of the actual devices, tools, machinery, or other materials from the real world. The environment must simulate the real working situation. Performance is like the real world.[1]

Unfortunately, it is not possible to foresee all the various conditions that might face the course developer planning to use on-the-job, hands-on, or even simulations (mockups) for training. Each instructional situation will be different. You must rate it on its own peculiar set of learning requirements, logistics, and job environment. The use of mockups, as with OJT or hands-on training, will depend on such factors as:

- availability of commercially produced materials,
- skills of individual,
- product, or
- budgets allotted.

---

[1] Simulations of all types are discussed in Chapter 16.

Relating Physical Objects to Instructional Objectives

Class of media: Instructional aid and instructional medium.

Characteristics: Can present audio, visual, and tactile stimuli.

Application to types of learning:

Cognitive objectives. These kinds of training can teach recognition and discrimination of relevant stimuli. Some examples are:

- to demonstrate the sound and appearance of a machine, or other equipment with which the student is working,
- to aid the student to discriminate among sounds and visual cues that show malfunctions, and
- to show proper and improper methods or techniques used in manipulating tools, equipment, and materials.

The training can also teach rules, principles, or sequential steps in operating various tools and equipment.

Psychomotor objectives. These methods are useful for providing student practice. They are also good for testing student performance in manipulating tools, pieces of equipment, devices, and materials of the job. You can also use them to demonstrate and measure student performance when in the actual work environment.

Affective objectives. Using actual tools or equipment from the job, increases the likelihood of job satisfaction. Students can develop a positive attitude toward their work early in the training period. You can positively reinforce attitudes by recognizing that their skills develop with the instruction. Also, you can reduce the students' apprehension about leaving the classroom environment to face real working situations.

Advantages and Disadvantages of Using Real Things for Instruction

Advantages:
- + Can provide students with maximum amount of realistic job or task simulation, reducing the need for transfer of learning.
- + Can display all or most of the relevant stimuli from the work environment, yet often with markedly reduced cost.
- + Allows students to experience and practice manipulative skills using their tactile sense.
- + Permits easy measuring of student performance when job tasks need physical dexterity or coordination skills.

Disadvantages:
- Often, can present safety hazards to students or others in the work environment.
- Can be costly because of the cost of the equipment and possible damage to it.
- Cannot always present all necessary views of actual objects, such as enlargements, cut-away, and sectioned views. Other media must then support the lesson content as needed.
- Often, it is difficult to find or to hire subject matter experts to conduct on-the-job training.
- It can reduce overall productivity by taking skilled personnel off their jobs to train others.
- It can be difficult to control learning because of conflicts with the job environment.

✔✔✔
Checklist of Considerations for Selecting and Using Real Things for Instruction

(Consider adapting these checklists to fit the local situation.)

Using actual tools, devices, equipment, and other materials from the real world can provide many advantages to the learning process. However, you must temper choice of this medium by a large number of constraints. These include: safety, availability of materials, and expense. Course developers contemplating the use of this medium can meet with many unique conditions. The following abbreviated checklist has only two segments. Part A is to help in the selection process. It presents only the most *critical* decisions that should apply to the choice of physical objects or simulators. We have also divided the selection process into three separate parts. These deal separately with each of the forms of instruction: on-the-job training, hands-on training, and simulation or mockups.

Because of the many differences in local production facilities, and availability of local commercial suppliers, Part B will simply present some critical suggestions that should apply to the developmental process.

A. Review the decision to use physical objects as a part of the lesson material.

ON-THE-JOB TRAINING: All answers should be YES.

	Yes	No
Will the student (and others) be safe working in be real environment with the actual tools or equipment?	❑	○
Will the environment be conducive to learning (for example, are the levels of noise and traffic low enough to allow learning to occur efficiently)?	❑	○

	Yes	No
Will the trainer be able to maintain control over student performance?	❏	○
Will it be economical to use on-the-job training?	❏	○
Is it impossible or at least difficult for the student to damage costly equipment or severely hurt customer relations?	❏	○
Will repair or replacement of equipment be inexpensive?	❏	○
Will the student become productive sooner by on-the-job training than by another method?	❏	○
Will the work group's productivity and quality of work maintain an acceptable level?	❏	○
Are there subject matter experts available and capable to train new students?	❏	○

HANDS-ON TRAINING: All answers should be YES.

	Yes	No
Will the student (and others) be safe working with the tools or equipment?	❏	○
Will the purchase of added equipment or tools be economically sound?	❏	○
Will the classroom environment be conducive to learning?	❏	○
If demonstrating equipment, will the area be large enough to permit viewing?	❏	○
Will the objects shown be large enough for students to see them? (It may be necessary to provide an example for each student. Another possibility is to use TV for image magnification, or to use correlated projected still visuals.)	❏	○
Will the noise and traffic levels be low enough to avoid distraction?	❏	○
Will there be ample tools or equipment available to prevent excessive student idle time?	❏	○
Will any expensive equipment or tools be in a secure location to prevent loss?	❏	○

Are enough qualified trainers available to conduct classes?

Will students become productive sooner by hands-on
training than by another method? ❏ ◯

SIMULATIONS or MOCKUPS: All answers should be YES.

	Yes	No
Does the mockup's design allow the students to be safe?	❏	◯
Can you produce and maintain mockups economically?	❏	◯
Will the classroom environment support learning?	❏	◯
Will the mockups be large enough for the class to see them? (It may be necessary to provide a separate mockup for each student or to use projected visuals for image clarity.)	❏	◯
Can a mockup present the student with the necessary stimuli? (Will the instruction need sound, visual, and tactile cues or will some emotion raising stimuli be necessary? For example, heat, fire, and motion.)	❏	◯
Will there be enough materials available to prevent excessive student idle time?	❏	◯
Will students become productive sooner using mockups, instead of another method of instruction?	❏	◯

  B. Start the developmental process. Consider the following items
during this process. All answers should be YES.

	Yes	No
Did you plan to provide proper safety equipment for the students while in class or on-the-job?	❏	◯
Will you check the training equipment before class starts to be sure it is in proper working order?	❏	◯
If using mockups, have you checked for commercially produced items already available?	❏	◯
If using other media to support lesson content, have you checked to be sure the necessary equipment and visuals are available (For example, to provide enlargements, sectioned, or cut-away views) ?	❏	◯

Have you made plans to tell other workers of the new students' starting date? This is imperative if the instruction will use real equipment and the real environment. ❏ ○

Have you budgeted for maintenance or replacement of the tools or equipment, if necessary? ❏ ○

CHAPTER 6

Printed Materials

To most of us, the term "printed materials" usually means professionally produced publications. These include items like books, magazines, and manuals. However, there are several other materials often produced in-house that we call "printed." These include: photocopy and offset reproductions, flip charts, white boards, placards, and photographic prints. These items find wide use in the fields of developing human resources. It appears clear that printed materials will always have an important role in training and education.

People working with training programs can distribute inexpensive textbooks, learning activity packages, workbooks, and illustrated booklets more conveniently than ever before. Print, in its many forms, is highly transportable. It is suitable for use by individuals in the most remote locations on a self-instruction basis. The advantages of print expand as technology continues to evolve means of reproducing attractive publications.

We course developers and writers must recognize the trends in design for instruction and training. A Ford Foundation report said this:

> Only within the past two decades have there been serious efforts to evolve a process of textbook development. . . . From these efforts has come the realization that textbooks must be developed in a reiterative process of testing and revision, like . . . instruction and instructional television. And, as in the case of these two other technologies, it has been found that the development of effective textbooks requires a team effort.
>
> Since, for the next few decades at least, the book will continue to be the most widely used instructional technology device, it

makes sense to assume it will be possible to make major improvements in the book as a learning tool and to invest extensively in the search for improvements.[1]

There is a greater emphasis on so called "information mapping" techniques as a way of improving the communication of ideas using printed materials. The following strategies help reduce the problems of poorly organized information, overload of jargon, and other errors:

- chunking
- labeling
- relevance
- consistency
- hierarchy of labeling and chunking—integrated graphics
- accessible detail

Desktop Publishing

The public finds the new electronic publishing fascinating. Eventually, printed and other communication media will share responsibilities for supplying content and directions for student learning. The development of new, rapid, economical, and eye-pleasing printing processes have positively streamlined instruction and can only help student learning.

Today's simplified electronic production techniques have blurred the line between designer and producer. Increasingly, course writers are producing their own print and graphics, bypassing the organizations "repro" section. We value the control we have over our materials, and save time in the process. Technological advances continue to provide improvements that support the use of printed materials in training. For example:

- Word processing and other computer applications allow easy development of printed materials including manipulation of text, quality printing, and electronic dictionaries and thesaurus
- Scanners allow the transformation of printed materials into electronic form, without the need for time consuming manual typing, allowing printed materials to be quickly modified.
- Desktop publishing and laser printers allow amateurs to produce professional styled printed materials.
- Telecommunications, including modems and facsimile machines, allow printed materials (or in electronic form) to be quickly transferred to long distance locations (considering they have the appropriate receiving resources).
- Computer can output transparencies with plotters and Polaroid® overhead transparencies.
- As this book goes to press, color reproduction is not yet common at the training level of most organizations. It will be.

This technology has made high quality print materials available for everyone, and has brought about a commensurate number of abuses as

---

[1] *An Inquiry Into the Uses of Instructional Technology.* Ford Foundation, 1973.

well.[2] The principles of developing clear objectives and appropriate methods of testing and evaluation, the techniques of feedback, reinforcement, prompting, fading, and branching apply to the instructional design of text. They apply to the use of all types of media. For our purposes here, we will consider text as a valuable form of learning support to be incorporated with an instructional program using a variety of media. Again, you can identify objectives for which text is the ideal medium for brief, pertinent, and efficiently used instructional units. ■

Some Rules of Thumb for Printed Materials

1. Give printed material the same consideration you would other media when planning the design and content. Take time to analyze your target population, their age, command of the language, and reading styles or habits.
2. You may be not be familiar with type styles, page layout, and design. If so, consult with someone who is. There are type fonts and page designs that can make your material look cold and formal, if that is what you want. Others can make the material look warm and informal. It is common to publish the type styles and sizes used in a text. Trainers can relate better to this information now, because they face the same choices. For those interested in the type in this text, it is 11/12 Galliard.
3. Follow good rules of typography. A partial list of such rules is:
   * Use only one space after a period and colon,
   * Use quotation marks (") and apostrophes (') not inch (") and foot (') marks,
   * Use a dash (—) not two hyphens (one hyphen was never correct),
   * Use italics not underlines for emphasis,
   * Use bold not all caps for emphasis,
   * Only use justified margins when the line length is sufficiently long,
   * Never use more than two typefaces on one page (never both serif or sans serif).[3]
4. Sequence information logically within topics and units. For example: from general to detailed, simple to complex, or beginning to end.
5. Always test your drafts on someone unfamiliar with the subject. Make notes for changes in *both* the content and the design of the material for its clarity and convenience of use.
6. Avoid using big words, jargon, and complex sentences. Don't make students stop to search out words or reread sentences to grasp what you mean. When possible, use active voice, short sentences.

---

[2]The professional graphic artist may still be nevcessary to ensure use of proper graphic design principles. The goodness of the graphic design should be equal to that of the instructional design.

[3]For additional advice on these and additional rules of good typography, see the excellent little book by R. Williams *The Macintosh is Not A Typewriter*, Santa Rosa, CA: Performance Enhancement Products—The Press, 1990.

7. Ensure that sub-points of an outline support respective major points.
8. Design frequent student response to the material.
9. Define unfamiliar terms in text. Explain unfamiliar abbreviations and acronyms.
10. When planning type size and page layout, consider your target audience. For example: You may want to provide a large margin for students to make notes.
11. If you have an older student population, you should use larger type with more space between lines to ease reading.
12. AVOID USING ALL CAPITAL LETTERS IN LONG PASSAGES FOR EMPHASIS. RESEARCH SHOWS SENTENCES WRITTEN IN ALL CAPITALS ARE THE MOST DIFFICULT TO READ AND COMPREHEND.
13. Avoid using all italics in long passages for emphasis. *Research shows that sentences written in all italics are also difficult to read and comprehend.*
14. Ensure that instructional concepts are illustrated with specific examples and/or visuals.
15. Use familiar images in visuals.
16. Use sketches, photos, or other graphics whenever possible for clarity and to reduce reading time.
17. Ensure that visuals support the text.
18. Always use masters or "work copies" to copy materials. Making copies of copies degrades the image with each "generation." Even the most sophisticated photocopiers make bad originals look worse.
19. When using flipcharts, white boards, or wall charts, limit information shown to the class. Allow a great deal of space between lines. Check for legibility before using. If all students can't read it, don't use it. Consider using a projected visual like an overhead transparency instead.
20. Do NOT *overemphasize* with **type styles.** Excessive use of **bold type,** *italics, or other presumed* "attention getters" can easily lose their impact.
21. Do not rely on spelling or grammar checkers. All materials must be carefully read. Spelling checkers, in particular, cause embarrassing errors. A word, correctly spelled, can be obviously out of place. Today's sophisticated audiences will realize that it was caused by your total reliance on a spelling checker.

Suggestions for Page Layout or Composition

In recent years, educators have become increasingly aware of the importance of organization and display of information in printed materials. It is important to help maintain student interest and to attract student attention to information. However, many educational or training materials tend to look like Figure 6.1.

Figure 6.1
Plain Page Layout

```
        ABC DEFINE THIS
   iouho uihiuhiuhi uyh uad
  fhuh adfo uhouh ouhou hi
  ouh iuh jpihjb ouhou .
    iu iughi ugiuhi uhi puhiu
  hiuh iuh ubnoun ouijoij ii a
  hg uyg uoygo ljkn ljknm uy
  jy gOuyg ug ;kmpi pij [ji gg
  jhg uygy lkjn pim.
     ouioj oijoij oij p[ij [pij
  oij ij p[ij pij O8hj 97h 8yg
  7tf 86g80g yuuh ou iiug
  kiigy ippgp iug piug pi
```

```
          ABC DEFINE THIS
  iouho uihiu    iu iughi u
  hiuhi uyh      giuhi uhi pu
  uad fh uh      hiu  hiuh iu
  adfo uh ouh    h ubn oun
  ouhou hi       oui joij ii a
  ouh iuh        hg uyg uo
  jpihjb hou .   ygo ljkn ljk
    iu iughi u   rm uy
  giuhi uhi pu   jy gO uyg ug
  hiu hih 8yg    ;km pi pij
  yg iygiy       [ji gg
  iygiy iyg iy.  jhg uygy ln.
```

This layout can sometimes present problems when using illustrations or photographs, or when trying to hold students' attention. When planning a layout, develop *unity* by thinking of the lesson as an entire unit instead of page by page. Keep the following items in mind.

Variety. Printed materials don't *have* to look like the above examples. Sometimes you can maintain the students' attention by varying the layout or by using photographs or cartoons. Also, remember that facing pages make a total display, which can enhance or detract from the effect. Sometimes, facing pages can function as one wide display. A designed layout is shown in Figure 6.2.

Figure 6.2
Designed Page Layout

```
  ABC DEFINE
  THIS

             iouho uiiuhiuhi
             uyh uad fhuh adfo
             uhouh ou ghb hou
             hi ouh iuh jpihjb
             ouhou.
               iu iughi ugiuhi
             uhi puh viu hiuh
             iuh ubno fhi a un
             ou on mijoij ii a
             hg uyg uoygo ljkn
             ljk hu fac arm uy
```

Justification. Most type we see in printed books or manuals is justified. Depending on line length, especially when short, justification can create word spacing and hyphenation problems. It also opens excessive space. The proponents of flush left prefer that format because it avoids the problems just mentioned. All the extra space falls on the right. Sometimes only full words are used. If there is no hyphenation, the right edge can appear too ragged. When insetting art in the flush left side format, place it to the left side for a more polished look.

Balance. You can use balance to draw attention or break monotony. Formal balance is identified by an imaginary line drawn vertically or horizontally through the center of the page. This results in a "mirror image." One side of the page looks like the other.

Figure 6.3
Page Balance

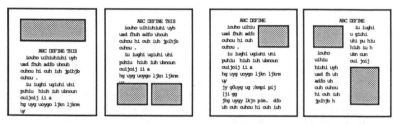

Simplicity. This is another key to good layout design. To achieve it:

- Use clean, clear type for copy of even dark intensity.
- Use clean, clear, and sharp photographic prints (black and white glossy originals reproduce best).

Simple, one-color line drawings are often better than photos. They eliminate unnecessary detail, permitting the learner to focus on the essentials being shown. Consider shading instead of color.

Don't use the original (copyrighted?) artwork. You can use non-copyrighted clip art for satisfactory display, and it is inexpensive.

Use dark ink on white paper. White type on black reduces reading speed by 40 percent. If you want to attract attention, use color combinations that have high contract and visibility, for example, black on yellow paper.

DO NOT:

- clutter or crowd type copy, or illustrations (You should leave plenty of white space.),
- mix type faces unnecessarily except for emphasis, or
- make titles so large and bold that they overpower the text content.

Relating Printed Material to Instructional Objectives

Class of media: Instructional medium or instructional aid.

Characteristics: Capable of displaying verbal symbols and still-visual representations, such as artwork, graphics, and photographs.

Application to types of learning:

Cognitive objectives. Printed materials can be used to:

- provide factual information (For example: policies and procedures, or to describe work functions.),
- teach recognition and discrimination of relevant stimuli,
- present vocabulary used in work functions,
- describe work flow,
- provide direction, and
- provide a representation of the working location, position, and situations that students will face in the real world.

Psychomotor objectives. Limited application. Use still visuals to teach principles or steps in psychomotor skills. Still visuals also show positions of things during motion or the way objects are manipulated. However, the display of motion is difficult to represent in this medium.

Affective objectives. Normally does not apply. Some books can stir the emotions and can be very interesting. Even though there are many talented training designers, it is unusual to find attitude changing training materials effectively prepared in this manner.

Advantages and Disadvantages of Printed Material

Advantages:

- + Print can and should augment other media formats. It does so economically and well.
- + Students can stop at any point in the material to refer to other sources. For example, dictionary, reference text, or use a calculator, and continue.
- + Students can proceed at their own pace. Lesson material can provide a variety of ways to allow self-paced instruction. This technique permits varying learning speeds, dependent on the student's reading level and entering level skills.
- + Material is usually very portable. Students can study materials where and when they choose.
- + The student or instructor may easily review the lesson material. The student can keep the material for reference on the job.
- + Black and white artwork or photography adapts easily to the printed page. High need to communicate important information to the student may justify the cost of two color (or more) printings.

+ The lesson content is "locked in" but can be resequenced easily by student or instructor, or by revisions of the materials.
+ The lesson materials can be: produced economically, distributed easily, and updated or revised as easily. They can display still visuals in either color or black and white. They serve as either an instructional aid or an instructional medium. You can easily move them from one location to another.
+ Similar to self-paced instruction, printed materials allow individualized instruction including quick and easy return to bookmarked sections for review and reference
+ Learning occurs more efficiently through visual means than aural means
+ Large public databases are available for subject-matter reference.

Disadvantages:

− Normally colored artwork or color photography is costly to adapt to printed material.
− Motion is difficult to show on the printed page.
− Extensive lessons presented in word copy alone tend to turn off and bore students. A similar serious problem can happen with long units of programmed instruction. Spans of study time and design of material need careful attention.
− Unless given care, the material can be damaged, lost, or destroyed.
− Large jobs sent out, or even done in-house, may take from several days to much longer. Depending upon the complexity of the material and local services, times can be better or worse.

✔✔✔
Checklist of Considerations for Printed Materials

(Consider adapting these checklists to fit the local situation.)

We divided the following checklist into a series of eight segments listed in sequence. Part A of this list is a "mind-jogger" to help you review your media selection. Parts B through H will help you plan the production of effective lesson materials

A. Review media selection. Analyze the proposed lesson content to determine if this medium is the one best suited to your needs. All questions should be answered as indicated in parentheses, *unless* the printed material is for use in combination with another medium.

	Yes	No
Is the recording of student performance important?	❏	◯

Is the material aimed at cognitive learning instead of
psychomotor skills or attitude change?
(Answer should be YES.)   ❏   ○

Is the display of motion necessary? (Answer should be NO.) ❏   ○

Is it necessary to present an audio stimulus?
(Answer should be NO.)   ❏   ○

Will it be necessary to package and distribute multiple copies
of the lesson material? (Answer should be YES.)   ❏   ○

   B. Rough draft lesson content. All answers should be YES.

	Yes	No
Was the rough draft typed in double-spaced copy with large margins to ease editing?	❏	○
Did you use simple words and avoid technical jargon when possible?	❏	○
Did you keep the sentences short and directed at the student?	❏	○
Did you consider the students' reading level and comprehension?	❏	○
Did you consider students' background and cultures?	❏	○
Did you mark the space planned for illustrations or photos?	❏	○
Have you reserved enough area for placing the illustrations or photos so they will be legible?	❏	○
Have you created headings, captions, footnotes, and references where necessary?	❏	○
Have you had someone proofread the copy to determine if they understand it? This is also a part of your developmental testing.	❏	○
Have you edited to minimize unnecessary verbal content?	❏	○

   **C. Have printed or retyped (single-spaced) and re-edit until you are
satisfied.**

D. Plan page layout after reviewing the suggestions at the beginning of this chapter. All answers should be YES.

	Yes	No
Is page layout simple and uncluttered?	❏	O
Is the format consistent—all-vertical or all-horizontal? (Keep the format consistent so the student doesn't have to turn the book around.)	❏	O
When using illustrations or photographs to support verbal content, were both formal and informal layouts considered?	❏	O
Are you planning to use black and white glossy photographs and simple line drawings when possible?	❏	O
Did you set margins to leave at least 1-inch margin on the top, side, and bottom of the paper and at least $1\frac{1}{4}$-inch margin on the side to be hole punched or bound?	❏	O

E. Test and revise the materials until acceptable for final copy. (Review Chapter 3 on developmental testing.)

F. Prepare for printing the final copy. All answers should be YES.

	Yes	No
Have you avoided using multiple colors unless meaningful?	❏	O
Have you selected the design and size of type for the final product based on how they can help convey your message?	❏	O
Have you avoided using a format with a justified right-hand margin unless necessary?	❏	O
Do the title sizes complement the text print? (Have you avoided too bold titles that overpower text material?)	❏	O
Are words that need emphasis underlined or placed in boldface type? (Do *not* overemphasize, or you will lose impact.)	❏	O
Did you check all verbal information for accuracy of spelling and grammar?	❏	O
Have you avoided cluttering the printed copy with illustrations? (Leave white space.)	❏	O

Is there enough space between lines to make the text
easy to read? (Be careful not to spread the lines out too
much and get a washed out or gray-looking page.) ❑ ○

Have you avoided using shocking or distasteful graphics,
or pictures for effect? (This also applies to humor. Consider
your students' backgrounds.) ❑ ○

Is the message printed on both sides of the page when
possible? (Printing both sides may reduce cost and
save paper.) ❑ ○

If necessary, have you placed a proprietary statement at the
beginning of the text? ❑ ○

If needed, have you prepared a title sheet? ❑ ○

Are the page numbers correct? ❑ ○

Are the headings and captions accurate? ❑ ○

Is the final copy clean and neat with good, black
illustrations and photographs? ❑ ○

Is the material organized and collated into its proper order? ❑ ○

G. Order printing and materials. All answers should be YES.

	Yes	No

Have you determined the specifications in coordination
with your printer? (Use of non-standard sizes requires
trimming and wastes a great deal of paper.) ❑ ○

Have you considered the weight of the paper stock needed
before ordering? (For example, 20–lb. bond stock may be
satisfactory for most materials. However, some material
with embedded tests may call for 60-lb. bond stock to
prevent answers from bleeding through.) ❑ ○

Have you determined the unit cost of your printing?
(A disproportionate share of printing costs comes from
setting up the job. Once the presses are set to roll for a
5,000 copy roll, the additional cost of 1,000 more copies
will be far less than one-fifth of the original cost.) ❑ ○

If necessary, are tabs sizes considered? ❑ ○
(Tab sheets are 1/4 inch wider than text sheets.)

Have you considered the color of paper? (Colored paper for text material is acceptable when there is a reason to use it. Black ink on white paper or soft green paper gives comfortable readability. This is not true of all paper colors.) ❑ ○

Have you considered folding and binding? (Some high volume presses can fold the paper automatically, as long as you use a standard fold.) ❑ ○

If material will require periodic update, have you considered a looseleaf binder? ❑ ○

If you will use hole-punched paper, have you determined the number of holes? ❑ ○

Have you considered the type of binder? (If you plan ringed binders, order standard sizes if possible. Unusual sizes cost more.) ❑ ○

Have you determined the required capacity of the binder? (A $\frac{1}{2}$ inch ring binder holds about 40 pages comfortably. A 1-inch holds about 80 pages.) ❑ ○

Have you determined the cover and spine design? (Remember, color, unless necessary, may add to the cost.) ❑ ○

Have you determined the appropriate logo, trademark, or other necessary or appropriate organizational identification for the cover? ❑ ○

Have you determined the copies needed for distribution, record files, and replacement? ❑ ○

Have you established printing cost estimates and promised delivery dates? (Always allow enough lead time for printing and for reprinting, if necessary.) ❑ ○

H. Proof Materials Before Distribution.

Have you considered having someone unfamiliar with the material proofread? ❑ ○

CHAPTER 7

Audio

F ROM THE PERSPECTIVE OF A COURSE DEVELOPER, AUDIO materials provide an economical and convenient source of instructional content. Normally, audio is readily available for students. Once packaged, lesson content and sequence are locked in—and can function as an instructional medium for independent study.

When appropriately prepared and well-used, audio programming has a relatively low production and distribution cost. When inappropriately designed or poorly used, audio programming can be a costly disruption to student learning. Audio instruction development must include the same skill, artistry, care, and planning as any other medium.

Evolution from analog-based to digital audio in entertainment will "trickle down" to future training use. That was exactly what happened with VHS format videotape. Analog audio quality decreases with each successive generation or reproduction. However, digital audio deals with numerical data: a reproduction is an image of numerical data describing the sound waveforms. Copies are as good as masters. Examples of digital audio include:

- CD-Audio, a read only medium
- Read/Write optical storage, desktop digital productions
- DAT (digital audio tape) recordable, compact disc quality on tape

Most course developers write materials intended for *students*. Their writing habits are normally developed on a basis of rules that produce an acceptable *literary* style. After establishing lesson content and sequence, the writer's concern is about the end product—printed words on a page.

This includes: associated rules governing grammar, sentence structure, paragraphing, punctuation, conciseness, and spelling. Techniques associated with writing lessons students will *hear* need unique skills and have different measures of quality. Rules of good grammar and clear expression do apply fully in writing spoken lines. But spoken words are not delivered as written. Beyond that, to produce lines that can be spoken naturally and clearly involves attention to such characteristics as:

Rhythm. Combinations of words and sounds with easy, clear, and smooth articulation.

Structure. Placement of *key words* in places where the listener can be sure to hear them. For example, the student may not hear, with certainty, the first words spoken. We may need to focus listener's attention to receive important message words. We may begin the sentence structure with attention-getting words that lead to a key word or statement.

Sentence structure. Use sentences that are most often sh*ort and not complex.* (That is, you package the ideas in complete statements, or in short phrases with clearly presented ideas.) A narration, unlike material for reading, marches along at a pace not controlled by the listener. The writer must be careful to package the ideas presented for easy, quick, and accurate acquisition by the listener.

Active voice. Use the active voice, when possible, to keep listeners' attention and to reduce confusion.

These sample characteristics show the complexity of the writer's job. Unfortunately, in this brief guide, we can only give general suggestions. We urge you to practice, read your own writing aloud into a recorder, listen, and self-rate your work. Even more important, have others listen to your recording. Let their reactions help you improve your work.

These guidelines are not a panacea for the woes of script writers. They simply present a systematic and time-tested approach used by professional writers to produce good audio material. The technical and procedural suggestions in this material for recording master tapes and duplicates are to ensure the best quality transmission to the student.

As with most specialized skills, the ability to write for the listener varies from individual to individual. For example, it may be difficult for some people to think visually. They have difficulty preparing a lean supporting script for a visual presentation. That skill deficiency, however, is not an excuse to give up. Nor is it an excuse to choose another, less appropriate medium. Help is usually available if you look for it. With time and patience you can develop adequate skills.

You must carefully avoid illegal activity when adding music to your presentations. Recorded music for personal use is generally allowed as an exception to the very restrictive laws governing the recording of copyrighted material. Even though the fair-use doctrine allows for educational use, recording to a tape, or computer drive, is considered mechanical reproduction.[1] Copyright law does make a distinction between public and private exhibition. A one-shot use of a song in a multimedia presentation for your company's meeting might cost under $200.[2] Here is the rule of thumb: If someone else's music is used in your instruction (regardless of the medium in which it is presented) and the copyright holder isn't getting any royalty from it, you're guilty of copyright infringement. Getting permission from the copyright holder for legal use is easy.

You can use the audio medium in several different ways. Students can use it alone, or with printed materials, slides, or some other still visuals. Each use calls for very different techniques for developing the audio script. To accommodate this situation, we divided this chapter to address script development in the following subsections for:

- audio only (or audio used with printed material),
- audio supported by still visuals, and
- audio materials supporting still visual presentations.

Most current instructional audio materials are produced in a tape format. Therefore, the checklists will deal only with that medium. Scripts for live radio or teleconference use are not specifically addressed. However, you can use the same developmental techniques and procedures for these and other types of audio media. ■

Relating Audio Materials to Instructional Objectives

Class of media: Instructional medium.

Characteristics: Capable of presenting audio stimuli.

Application to types of learning:

Cognitive objectives. You can use audio tapes to teach recognition and discrimination of relevant *audio stimuli*. Some examples are:

- To present the sound of a machine (or tool) with which students will be working. Or to present sounds identifying malfunctions of the machine or tool to permit student discriminations among proper functions and malfunctions indicated by sounds.
- To present the sound of specific alarms or other devices from which students should take specific actions.
- To teach recognition of dialects and accents associated with a job. Or, to present voices as they will sound on the job accompanied by

---

[1] If you are laboring under the impression that it is legal to use four bars or seven seconds of music, whichever is less, you are grossly mistaken.

[2] As a rule, until the year 2010, you can safely assume any song written before 1915 is in the public domain. Also consider the Library of Congress. Much public domain material is available at little cost.

shop noise or other interference, or customer voices on the telephone.
- To present audio drills for learning to recognize or pronounce foreign or unfamiliar words or phrases.

Audio can also teach rules and principles. When used for these purposes audio recordings usually are a substitute for, or used with, printed matter or still visuals. Such use adds variety to the training or ensures exact content.

Psychomotor objectives. You can use audio to teach verbal skills, such as to:

- permit the learner to hear and to imitate and practice the sounds of foreign or unfamiliar words,
- provide drills for the student to be able to recognize and practice sounds of words to overcome speech difficulties,
- give practice in making responses to spoken requests,
- present recorded drills in practicing to take orders or directions, with increasing rates of speed, and
- present taped drills for practicing responses to alarms or signals or other emergency audio communication or instructions.

Affective objectives. You can establish moods or attitudes through use of background music, sound effects, and narrators' voices. Radio serial programs and advertisements (either live or taped) best demonstrate these techniques.

Advantages and Disadvantages of Audio[3]

Advantages:

- + Lesson content is fixed and exactly reproducible.
- + Production and program reproduction are economical, and distribution is convenient.
- + Equipment for using audio programs is among the least costly of any of the audiovisual media. With continued advances in digital audio and new technologies introduced into the consumer market, equipment may no longer be too inexpensive for training use.
- + The use of various audio tape recording techniques permits use of individualized instruction formats. They allow self-pacing by the students, reinforcement, and immediate knowledge of performance.
- + For sophisticated self-instructional program formats, devices are available to synchronize visuals with the recorded audio program. They provide automatic stop features to give students time to interact with the program and to proceed when ready. Other devices are

---

[3]August Spector, of the Nuclear Regulatory Commision, made valuable suggestions for this chapter.

especially designed for audio comparator techniques. These permit students to hear a model performance, to respond, and then to compare their performance with the model.

+ Moods or student attitudes can be affected by background music and sound effects.

Disadvantages:

- Be careful when using the audio channel alone for long periods without supplying the student any visual stimulus. This can make lessons boring and can inhibit self-paced instruction. (A 15-minute tape requires 15 minutes of student time, regardless of the student skills.)
- Revisions usually require production of a new master and issue of new copies. This is time-consuming and can lead to considerable cost.
- Producing synchronized visuals with audio tape can generate distribution problems. This is because of the variety of hardware devices available and used in different training locations. Course developers must know what equipment is available to provide compatible software.
- Development of quality scripts (particularly those intended to support visuals) can be time-consuming and need specialized skills.
- Exercise caution in pacing verbal content. The student may become lost or confused if forced to listen to material at too fast a speed. The same is true of complex instructions presented too rapidly.
- It may be prudent in some cases to provide redundancy through visual reminders (for example, restatements in workbook materials or displayed on still visuals). You can usually determine this during developmental testing.[4]
- Student review of audio materials synchronized to still visuals can be difficult and confusing if the audio and visual materials get out of synchronization.

✔✔✔
Checklist of Considerations for Audio Only

(Consider adapting these checklists to fit your own situation.)

The following checklist is for use as a mind-jogger when viewing your media selection and developing lesson materials. Segment A is to help you

---

[4] Several makes of variable speed audio players are available providing both fast and slow speed playback. The sound is generally excellent with little or no distortion of voice quality. Although an expensive investment, these devices can be most useful in limited situations—for example, instructing students with English as a second language, or when frequent quick reviews may be required of lesson materials.

confirm this choice of media. Segments B through G are to help in planning, developing, and producing your own instructional materials.

A. Review media selection. Consider lesson objectives and contents; The audio medium must satisfy at least one of the following criteria:

	Yes	No
Are students unable to read, or do they have difficulty comprehending printed materials?	❏	⭘
Does lesson material contain appropriate audio stimuli for presentation to students? (See examples in the sample scripts at the end of this section.)	❏	⭘
Does the lesson teach verbal skills or responses to verbal stimuli on the job?	❏	⭘
Can audio be a practical way to add variety to instruction by changing media?	❏	⭘

A Word of Caution:
Audio materials have a fixed time frame for presenting instruction. This suggests that you must design self pacing aspects of instruction and *choice of content* into the lesson materials.

B. Prepare first draft. Check script for the following criteria. All answers should be YES.

	Yes	No
Is the rough draft script either clearly written or printed double-spaced? Does it leave a wide left-hand margin for notes?	❏	⭘
Have you used active voice when possible?	❏	⭘
Have you used "spoken" language? Have you used a colloquial style normally used in conversational speech?	❏	⭘
Have you used contractions whenever appropriate? We normally use such statements as: I'm, you're, haven't, and won't, instead of I am, you are, have not, and will not.	❏	⭘
Have you avoided big, complex words? (The students don't care how smart you are and may not have a dictionary handy. Besides, you should make it as easy as possible for the narrator to speak clearly)	❏	⭘

Have you considered what sound effects and background
noises may be necessary or desirable to establish realism
or moods?   ❏   ○

Did you consider students' background, cultures, etc., and
avoid insulting or shocking phrases?   ❏   ○

Have you avoided jargon and technical terms when possible?   ❏   ○

If you had to use some technical term did you spell the word
phonetically in parentheses, so the narrator can pronounce it?   ❏   ○

Is the number of voices (characters) at a minimum for ease of
production and to reduce cost?   ❏   ○

Have you had a subject matter expert check the lesson
content to ensure relevance and accuracy?   ❏   ○

If script is for use with printed (workbook) material, have you:

  • Planned to present examples when possible, to allow the
    student to practice interacting with the instructional
    materials?   ❏   ○

  • Compared the printed material with the script to be
    sure they are compatible?   ❏   ○

  • Planned to have the audio and printed materials com
    plement each other. For example, have the audio tell
    the students to turn to the printed material and the
    workbook refer them back to the audio portion?   ❏   ○

    C. Tape first script on a cassette recorder. Preferably someone other
than the writer should record the script to help you be objective. As you
listen to the tape check for these points. All answers should be YES.

	Yes	No
Was the script read *exactly as written?*	❏	○
Were the messages clear?	❏	○
Did the script sound natural, as though it was conversational—and not being read?	❏	○
Were there enough built-in pauses to give the narrator time to breathe?	❏	○
If there were any tongue-twisting phrases, did you revise them?	❏	○

Did you remove needless technical words or jargon
when possible?   ❏   ○

If the audio material is for use with a student workbook
(interactively), did you check the instructions to the student
in both media to be sure they complement each other?   ❏   ○

Was the pacing correct? (Did you consider the student's
ability to understand the language?)   ❏   ○

   D. Revise your first draft and then re-record on a cassette recorder. Play
back and check the following points. All answers should be YES.

	Yes	No
Was it read (preferably by someone other than the writer) *exactly as written?*	❏	○
Does it meet the qualifications outlined for preparation of the first draft script?	❏	○
Is the pacing correct for the intended students?	❏	○
Has the number of characters (or voices) been minimized for efficiency of recording?	❏	○
Have you noted the necessary sound effects? (Is it desirable to establish realism of location through background sounds, for example, office or street noises and telephone voices and echoes?)	❏	○

If the tape is for use with a student workbook, have you:

    • Emphasized brevity and clarity on the recorded
      instructions for the student?   ❏   ○

    • Tested the audio product with the written material
      for ease of interaction?   ❏   ○

    • Tested the length of the pauses to confirm adequate
      time for the students to perform?   ❏   ○

Have you indicated how they will know when to restart a
stopped tape?   ❏   ○

Have you checked the section, "Developmental Testing"
for testing the material?   ❏   ○

E. Developmentally test the material and revise the script again. Then, if necessary, re-record and play back. Check for the following criteria. All answers should be YES.

Did you underline words that need stress?	❏	◯
Did you note pauses correctly? And, when necessary, did you state the length of the pause in numbers of seconds?	❏	◯
Did you check to determine if music is really necessary? (Avoid breaking copyright laws!)	❏	◯
Does a student or instructor have to adjust the volume?	❏	◯
It is desirable, or necessary, to set a mood through music (for example, suspense, humor, period in time, etc.)?	❏	◯
Did you check to determine if you left out any relevant audio stimuli (for example, sounds such as warning signals, shop noises, and engine or equipment sounds significant in the lesson)?	❏	◯
Did you have a subject matter expert check for the accuracy and realism of the audio presentation?	❏	◯

F. Write the final draft. Check typed copy as below. All answers should be YES.

	Yes	No
Are sentences complete at the bottom of the page? (no sentence carried over to the next page)?	❏	◯
Are words spelled correctly (so they will not be mispronounced)?	❏	◯
Did you give instructions for the sound technician at the beginning of the script? (These include the sound effects required, music, and number and types of voices used. See the sample scripts at the end of this chapter).	❏	◯
Did you number all pages correctly?	❏	◯
Did you underline words that need stress?	❏	◯
Have you given directions for pronouncing unusual words?	❏	◯
Is speed of pacing indicated for narrator?	❏	◯

Is the draft double-spaced? Is it in the format shown in the
samples at the end of this section? ☐ ○

Have you avoided stapling the draft? (The sound of turning
pages may also be recorded.) ☐ ○

G. **Consult with production personnel for requirements of master tape,
protection copies, and duplicates for release.** See the suggestions at the
end of the section.

	Yes	No
Have you allowed enough lead time for production and distribution?	☐	○
Have you arranged for storage of master or "work copy"?	☐	○
Have you determined how many copies to order?	☐	○
Have you determined in what format(s) you will release the audio program, standard cassettes or DAT?	☐	○
Have you planned for packaging and labeling?	☐	○
Have you prepared copies of script for use at the recording studio?	☐	○

Audio Scripts with Visuals

The two basic types of cued audio scripts described in this section are
scripts using dialogue to support a visual message, and scripts using visuals to support a verbal message.

Preparing a visual message *supported by narration* or dialogue is more
difficult to develop and is best compared with producing motion visuals.
This method has developed many effective slide-tape or filmstrip presentations. But, for a writer to maintain a lean dialogue is a challenge. Writers
have a tendency to write to be either heard or read. In doing so, they ignore
the primary message-carrying power of visuals.

Scripts using still visuals *to support verbal content* are more common
and presumably more natural for course writers to develop. An example of
this method is narrated instructions using visuals as reference or to create a
mood. In these cases, visuals are most commonly used as support to:

- occupy the audience's visual sense to keep its attention,
- clarify some verbal abstraction ("One picture is worth a thousand
  words."),
- represent pictorially some object or thing about which the audience
  is unfamiliar (See Chapter 9 "Still Visuals"), or

- elicit some emotional response from the audience.

Final script format. When you use visuals with audio materials, the final draft must follow the same format shown in the samples that follow this chapter. This is true, despite the type of program being written. However, the development process varies. We will deal with it separately. The *important* fact is that the writer must determine *which* medium is carrying the principal message. You must determine this at the beginning of the project. Otherwise, you run the risk of creating interference between the two media and inevitably impairing student learning.

Determine which channel (audio or visual) to use chiefly to communicate the instructional content. Once you have, you can use the following checklist sections to develop the lesson script.

✔✔✔
Checklist for Scripts Using Visuals to Support an Audio Message

(Consider adapting this list to fit your own situation.)

A. Prepare the first script following Steps B through D of the guidelines in the previous checklist for audio only.

B. Read the script and note those points where visuals may help, support, or are needed to clarify the lesson. Use the following checklist:

	Yes	No
Is the audio message in an active voice, short, clear, and simple?	❏	○
If your audio message is long or complex, will visuals help keep students' attention and clarify the verbal message? (If YES, identify places where you will use either reinforcing or clarifying visuals.)	❏	○
Does your message deal with objects or things?	❏	○

If YES, consider the following requirements:

	Yes	No
• Are the students familiar with the objects or things in the lesson? (If your answer is NO, you *must* use visuals.)	❏	○
• Is it practical to show the students the real thing in the classroom? (If the answer is YES, you should use the real thing, and support the lesson, if needed, with still visuals.)	❏	○

• When necessary, will a visual show the students items
(size, color, and relationships) in comparison with
something they know?   ❑   ○

• Will the visuals show students objects from the
subjective viewpoint (as they will see the objects when
they are working with them)?   ❑   ○

C. Prepare visuals for the lesson. (See Chapter 9 "still visuals.")

	Yes	No

Have you checked the Chapter 3, "Developmental Testing"?   ❑   ○

Have you discussed your rough draft and rough visuals
with a subject matter expert to ensure accuracy?   ❑   ○

Have you considered your student's backgrounds when
planning the visuals (culture, expectations, etc.)?   ❑   ○

D. When rough visuals are complete, record the script on an audio cassette. Play it back while viewing the rough visuals. Check the following points. All answers should be YES.

	Yes	No

Are the visuals clearly and directly germane to the narration?   ❑   ○

Are the visuals legible?   ❑   ○

Does the speech sound natural (conversational)?   ❑   ○

Have you avoided "cute," shocking, unrelated, or too
elaborate visuals that may detract from the verbal message?   ❑   ○

Have you cut unnecessary narration or dialogue that could
be replaced by visuals?   ❑   ○

Have you had a subject matter expert check the accuracy
(or realism) of your message content and the correlation
of voice and pictures?   ❑   ○

Is the pacing correct for student learning?   ❑   ○

Is the verbal message clear?   ❑   ○

E. List the number of each visual down the left-hand column of the script giving a brief description or simple drawing of each. When using slides, start with slide number 1 as a black slide. (In some recent projectors this may be unneeded because of their blocking light on the screen when no slide is projected.)

F. Developmentally test the materials until the lessons work and the students learn. Check Chapter 3, "Developmental Testing.")

G. Were final scripts printed or typed according to the standard format at the end of this section? Check for the following characteristics. All answers should be YES.

	Yes	No
Are all cues marked properly?	❏	◯
Are all pages correctly numbered?	❏	◯
Are all pauses indicated?	❏	◯
Are all words to be stressed *underlined*?	❏	◯
Are sentences at the bottoms of pages complete (no sentence carried to next page)?	❏	◯
Did you give special instructions for music and sound effects at the beginning of the script?	❏	◯
Is pacing indicated for the director or narrator?	❏	◯
Is the script double-spaced and arranged in the correct format?	❏	◯

H. Have several copies made of the script for use by performers and production personnel. Order any necessary materials.

	Yes	No
Have you allowed enough lead time for preparation of all materials?	❏	◯
Have you checked the production suggestions outlined at the end of this section?	❏	◯
Have you considered possible requirement or advisability to copyright materials?	❏	◯
Have you determined the format? Have you determined how many copies of release tapes or cassettes to order?	❏	◯

✔✔✔
Checklist for Scripts Using Audio to Support a Visual Message

(*Consider adapting these checklists to fit your own situation.*)

A. Outline the message content in rough form stating what you wish the student to see. Consider students' backgrounds and cultures.

B. Prepare a rough storyboard of the lesson starting with visual notes or rough sketches. If you have not worked with the storyboard technique before, it might be wise to seek help at this stage.

C. Rough draft the script on the storyboard cards.[4]

D. Prepare a rough draft of the script. Check it for the following. All answers should be YES.

	Yes	No
Have you avoided complex words? (The students don't care how smart you are and may not have a dictionary handy. Besides, you should make it as easy as possible for the narrator to speak clearly.)	❏	○
Have you avoided jargon and technical terms when possible?	❏	○
Have you considered students' backgrounds and cultures?	❏	○
Have you considered what sound effects and background noises may be necessary or desirable to establish realism or moods?	❏	○
Have you had a representative from your target audience check for proper pacing?	❏	○
Have you had a subject matter expert check the lesson content to verify relevance and accuracy?	❏	○
Have you used active voice whenever possible?	❏	○
Have you used contractions whenever appropriate? (We normally use such statements as I'm, you're, haven't, and won't, instead of I am, you are, have not, and will not.)	❏	○

---

[4] J. Kemp gives a good description of working with storyboarding in *Planning and Producing Audio Visual Materials*. Refer to the Selected Readings at the end of this book.

Have you used ordinary spoken language; using a
colloquial style normally used in conversational speech? ❑ ○

If you *had* to use some technical term, did you spell the
word phonetically in parentheses so the narrator can
pronounce it? ❑ ○

Is the number of voices (characters) at a minimum for ease
of production and to reduce cost? ❑ ○

Is the rough draft either written or typed double-spaced;
leaving a wide left-hand margin for notes? ❑ ○

E. **Revise the script as necessary and record it yourself or have someone else record it on a cassette recorder.** Play it as you review the storyboard visuals. Check for the following. All answers should be YES.

	Yes	No
Did you avoid big words, jargon, and technical terms when possible?	❑	○
Did you include music or sound effects when necessary?	❑	○
Did you use conversational (colloquial) language?	❑	○
Does the narration discuss *only* what is in the visual and not wander to other topics or content?	❑	○
Does the narration or dialogue support and reinforce the messages in the visuals?	❑	○
Have you checked the script and planned visuals with a subject matter expert to ensure accuracy?	❑	○
When you *had* to use technical terms, did you spell them phonetically (in parentheses) for the narrator?	❑	○
Will the visuals convey the intended message?	❑	○

F. **Review Chapter 3 "Developmental Testing."**

G. **Produce the rough visuals and sequence the master set.**

H. **Developmentally test the material.** (See Chapter 3 "Developmental
Testing.")

I. **Edit the script and revise according to the results of testing.** Re-tape
the script yourself or have it re-narrated by others exactly as written.

J.   **Play back the tape.** Marking words to be stressed and note pauses on the script. Check for the following. All answers should be YES.

	Yes	No
Are pauses indicated?	❏	◯
Are the stressed words <u>underlined</u> or printed **bold** or *italics?*	❏	◯
Are the visuals properly synchronized with the narration or dialogue?	❏	◯
Have you checked materials again with a subject matter expert?	❏	◯
Have you indicated pacing instructions for the director or narrator?	❏	◯
Were necessary sound effects and music noted?	❏	◯

K.   **Prepare the final draft by first checking the visuals and marking cues for change of visuals on the script.** See the sample script at the end of this section. Before typing it, check the final draft for the following. All answers should be YES.

	Yes	No
Did you finish sentences at the bottoms of pages (no sentences carried over to the next page)?	❏	◯
Did you include instructions for pacing, sound effects, music, types of voices, and other production directions at the beginning of the script?	❏	◯
Did you mark the cues with an asterisk or large dot for changes of visuals at the *ends* of sentences? If a cue fell in the middle of a sentence, did you leave space for it to be noticed?	❏	◯
Did you number the pages correctly?	❏	◯
Have you left a wide left-hand margin to add descriptions of visuals?	❏	◯

L.   **Number and briefly describe visuals in the left-hand column to correspond with the script.** An example is shown in the sample script for tape and visuals that follows.

M.   **Have the script printed or typed.** Check for the following. All answers should be YES.

	Yes	No
Are all pauses indicated and noted with time?	❑	○
Are cues marked with asterisks or large dots in the proper places (ends of sentences or wide space in the middle of sentences)?	❑	○
Is the final copy double-spaced?	❑	○
Is the format like the one used in the sample?	❑	○

N. Have enough copies of the script prepared. Arrange for production of the master tape and duplicates with local production personnel.

	Yes	No
Have you allowed adequate lead time for production of both audio and visual materials?	❑	○
Have you determined the format? Have you determined how many copies of the tapes to order?	❑	○
Have you planned for packaging and labels?	❑	○
Have you planned for storage of masters and work copy?	❑	○
Have you reviewed the suggestions for producing master copies at the end of this section?	❑	○

O. At the session, consider the following.

	Yes	No
Have you brought two sets of your materials?	❑	○
Have you checked the sound quality?	❑	○
Have you set the volume and sound controls to an appropriate level? (Use someone at the opposite end of the room to verify the adjustments)	❑	○
Have you, prior to the start, cued the tape to the starting point (or the portion to be played, if different)?	❑	○

Sample Script for Audio Only

Supervising Work Operations

Script Instructions: Miles' voice on phone filter
                                         throughout script.
                                         Sound effect: Telephone ring.
                                         (Two rings only)

Narrator: If you have answered test problem number 1 / you are
                ready to listen to the *first* conversation associated with test
                problem number 2.

                (telephone ringing)

Hillman: Garage / Hillman.

Miles: Yeah Ray / Miles // Good thing Swenson's wife called in
                early to say he wouldn't be in / It gave me time to get rid of
                his workload before the fellas leave.

Hillman: Right Rog / I've got my load sheet here / What are the
                changes?

Miles: First // cancel Lynch's day off and give him all of
                Swenson's morning work orders.

Hillman: OK.

Miles: Then give the afternoon appointments to Johnson.

Hillman: Right.

Miles: That covers the repair orders Ray / I'll give out the *rest* of
                the orders as the men are free.

Hillman: OK Rog / After the guys leave / Lewis and I are going down
                to Hillwood // I'll call you about ten o'clock?

Miles: Talk to you later / So long.

Narrator: Now answer the question for test problem number 2.(pause
                20 seconds). The next conversation you hear is the one for
                test problem number 3.

                (telephone ringing-two rings)

/ means pause. // means pause a bit longer.

Sample Script for Tape and Visuals

TITLE
PLANNING AND PROGRAMMING

Visuals	*Voice*
1. Black slide (note: this slide is advanced before tape is started.)	Music up 3 seconds — (Fade at slide 4 to voice over.)*
2. Title: THE "WHY" & "HOW" OF PLANNING & PROGRAMMING	///* (4 seconds)
3. Company logo.	///* (3 seconds)
4. Young girl on chair with a questioning look on face. (music fades)	///* (3 seconds) *Narrator:* *Planning* is deciding in advance what needs to be done / and *
5. Young boy holding sheet of paper entitled "WHEN"	*Programming* is the scheduling of those plans.*
6. Young girl asking "WHY" PLAN & PROGRAM?	*Girl:* Well / That sounds good // But is it *really* all that necessary? // Most managers *know* what they have to do // *Why* should they waste their valuable time *planning* that time // Why not let them get on with doing all the things they have to do?*
7. Story title: THE CASE OF THE WELL INTENTIONED FARMER	*Narrator:* /// (3 seconds) Perhaps that can best be answered by a story I heard many years ago // It made sense to me and it may help explain the reason to *you* // The story goes like this.*
8. Farmer and wife in front of fireplace	A farmer told his wife "I'll plow the south 40 tomorrow."*

Cue tone indicated by *

Suggestions for Producing and Storing Audio Tapes

Producing Master Tapes

When arranging for production of an audio tape master, provide the following information to the production personnel:

- Type of master and speed at which it will be produced. When possible, all masters should be produced on high-quality professional equipment and high-quality tape.
- Number of channels to be used. When producing audio tapes with cue tones for visual displays, the master should be in a two-channel format. Record the voice on Channel A, and cue signals on Channel B. This provides flexibility in reproduction and editing.
- Select frequency of cue signals to be used. There are currently several standards inaudible cue signals used to control hardware devices. The AV equipment industry is tending to acceptance of ICIA standards of: 1 kHz for advance and 150 Hz for stop signals.
- List of music and sound effects required. Avoid using home recorded or pirated music. Select music and sound effects from a studio library or buy stock resources cleared for use.
- Number and types of talent voices (male and female) and arrangements to be made for hiring professional talent.
- Date master must be completed. Leave enough lead time for final editing and checking.
- Number of copies of script to be supplied to the production personnel. Allow one copy each for the sound recording technician, engineer, voice talent(s), the director, and for filing for future reference.

Storing Tapes

- Make clear arrangements for storing of master and work copy, including filing number and who will have access to materials.
- Label all tapes clearly. Label the counter number on the tape for easy access to the correct spot on the tape.
- Store all tapes on wood or plastic shelving to avoid demagnetizing.
- Rewind all tapes. Be sure tape is not loose in cassette before storing.
- Store tapes in plastic cases, or at least with some form of dust protection.

Ordering Duplicates for Release of Audio Programs

- Be sure to order production of a high-quality duplicate (protection) copy before any work is done.
- Specify the number of release copies and the format (either reel or cassette).
- Specify cue tones (if needed) to be audible or inaudible.
- Specify the date you will need copies.
- Specify label information.

CHAPTER 8

Guidelines for Visuals

SIGHT IS BY FAR THE MOST POWERFUL OF THE SENSES. WE perceive the world around us based largely on what we see. Research supports this flat statement, although the relative contribution of sight in comparison with the other senses varies according to many circumstances. Yet, in this discussion we accept as fact that most people depend upon sight as their primary source of information.

People keep their visual sense occupied during most waking hours. They continually watch for information, cues, alarms, and items of interest. This primacy of sight has important implications for teaching and learning. You must consider the visual channel, without fail, when planning training strategy and in developing course materials. Studies conducted by the Wharton School's Applied Research Center and the University of Minnesota conclude that visual aids do increase the effectiveness of presentations. According to the University of Minnesota study visuals increase retention by 10 percent when added to an oral presentation. They also make it up to 43 percent more persuasive.[1] If the course developer doesn't plan to use the visual sense, something or someone else will.

There is always the exception. An exceptional person—an orator, perhaps—can catch and maintain audience attention for long periods of time. These rare people have a special talent for generating visual imagery in the minds of their audiences. But, even the "golden-tongued" Greek orator

---

[1]Studies examined the impact of overhead projection and computer-generated visuals on presentations and business meetings. See Johnson, V. Picture Perfect Presentations. *Training and Development Journal*, May 1989.

might find it difficult to keep an audience attentive when lecturing on the history of the drill press without some visual help.[2]

Think of your experiences listening to lecturers who talked *at* you, failing to command your visual sense. When a live lecturer, or a voice on an audiotape, bombards the sense of *hearing only,* you—or any audience— will become distracted. Students avoid such punishment. They sleep (turning off the senses of sight and sound) or daydream (allowing irrelevant images, real or imaginary, to occupy the mind).

The visual sense is highly discriminating, constantly analyzing visual events to accept or reject new information based upon what we already know. We may summarily reject any visual image that conflicts with our own real world. This obviously presents a barrier to learning.

Sight is sensitive to punishment. We are unwilling to tolerate any strain, including illegible or ambiguous visual images or sudden and extreme changes in illumination. We are also turned off by shocking, culturally inappropriate, or boring visual displays. This also applies to materials in books and other forms of print. Although these are not of *principal* concern here, we use visuals continually in all kinds of printed matter. The characteristics of printed type displays and page layouts can be motivational and effective in communicating to students. When done poorly, they may confuse, bore, or punish.

Therefore, be alert to the problems that may arise because of mistreating the sense of sight. It will always be to the detriment of student learning in any instructional situation. ■

Some Rules of Thumb for Visuals

Here, then, are some rules of thumb to consider when you are designing visuals for instruction. Remember, these are neither laws nor absolutes, but reminders for you. As you conduct developmental testing of your program, watch for causes of failures because you did not follow one or more of these guidelines.

Visuals used simultaneously with audio materials must be directly connected to the audio content.

If the audio presentation carries the principal weight of the content, visuals can inhibit learning if:

- they conflict with what is presented verbally,
- they are trivial visuals; for example: a visual used simply to have something on the screen; or a simple, instantly grasped visual left on the screen while the verbal presentation continues on and on, beyond the content of the visual,

---

[2]Remember Demosthenes, the great Greek orator that, according to legend, practiced by speaking with pebbles in his mouth?

- they are flashy, arty visuals presented to impress or challenge, but cause the student to be diverted to irrelevant thoughts or emotional reactions.

Avoid excessive redundancy between visual and audio components.

- If you display words visually, provide the viewers time to read them before you comment or rephrase the projected message.
- If the print on the screen is brief, control group reading by repeating the printed words exactly. Reserve identical or parroted visual and audio verbiage for very brief or important messages. Consider the procedure the same as underlining or highlighting.

Visual displays should not be punishing.

- Projected visuals must be legible to reduce student discomfort and frustration. Legibility involves both clarity and brightness of images.
- Use few fonts and sizes. A good guideline is not more than two fonts and three sizes.
- Use appropriate type size. For example, at least 18 point ($\frac{1}{4}$inch) for overhead projection. (Although we still see it all too often, typewriting is *obviously* too small.)

Visuals should not be ambiguous, which means:

- Graphics should be as simple and bold as possible.
- As early in the lesson as possible, display unfamiliar objects in relation to familiar objects to provide information about size and shape
- Visuals should not be busy or cluttered, to be sure that the intended communication is clear to the viewers.
- Use key words, not entire sentences.

Visuals should not be distasteful to students or to any audience.

- Since we assume that we want to encourage people to change their behavior in desirable ways, we don't want to alienate them. Quite the opposite, we want to encourage them and attract them to the subject. Avoid, or at least use with great care, display of scenes that some students find either morally or emotionally shocking. Check the results. You may have objectives that you believe require jolting your audience; in such cases you may have serious problems. Use humor with care and judgment, and test the results *before* including it in your material. Check your student analysis carefully regarding age, sex, cultural background, etc., before planning to have an impact on their emotions. You won't regret it.
- We consider motion visuals (film and video) effective media for producing attitudinal changes. Because they are also costly, we may deeply regret errors in judgment in their use. One of many factors that we must bear in mind when planning scripts is to account for the audience's attention span. The "talking-face" is not, in itself, bad if

the face is interesting. But, you must to change views periodically to accommodate the students' natural tendency to shift their attention.

Visuals representing on-the-job situations must be acceptably realistic.

All instructional situations should:

- accurately reflect company or institutional policies and practices in such matters as dress, demeanor, work and safety rules, and models of performance;
- show views of persons using tools, instruments, and control equipment, for example, from the viewpoint of the person using them on the job. Work environments and situations should, to the greatest degree possible, represent the real world. This does not mean that lesson materials and the learning environment must be carbon copies to effect desired learning. But, we should provide conditions representing typical factors that control performance of personnel.

Usually, we design projected visual materials for display in a horizontal format.

- The lower part of viewing screens in many classrooms is difficult to see from the back rows of seats. To overcome this problem, design visuals in horizontal format to keep the bottom of the image as high as possible.
- The entertainment media has conditioned students to expect horizontal visuals. Avoid including an occasional vertical format in a series of horizontal visuals—it can be distracting.
- Motion visuals, both film in all sizes and video, have a horizontal format. The proportions are rarely altered, except wide-screen pictures or multi-screen slide presentations.

Avoid references to time and dates, unless applicable to content.

- This avoids problems such as students daydreaming about where they were then, signs of antiquated material, or conflicts with visual time setting.

Color, unless needed for content, usually adds very little to learning.

- Nevertheless, people in our society today are increasingly accustomed to color. Black and white presentation may receive less attention.
- The addition of color in some media such as print can result in increased cost. Consider avoiding needless expense.

Placement and color of information on visuals should be consistent.

- For example, titles, content, and instructions should appear consistently in the same place and color as other visuals. This decreases

frustration and time needed for students to extract important information.
- Choice of type style can be as important as choosing the color.
- Consider color fidelity. Currently, many training people are becoming acquainted with the Pantone® standard colors. Specification of these shades ensures that a final color will be the one expected.
- The palette of colors used in different visuals is not constant. For example, a smaller palette of colors will ordinarily be used for overhead transparencies than slides.

Background and foreground colors should contrast but be pleasing to the eyes.

- Some color combinations are very distracting and sometimes may hurt the eyes. Obviously, pure blue on black is a bad choice. High contrast between the colors adds to legibility. Avoid combinations of very light shades or colors that complement each other closely. For example, dark blue background with white lettering is good. Red on green is poor.
- Be very careful in planning multiple background colors. They can have unexpected effects. As the foreground color crosses the background it may appear to recede and project depending on the particular background. A straight line may appear thicker or thinner for the same reason.

Visuals should be as natural and normal as possible.

- Just as too polite or unnatural conversations may appear fake or even comical to students, the body language of persons in visuals should be relaxed but appropriate.

Check all visuals for careless and unthinking errors.

- Check for typographical, grammatical, or spelling errors.
- Check for sexist, racist, or culturally inappropriate language.
- Check for appropriate use of colors, symbols, equations.

Use visuals appropriately. Use them to:

- draw comparisons,
- emphasize key points,
- explain concepts,
- present statistics or other data in an understandable way,
- show items to large or small to see clearly otherwise,
- show relationships, or
- state rules or formulas.

Guidelines for Legibility for All Projected Visuals Except Video[3]

To determine the size of the projected image in relation to the viewing distance (called aspect ratio), use the "6W" formula. All projected visuals—excluding video—are based on the premise that 1 foot of screen width is required for each 6 feet of viewing distance from the screen. To state this another way, the audience should be no further away than six times the width of the projected image.

Figure 8.1
The 6W Formula

Formula for
Projected Visuals—Excluding Video

6W

1 foot of screen width is required for each
6 feet of viewing distance from the screen.

This formula determines the proper screen-size-to-room-length ratio in the design of auditoriums, theaters, and classrooms. For our purposes we will assume viewing screens or projection walls of adequate size exist in instructional areas.

Test preliminary artwork or graphics for screen projection *before* they are put on film. Here is the way to make the test:

1. Measure in inches[4] the width of the artwork or lettering display for projection.
2. Divide your answer by 2.
3. Hold the artwork or display that many feet away from a viewer and ask the viewer to read the content or to describe the image. If the viewer is successful, your design is adequate for projection.

For Example: Your artwork is 10 *inches* wide, divide it by 2 = 5 *inches*. In this case 5 *feet*. is the distance from which the viewer should read the display. [5]

---

[3]Guidelines for video will be covered later in this chapter.
[4]The 6W formula is not specific to *inches*. Any constant measure will work. If using the metric system, you can use whole meters or any convenient measure.
[5]When using the metric system, multiply the total width of the artwork by 6 and hold it that distance from the viewer.

Caution: Do not read or test the visual yourself. Your memory may help you read things that are not truly clear. Pick someone with normal vision to make the test. Preferably, that person should be completely unfamiliar with the work.

Figure 8.2
Application of the 6W Formula

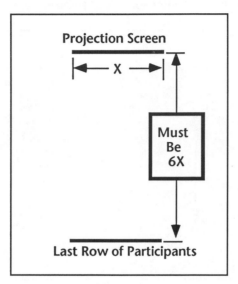

Image clarity and brightness. Obviously, the clarity and sharpness of the original artwork or graphic display affects the quality of the reproduced product—whether on film, in print, or on a video screen. No amount of camera magic can turn a poor quality image into a good one. Simply put, the idea is—garbage in . . . garbage out. One major contributor to unclear, distorted, or even weak visuals is *generation loss,* that is, the degradation of image by duplication. The original quality decreases in each succeeding generation. When converting artwork or graphics for projection, bear in mind the following:

- Avoid using art or graphics that have obvious flaws. If you think a small smudge or erasure mark won't matter, remember it will be much more obvious when enlarged on a screen.
- When possible, use original artwork or graphics, or slides, to make a master copy, or for short runs, use the original for making each copy.
- If the original artwork is not available, use a first mastercopy, master slides, film internegative, or filmstrip master for duplicating. Avoid using release prints or other late generation products for duplicating.
- When working with slides mounted in glass, or slides for rear projection, inform your photographic personnel or laboratory. Often, they can compensate for these conditions and adjust to provide best image brightness.

- If you do not know the location where your visuals will be used, make them to be legible 50 feet away.

Suggested seating for screen legibility is shown in Figure 8.3. Lens focal length in relation to screen width and projection distance is shown in Figure 8.4.

Figure 8.3
Suggested Classroom Seating for Screen Legibility

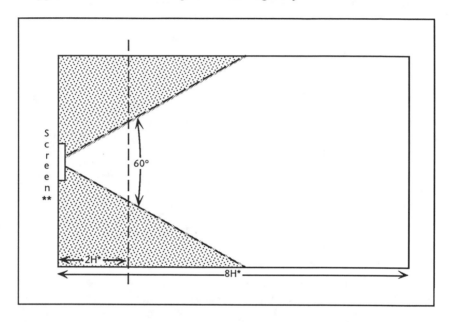

*For maximum legibility, students should be seated within the white area. Students should *not* be seated closer to the screen than two times, nor further than eight times, the *height* of the screen.

**The bottom of the screen should be *at least* four feet above the floor to avoid obstructing the viewing of the students at the back of the room. When a room is arranged for theater-style seating, aisles should be placed at the sides and back of the room to maximize viewing area.

A proper sized screen must be provided to ensure 6W legibility standard, and one foot of screen *width* must be allowed for each six feet of viewing distance from the screen. For example, a room 25 feet long requires a 50 inch screen, a room 30 feet long requires a 60 inch screen, etc.

(Reprinted by permission of the International Communications Industry Association from the *Audio-Visual Equipment Directory*.)

Figure 8.4
Lens Focal Length in Relation to:
Screen Width and Projection Distance *

Overhead Projection

Screen Width (inches)

Lens	50	60	70	84	96
3"	5.5	6.4	7.3	8.6	9.7
4"	6.3	7.3	8.4	9.8	11.1
5"	6.5	7.6	8.7	10.3	11.6
6"	7.0	8.2	9.4	11.1	12.5
7"	8.1	9.5	10.8	12.7	14.4

16mm Motion Pictures

Screen Width (inches)

Lens	40	50	60	70	84	96
$\frac{1}{2}$"	4.5	5.7	6.7	7.8	9.3	10.6
1"	8.9	11.1	13.3	15.5	18.6	21.2
$1\frac{1}{2}$"	13.4	16.7	20.0	23.7	27.9	31.8
2"	17.9	22.3	26.7	31.0	37.2	42.4
$2\frac{1}{2}$"	22.3	27.8	33.3	38.8	46.5	53.0

35mm Single Frame Filmstrips

Screen Width (inches)

Lens	40	50	60	70	84	96
3"	11.8	14.6	17.5	20.3	24.2	27.6
4"	15.7	19.5	23.3	27.0	32.3	36.8
5"	19.7	24.4	29.1	33.8	40.4	46.0
6"	23.6	29.3	34.9	40.6	48.5	55.2
7"	27.5	34.1	40.7	47.3	56.5	64.4

*The lenses listed are selective and do *not* include all the various sizes available. Because of lens manufacturing tolerances, projection distances shown may vary 6" either way.

(Reprinted by permission of the International Communications Industry Association from the *Audio-Visual Equipment Directory*.)

Large Screen Data/Graphics Projection Systems[6]

How to Prepare Your Facility

Today, large screen data/graphics video projection systems are an accepted business tool in many companies and organizations. Projection systems are used worldwide for a wide variety of purposes. Uses include: to train employees, handle customer and sales support, market product at trade shows, and present company financial results to the board of directors. As important a task as choosing the right projection system for your needs is preparing your facility for its arrival. Evaluation and choice of room decor and the necessary components, such as screens, cables, and interface, are important to the performance of the projection system. Carefully planning for a projection system will benefit in its best performance and user satisfaction.

Portable or Fixed Installation

Most color data/graphics and video projection systems are based on a CRT design with three lenses. With three lens systems, colors from separate red, green, and blue CRTs must converge or align on the screen several feet away. An important consideration for organizations that will use their projection system in different locations or move them from room to room is the ease of set-up and convergence. There are now projection systems available with an automatic convergence feature that will accurately align the image in minutes via the infrared remote control. This feature is also beneficial to fixed installation for quick alignments when changing input sources to ensure your image is clear and crisp.

When having a projector permanently installed, carefully follow the manufacturer's instruction for distance from the screen and secure mounting to ensure safe and proper operation.

Projection Room Treatment

When planning on where to use your projection system, avoid light colored or reflective wall, ceiling, and floor treatments. Use muted colors such as grays, dark roses, or browns. Avoid white, silver, reflective, or bright colored treatments. They will reflect light, causing the screen to lose contrast or appear "washed out."

Lighting

Proper lighting control in the projection room is another essential factor for the satisfactory performance of the projection system. The following are guidelines to reducing ambient light:

- Avoid direct light reflection on screen surfaces.
- Fluorescent lights typically disperse light over a wide cone—usually causing the image to wash out. You can reduce or virtually eliminate wash out by installing rheostat (dimmer) controls. They can reduce

---

[6]Large screen data/graphics projection system information adapted from information prepared by Tom Sutherland, Product Manager, Electrohome Limited, Kitchener, Ontario.

light and lens filter panels to control dispersion of light downward from the fixture.

- Recess incandescent lighting and control it with a rheostat .
- High intensity spot fixtures on rheostats similar to those in airline cabins over work areas are the best to concentrate light and avoid washing out the screen image.
- Take care to avoid external light from windows or doors reflecting on the screen surface. Use blackout window shades or drapes to control external light.

Screens

The choice of the proper screen type is critical to ensuring optimal projected display performance. If you are considering using the glass beaded screen used for 35mm slides and the overhead projectors—don't. We do not recommend them for video projection. The next decision is front or rear screen projection.

Front. If you are setting up for front projection in your facility you have a choice of rigid curved or flat screens. Curved screens usually have a high gain (8 to 15) and provide excellent resistance to ambient room light but limit the horizontal and vertical viewing angles. These are best used for portable applications or rooms where lighting cannot be controlled.

Standard matte white screens are the most common type of screen offering the widest viewing angle, and are ideally suited for 35mm slide and overhead transparency projection, and video projection. This type of screen is most affected by ambient room lights. So, lighting control is important. Some manufacturers of screens now offer a flat screen material with a gain of 2.2 for increased brightness.[7]

Flat screens are available in many different styles. These include manual or electric roll down, snap frame, rigid, or material applied directly to the wall.

Rear. Installing your projector for a rear screen calls for the construction of a dedicated projection room where the projector is installed. The image can be projected directly at the screen. Or, if limited by space, the image can be "folded" in one or two first surface mirrors to reduce the space required.

Rear screens are most resistant to ambient light and are available in rigid or flexible membrane material. Lenticular rigid screens are also available and offer a high gain image (brighter). Rear screens offer a less cluttered look but require more preparation. For maximum image contrast on rear screens, it is important that the projection room be completely dark with no light leaks. The walls and support structure should be painted flat black to eliminate light reflections.

Some projection systems feature microprocessor control of all major functions including digital zone convergence through an infrared keypad to simplify set up for rear screen applications.

---

[7]For comparison, white bond paper has a gain of 1.

An alternative to the rear projection room is a "Retro Box" type projection enclosure. This Retro Box combines a projector with a high gain lenticular screen (typically 67 inch [1.68 meters] diagonal) installed on casters. This provides a rear screen room without costly construction and offers portability.

Human Factor Considerations

In addition to the guidelines above, adequate consideration of human factors is essential for the effective use of large screen projection.

Resolving Capabilities of the Human Eye. Character (alphanumeric) height should be no more than 1/150 of the distance from the viewer(s) (i.e., viewers seated 20 feet from the screen—minimum character height 1.6 inches [4 centimeters]).

Information Density. Ideally, there should be no more than 15 lines per display height and 40 columns per display width (typical of 35mm and overhead transparency presentations).

Alphanumeric Legibility. Alphanumerics are most easily read for black on white displays when the ratio of character stroke width to height is about 1:6 to 1:8 (reverse video). For white on black displays, a somewhat higher 1:10 is acceptable. Ideally the character width should be at least $\frac{2}{3}$ of the height.

Color Graphics. Incorrect choice of foreground and background colors will diminish readability. For example, green or white text on a black background is generally harder to read than black on white. Any dark color on a black background is not recommended.

Normally, the eye cannot focus on all visible color wavelengths simultaneously and must slightly change focus for each color. Blue tends to be the hardest and appears fuzzy and out of focus. Many terminals and projection interfaces provide "enhanced blue" by adding green to increase readability.

Interfacing

When the room is complete and the projector installed, it must be connected to the computer terminal, PC, VCR, or other video signals. These sources produce a myriad of signals and need an interface to convert the information for use by the projector. In more elaborate systems where several sources or projectors are used, they may be connected with a complex switcher signal.

Interfaces and switchers designed for most video sources are available from some manufacturers of large screen data/graphics projectors. A competent dealer will help you in designing a system for your needs.

Companies and organizations looking for a large screen data/graphics projection system have many choices. Take time and care to choose a product that provides the features and flexibility to meet your needs now and in the future. Local dealer support is also important to provide installation advice and assistance, set up, and training.

Figure 8.5
Visual Formats
Projected Visuals and Computer Displays

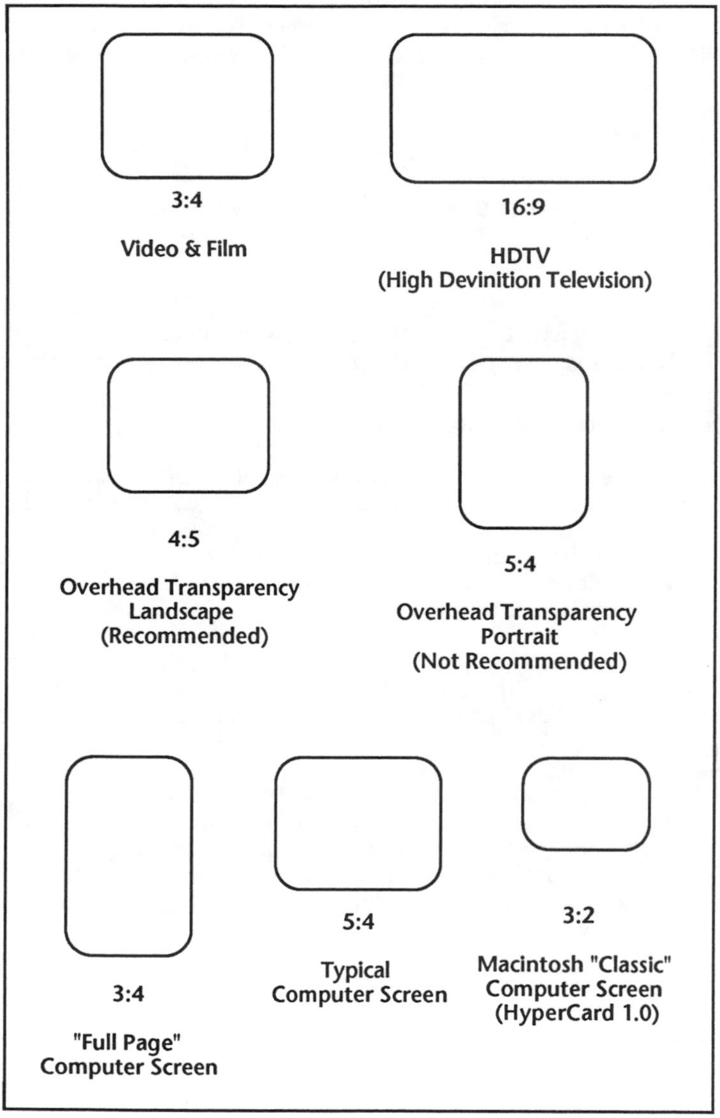

3:4

Video & Film

16:9

HDTV
(High Devinition Television)

4:5

Overhead Transparency
Landscape
(Recommended)

5:4

Overhead Transparency
Portrait
(Not Recommended)

3:4

"Full Page"
Computer Screen

5:4

Typical
Computer Screen

3:2

Macintosh "Classic"
Computer Screen
(HyperCard 1.0)

Guidelines for Legibility of Video Materials

To determine the size of the projected image in relation to the viewing distance, use the 12W formula. For television, the ratio of screen width to viewing distance is different from that for other projected visuals. To test for legibility of visuals for use on video displays follow this procedure:[8]

Figure 8.6
The 12W Formula

Formula for Video Display Visuals

12W

**Must be legible to a viewer located
12 inches (use 1 foot) distant from the visual for each
1 inch of screen width.**

---

1. Measure the width of the artwork or graphic display *in inches.*[9]
2. Hold the artwork or graphic as many *feet* away from the person or persons chosen to test your visuals as the number of inches measured for the art or graphic. If the materials can be read or explained by the viewers, they should be legible when viewed as television images on a well-adjusted receiver.

For example: The original artwork or graphic display measures 12 *inches* wide (including the necessary margins); the evaluators will view the materials from 12 *feet*. Remember, don't trust yourself as a test subject.

Image clarity and brightness.
- Avoid bright, shiny surfaces that can create glare when lighted.
- As with other media, quality reproduction is possible by duplicating from master tape to the same size or smaller tape. Avoid, if you can, duplication to tape wider than the original.
- When transferring between film and video, you can usually get the best quality by going from film to video, not from video to film (Kinescope). There are, however, special processes that will produce satisfactory results under the opposite conditions, but they are costly.
- Remember conversion of video to videodisc is one generation. A barely adequate videotape image will blur when transferred to videodisc.

---

[8] When using the metric system, multiply measurements by 12 for viewing distance.

[9] The 12W formula is not specific to *inches.* Any constant measure will work. If using the metric system, you can use centimeters or any convenient measure.

• Store master tapes in a cool, safe location, preferably on wood or plastic shelves, and racked in a vertical position. See audiotape starage suggestions in Chapter 7.

Figure 8.7
Application of the 12W Formula

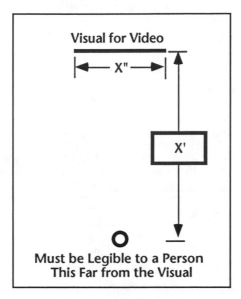

When working with artwork, graphics, and photographs for display in black and white video, you must consider the color spectrum. For example, some shades of red and green project as similar shades of gray. Learn to use a gray scale. Test all artwork with color content on a television system before making finished copy. When planning black and white video productions it is helpful to: use black and white and shades of gray for artwork and graphics. If you must use a colored visual, test it on a portable video unit before final showing. Unless you have broad experience, it is best to check *all* visuals on a system with a receiver similar to the one viewers use under normal conditions for them. Don't use a finely tuned high-resolution monitor to test visuals.

Guidelines for Visual Formats

You must understand visual formats to avoid problems: Although you should design all projected visuals in horizontal format, the ratio of height to width is not the same for all media. This fact can present problems when you will produce the same visuals with different media. For example, 35mm slide images are 2 units high by 3 units wide while 16mm film images are 3 units high by 4 units wide. As another example, the format of 35mm slides with a 2:3 ratio is different from the 3:4 television format, (3 units high by 4 units wide). A variety of formats are shown in Figure 8.5.

Legibility standards for television are different from those for projected media (see the 6W and 12W formulas). Since we often use visuals originally made for other media for television productions, we should foresee and avoid the problems that can arise at the outset of production planning. For example, 35mm slides designed for projection according to the 6W formula probably should be redone for satisfactory presentation on television.

A Note in Summary

These rules are ordinarily applicable to all visual materials. There are situations that call for "bending "the rules to achieve a desired effect. These happen particularly in the motion-visual field, and in attempts to make training materials for affective-attitudinal objectives. You must cope with each situation on an individual basis. Unfortunately, there are no cookbook recipes that will guarantee success under all conditions, and we often have to compromise. Check your student analysis, test, revise, and test; revise again, and test again.

When you are developing all types of media for instruction, the more time spent on preproduction planning, and the more revising and editing of rough-draft materials during developmental testing, the greater the chance for success. This is true especially for expensive and sophisticated media. Without adequate planning, even the most sophisticated medium available will not make poor lesson material good. In fact, the reverse effect will often result, and poor material will appear to be even worse than it is.

CHAPTER 9

Still Visuals

"WE HAVE THE VERY LATEST IN INSTRUCTIONAL SUPPORT equipment." That phrase was issued by an official in a large bank in the capital city of an Asian country recently. We were eager to see what device he meant. When it turned out to be an overhead projector it was not altogether a surprise or disappointment. Overhead and 35mm slide projection are the workhorses of instructional media. They got their popularity in the old fashioned way . . . they earned it!

Who among us has never used these devices to make our instruction better? They have earned our trust by "coming through" when we needed them. We have used the 35mm projector when we have slides that illustrate our topic. But the overhead projector is our servant. We are able to make transparencies that add a professional image to presentations—at a cost that doesn't cause hesitation even when we will only use them once. The ease of preparation, simplicity of use, economy, and effectiveness of overhead projection makes it more than a sentimental favorite. ■

Overhead Transparencies

The overhead projector is a perfect example of an instructional aid. It was designed for operation by an instructor at the front of a class or audience. As an aid, the medium is flexible, convenient to use, and when well-used, of great benefit to both the instructor and the students.

The overhead projector is possibly the only widely used piece of instructional equipment developed especially for the education field. Others were adopted from consumer or commercial entertainment products. It is useful for groups of any size. However, industry developed the overhead projector especially to project still visual images for many students assembled at one location. Several major advantages of overhead projection explain its increasing use at all levels of education and for many instructional situations: The instructor can face students in a lighted room and control the sequence of visual displays during a presentation. Elements in a visual can be pointed out; and various techniques permit manipulation of the elements to improve the visual communication.

Preparation of artwork for overhead projection is simple. Many instructors prepare their own transparencies, either manually or with mechanical lettering and drawing techniques, or on a computer, and with several available methods for making final transparencies. We can convert drawings made on paper into transparencies on transparent plastic materials by several processes: heat, electrostatic, or diazo. Each of these methods has advantages, but all produce satisfactory images in black and white or in colors.

When using overhead projectors, it is best to project the image on a screen tilted forward at the top. This will eliminate image distortion called the "keystone effect." There are times, however, when it may be necessary to project the image on a flat white wall and still have acceptable results. Viewing area, audience size, and the quality and content of the overhead visuals are all important considerations in choosing projected image size. Judging the legibility characteristics of a transparency by viewing it at handheld distance, instead of by projection, can be misleading in determining whether the image is appropriately designed for the audience. Review, if you need to, the material on viewing standards in Chapter 8, "Rules of Thumb for Visuals."

Despite the many advantages of overhead projection, often instructors and program developers want to use more sophisticated and costly media devices for instructional aids. Such devices can be effective. But, in situations when an instructor is the principal transmitter of lesson content, the overhead projector is far more effective. It is also dramatically less expensive than the attractive, but complex and costly, alternatives.

In this section, as in the others on various media, we present guidelines for course developers and instructors in selecting, planning, and producing overhead transparencies for specific purposes during instruction. Topics include: the class of the medium, characteristics, examples of applications, advantages and disadvantages, and checklists of considerations to help you plan the production and use of overhead projection transparencies.

Relating Overhead Transparencies to Instructional Objectives

Class of media: Instructional aid.

Characteristics: Still visual (limited capability for displaying or simulating motion).

Application to types of learning:

Cognitive objectives. Overhead transparencies can be used to teach recognition of, and discrimination among, relevant visual elements. Overhead projection visuals can:

- Teach recognition of unfamiliar objects by displaying to students visual representations—symbols, pictures, drawings, and forms.
- Teach discrimination skills by comparing and contrasting pictured objects, whether shown simultaneously or sequentially. By use of a pointer, directly on the transparency, critical differences among objects can be quickly and accurately shown on the screen.
- Enhance teaching of discrimination skills by exaggerating differences in objects that may otherwise be overlooked. This can be done using line drawings, enlargements, and color coding.
- Show such relationships as interaction of objects in motion, and changes in position by use of simple overlays of translucent, colored materials, or by polarized materials. (Actions are, for example, parts moving in a pump, pistons in an engine, or the flow of fluids.)
- Show principles of operation of objects that normally have working parts enclosed and invisible to observation.

They are also useful to teach rules, principles, or concepts. When used or these purposes, overhead projection can:

- Reinforce the comments of an instructor with visual representations of numerical values—percentages, amounts, or ratios—by such graphics as charts, diagrams, and scales.
- Display words or phrases to be stressed, or present an outline of points in coordination with the instructor's presentation. Clarify and reinforce the instructor's commentary by displaying elements of the lesson content.
- Provide visual cues for the instructor to follow in presenting lesson material—a visual outline that helps both instructor and students, and reduces the need for written script or stacks of notes.

Psychomotor objectives. Limited application. Used to show positions of things or people in motion before instructor demonstrations or student practice. For example, body positions for lifting heavy weights from the floor, in safety training.

Affective objectives.   Generally does not apply.

Advantages and Disadvantages of Overhead Projection (Transparencies)

Advantages:

+ Allows freedom for instructor to edit, sequence, and revise instructional material.
+ Allows instructors to face an audience in a lighted room to permit interpersonal exchange and to encourage questions and discussion.
+ Permits instructors to write on a transparency, use a pointer, or edit items during projection.
+ Provides opportunity for simple visuals in black line or in colors, or in combination.
+ Permits sequential disclosure of information by adding to an initial base visual using overlays, thus building the display.
+ Permits local production of transparencies by the instructor or semiskilled staff.
+ Permits inexpensive production of visual materials and when small quantities are needed for distribution, simple and economical distribution.
+ Permits display of transparent or translucent materials on the stage of the projector and enlargements for viewing on the projection screen.
+ Permits simulating motion (within limits) by translucent plastic cut-outs. Also, simulates by a more sophisticated and costly process of using polarized plastic sheets and a hand- or motor-driven polarized rotor in front of the projector lens.
+ Offers a variety of portable and permanent projectors with various lenses for adjusting picture size to projector-screen distance requirements.
+ Permits adaptation of transparency masters, by plan, for paper prints for use as handouts or for evaluation purposes.
+ Can display contents of a computer screen by using liquid crystal display devices. This may be especially useful if teaching computer skills or using computer graphics to support instruction.
+ The high level of portability makes the overhead projector popular. All can be carried with relative ease. Especially designed portable models are even more so.
+ The overhead projector is available at most business locations. Hotels that do not specialize in conferences often have one. Hotels often provide them without charge.
+ The copy machine permits the simple creation of high quality transparencies (if the machine is well adjusted and the master designed suitably).
+ Use of overheads with water soluble pens allows easy erasure of information
+ Overheads make it easy to refer to specific overheads for reference or review.

Disadvantages:

- Limited to use as an instructional aid by an instructor or by students for their presentations. Seldom used as an instructional medium.
- Widespread distribution of transparencies individually or in sets may be less convenient than the more compact slides or filmstrips, for example.
- Multicolored, commercially, or locally produced transparencies may be more expensive then 35mm slides.
- When using overhead projection, the flash of unfiltered white light on the screen while changing transparencies may cause mild distraction. (Accepted practice is to turn the projector off when changing transparencies.)
- Designed for front screen projection, the overhead is seldom used for rear screen projection, except in unusual circumstances.
- Overhead transparency formats may be transferred to 35mm slides or made into printed paper handouts. If so, we must give special attention to such matters as scale, proportions, lettering size, and border spaces around the pictorial image.
- Sometimes needs a special tilted screen to avoid extreme keystone effect that distorts the visual image. (Newer machines with variable focal length help prevent the keystone problem.)
- If you need many visuals, the size makes them cumbersome to work with or bulky for transporting.
- The simple creation of transparencies by anyone on copy machines permits making very "unprofessional" low quality transparencies easily. The copy machine may not be properly adjusted or the master not suitably designed.
- Space and location for front projection may be inconvenient for room set up.
- Multiple overheads may become a burden to instructor and cause confusion during presentation especially if instructor is spontaneously using them out of sequence.
- For best illumination and readability dimmed lights are needed. This may interfere with student note-taking or printed material reference.

✔✔✔

Checklist of Considerations for Selecting and Developing Transparencies for Instruction

(Consider adapting these lists to fit your own situation)

How To Use the Checklists

The following material is divided into five segments, listed in purposeful order, and is for use *after* the initial decision to use overhead projection has been reached. The lists and activities are mind-joggers to help you plan effectively for the production and use of your visual materials.

Segment A lists questions designed to help you confirm or reevaluate your decision to use overhead projection. Segments B through D will help you plan the content of the instruction you wish to visualize. Segment E is to help you in ordering the production of visual materials. (It also provides some suggestions for presentation techniques.)

A. Confirm or reevaluate your decision to use overhead projection techniques in the lesson.

	Yes	No
Is the lesson material to be presented by an instructor? (If the answer is NO you should not use this medium.)	❏	◯
Will *exact* reproduction of the *visual and oral* information be needed each time the lesson is presented? (If *exact* reproduction is called for, you should NOT use this medium; consider, for example, slide-tape techniques instead.)	❏	◯
Is the verbal message to be presented by the instructor long and complex, suggesting that visuals could help the audience concentrate and fix its attention on an orderly progression of ideas? (If NO, consider having the instructor ecture using a few simple handouts.)	❏	◯
Is it easier for students to learn what you want them to by showing them visual representations of objects or things as they are discussed?	❏	◯
Are there parts of the verbal message that can better be expressed visually or with visual support material than by words alone? ("One picture is worth a thousand words.")	❏	◯
Are there parts of the verbal message that need to be stressed by repeating them visually, or are there points to stress through a progressive (or sequential?) build up of images?	❏	◯

B. On separate sheets, make notes that describe the overhead transparency visuals needed. If a lesson outline or script has been developed, indicate on it the locations and code numbers of the visuals planned. (A good way to number is to make your system refer to the page of the outline or script, and to use a code representing the type of medium. Also, if more than one visual is listed on a page, provide sequence numbers. Here is one way to do it. The visual number is indicated: T-9-B, where T = Transparency, 9 = page 9, and B = the second visual used. Such a system helps keep visuals in order, and simplifies your numbering problem when you drop or add visuals.)

C. Review the sequence of learning points in the content to determine whether the contents should be re-sequenced. Re-sequence either to improve the logical appeal of the presentation or to better use the visuals. Plan transitions between visuals, and introductions to visuals, to be as smooth as possible to avoid distractions.

D. Make a sketch of each visual with pencil on 8 $\frac{1}{2}$ by 11 paper. Check the following questions. All answers should be YES.

	Yes	No
Have you reviewed the section on developmental testing in this book?	❏	○
If the lesson deals with objects or things, have you considered whether the students are familiar with them?	❏	○
If student are unfamiliar with the objects or things, have you provided visuals that show perspective and size scale, and in different views so students will recognize the items later in training or on the job?	❏	○
If objects to be shown are tools or equipment that students will use on the job, did you show them over-the-shoulder views as they will see them on the job?	❏	○
Have you reviewed the rules of thumb for visuals in this book to check points related to this project?	❏	○
Have you used a horizontal format?	❏	○
Are the graphics as simple as possible, yet clearly communicate your ideas?	❏	○
Did you check to determine if basic transparencies are already available for use in this lesson?	❏	○
Have you planned to use overlays and masks when appropriate to develop cut-away images, progressive disclosure, and identification symbols or words?	❏	○
Did you check the visuals for accuracy?	❏	○
Did you check for legibility of the visual? (Check again the 6W formula in Chapter 8 and suggestions for lettering in the of rules of thumb section.)	❏	○
Have you avoided overloading the visual with too many details?	❏	○

Did you avoid a busy, cluttered design? ❑ ◯

Are all the visuals really necessary? Does each one
fulfill a planned and useful function in the lesson? ❑ ◯

Have you resisted using too many visuals in the total
lesson, since changing visuals often and too rapidly can
become distracting both to students and instructor? ❑ ◯

Is the visual for the audience, not solely for the instructor?
(Notes for the instructor should be written on the paper
frame of the transparency, and not on the projection area.) ❑ ◯

Have you considered factors such as age, sex, cultural
values, etc. when designing visual content? ❑ ◯

    E. Place an order for production or produce your visuals. When requesting transparences from departmental or commercial production sources, check the following questions. All answers should be YES.

	Yes	No

If original artwork is needed, is this work clearly
described in the order? ❑ ◯

Have you left a wide margin? (The overhead glass is
about 10"x10" and the paper frame is about 1" wide,
so 7"x9" is about right.) ❑ ◯

Have you noted colors required, and have you
indicated exactly where they will be used? ❑ ◯

If original artwork is required, have you allowed enough
lead time for the job? ❑ ◯

Have you clearly indicated overlays, their number, the
sequence in which they will be used, and any other
technical details that require production attention? ❑ ◯

Do you plan to mark or write on the visual? (If you do,
order extra sheets of cheap, clear acetate to write on and
throw away. This will save your original visual for later use.) ❑ ◯

If you plan to use the overlay for a long period or
frequently, have you ordered protective envelopes? ❑ ◯

Storage of Transparencies and Masters for Overhead Projection

Store transparencies in protective envelopes or folders. Use them to continue protection for the transparencies when transporting the visuals. This is especially important for those made using the Thermofax® process. They will turn a dark color. Otherwise, separate transparencies with sheets of paper to avoid scratches or finger marks.

Avoid exposing transparencies to light and excessive heat for long periods. Keep the plastic surfaces clean and free from dust, grit, and fingerprints. Remove completely any color remaining after using removable felt pen markings. Provide clear, blank transparent plastic sheets for instructors who wish to mark on their transparencies. By use of the clear sheet for writing and marking the original transparency will keep original clarity.

Suggestions for Overhead Transparency Presentations

The following information is to help you prepare hints for persons who will use the transparencies in their presentations.

- Practice using your new transparencies.
- Face the audience, *not* the screen.
- Project on a screen of adequate size, tilted forward at the top enough to avoid an extreme keystone image. Avoid shiny surfaces, such as the metal "white boards." Viewers at an angle can't see the image.
- Check focus before use. Use a pencil and focus until the outline is sharp.
- Use pointers (a thin sharp pencil, pointed cocktail stirring rod, etc.) on the stage of the projector to indicate or point out items.
- For ease of operation, the overhead projector is best-used when the instructor is seated. Place the projector on a low stand alongside a table or desk with the top of the projector stage at the same level.
- Once the projector is focused on the screen, avoid turning around to look at the screen. This can be distracting to the audience.
- Avoid leaving the projector light on the screen while changing visuals, as the glare is distracting. Turn the light off between visuals.
- Use pastel colored backgrounds on transparencies to reduce eye glare.
- Use masks, overlays, and translucent objects to keep visuals to the minimum.
- Use masks to reveal points as you cover them.
- Use a sheet of cheap clear acetate for writing on to protect expensive or film transparencies.
- If you write, do so legibly with a marker designed for writing on transparencies.

- Do not read the transparencies directly. There can be specific exceptions to this rule. Generally, paraphrase or summarize the point.
- Use frames for transparencies that will be reused.
- Note points on the frame as prompts for your presentation.
- Mark frames to ensure they are in the right order and right side up.
- Consider including copies of the transparencies in your student handout.
- Check where the light switch is in case it becomes necessary to dim the lights.
- Provide help for instructors who want to learn to use transparencies, and encourage them to practice the presentation privately before facing a class.

Slides

The standard 35mm slide (also called 2" by 2"—the dimensions of the paper slide mount) is probably the most widely used still-visual medium on the market today. Its low production cost, compactness, and versatility appeal to many users and producers of instructional and informational programs. As stated in Chapter 8, "Guidelines for Visuals," *all* still visuals, including 35mm slides, are designed for horizontal viewing. Among novice course developers and instructors, there is a tendency to assume because it is *possible* to use vertical slide images it is *logical* to do so. All vertical image would ease the legibility problem when photographing original materials such as printed forms. However, the vertical format poses other problems for both instructors and students in a classroom designed for viewing horizontal images. The horizontal format for slides is strongly recommended.

One advantage in using slides is their flexibility of use for either front or rear screen projection. Formerly, many institutions were installing rear screen projection systems to reduce equipment noise, ensure security of equipment and materials, and allow instructors to point out information while standing in front of the screen. Unfortunately, some systems were poorly designed or used inferior equipment. In recent years, many reasons for installing (and maintaining) costly rear projection systems were eliminated by advances in equipment and cabinetry design. Therefore, it is prudent to check slide trays for proper assembly and projection quality with the system with which you will be working with *before* giving presentations to avoid any surprises.

A disadvantage of slides in the relative difficulty in pointing to a location on the projected visual. If you are far from the screen, flashlight pointers, or the newer laser pointers, must be used.

Course developers find compelling reasons to use slides for instruction. They can serve as both instructional aids to support an instructor's presentation or as an instructional medium when combined with recorded sound. Also, they can rearrange lesson materials, or make substitutions, with minimum delay and maximum economy. More examples of the advantages and disadvantages of slides are discussed in the following pages.

The principal purpose of this section, as in each section devoted to an individual medium, is to provide you with simple checklists that you can view when planning and developing visual instructional materials.

Relating Slides to Instructional Objectives

Class of media: Instructional aid *or* instructional medium (when used with audio or print).

Characteristics: Still visual (limited and expensive semi-motion capability).

Application to types of learning:

Cognitive objectives. Slides can be used to teach recognition and discrimination of suitable visual stimuli. For example, slides can:

- Teach recognition of unfamiliar objects by displaying visual representations (pictures or drawings).
- Teach discrimination skills by visually contrasting objects shown sequentially or simultaneously.
- Enhance the teaching of discrimination skills by exaggerating differences in objects through visuals such as line drawings and enlargements.
- Display principles of objects having internal working parts with cutaway views.
- Present a representation of the working location, position, or situations that the student will face in the real world.

We can also use slides to teach rules, principles, and sequences of events. They can:

- Reinforce an instructor's presentation by graphic representations such as charts, diagrams, and scales.
- Display words or points for emphasis in the instructor's commentary and thereby provide reinforcement .
- Clarify instructor's commentary by also displaying the lesson content.
- Provide visual cues as a guide to the presented materials.

Psychomotor objectives. Little, if any, application. Still-visual displays can point out static positions of moving items, ways to hold items for manipulation, or other critical incidents in the movement of objects.

Affective objectives. Slides used in combination with audio tapes can carry effective attitude-changing material. Even when well-done, slides still rank below motion video (film or video) for affective presentations. One especially attractive feature of slide and sound presentations is the low cost of production compared with sound and motion media. However, as with

any medium, the cost is low if the program gets results. If nothing con-
structive happens to the learner it is expensive.

Advantages and Disadvantages of Slides

Advantages:

+ Color visuals can be produced economically in slides.
+ Slides are easily reproducible in large quantities.
+ The small size of slides allows compact packaging and storage, ease
  of distribution, and convenient transportation for use in various loca-
  tions.
+ A slideprogram can be changed easily, compared to a video program.
+ Slides are very convenient if assembled in tray before presentation,
  transported to instruction site, and used with projector on-site.
+ Slide generation from computer graphics makes possible high quality
  personalized slides on short notice.

When slides are used as an instructional aid:

+ Instructors can adapt their lessons for different student groups or vary
  emphasis by removing or adding slides before each presentation.
+ Instructors can back up visual displays to review specific points.
+ The large visual display on a screen allows an instructor to point out
  critical items.

Slides can also serve as an instructional *medium* when used in combination with audio. For example: A pre-programmed sequence of slides can
provide exact visual content. It can inhibit the tendency of various pre-
senters or instructors to revise or improvise lessons. The compact size of
slides simplifies the production and distribution of individualized lesson
materials.
Versatility of display through slides allows:

+ Visuals to be designed for progressive disclosure of information.
+ Visuals designed to present special visual effects (for example, cut-
  away or enlarged views of objects and distortion of image for impact).
+ Economical (and realistic) visual representations of what the student
  will see in the real world.

Disadvantages:

− Effective projection of slides normally calls for lighting to be dimmed
  and controlled for an adequate visual display. Usually, this concern
  represents a problem only when slides are used as an instructional
  aid.
− Processing is seldom done locally. Depending on available laboratory
  services, you must wait from 24 hours to several days for commercial

film development and mounting of slides. Fast developing service is available, but usually with extra, sometimes hefty, charges.
- Artwork formats must be specially designed for slides to be used with video (see aspect ratio discussion in Chapter 8).

✔✔✔
Checklist of Considerations for Selecting and Developing Slides for Instruction

(*Consider adapting these lists to fit your local situation*)

Instructions. The following checklist is intended for use *after* you make the decision to use slides for visuals. The list is a mind-jogger to help you plan the production of the visuals for your project.

Group A is a series of questions designed to help you reevaluate your decision to use slides. Groups B, C, and D will help in planning the visual content of the instruction. Groups E and F will help in the ordering and organization of slide materials.

A. Analyze lesson content to determine what visuals are needed, if any. All answers should be YES. A NO answer indicates you should reconsider your choice of medium. These questions relate to slides used either as an instructional aid or an instructional medium.

	Yes	No
If the lesson is about objects or things that are unfamiliar to the student:	❏	○
Is it *impractical* to show the students the real thing due to size, cost, or safety reasons?	❏	○
Is it easier to display visual representations of the objects or things than tell them about them?	❏	○
Will a still visual displays satisfy learning needs? (Caution: Think over carefully. We often assume motion is critical when it is not.)	❏	○

Are there parts of the verbal message that can best be
displayed visually (for example: a description of an event
or a situation where "one picture is worth a thousand
words," or parts of the verbal message that need to be
stressed or repeated visually to enhance communication)?   ❏   ○

Is the verbal message sufficiently complex so that visuals
may help keep attention and help them follow the logic or
purpose of the presentation?   ❏   ○

If slides are used as an instructional aid only, is it feasible
to dim room lights for viewing?   ❏   ○

B. Describe the visuals needed on 3 by 5 inch or 5 by 7 inch storyboard
cards, either in longhand description or by a rough pencil sketch.[1] If
working with a script for a narration, write the ideas for the script on the
storyboard cards. To confirm your planning for the visual display, complete the following checklist. All answers should be YES.

	Yes	No
Have you lean programmed your visuals to minimize both production cost and student distractions? (See Chapter 3, "Developmental Testing.")	❏	○
Have you checked local art or slide files for ideas or materials you can use without new production work?	❏	○
If you need drawings or cartoons, have you checked available clip-art files?	❏	○
Have you reviewed the section "Rules of Thumb for Visuals" in Chapter 8?	❏	○

C. Review the storyboard visuals and the lesson content to see if you
should re-sequence the materials to best use visual displays. If student or
instructor is to work with various media, plan transitions smoothly to
reduce distraction.

D. Edit visuals in hand-drawn form and combine them with slides
already available for the lesson. Check the following items. All answers
should be YES.

	Yes	No
If dealing with objects or things, have you considered whether the students are familiar with them?	❏	◯
If students are *unfamiliar* with the objects or things, did you provide visuals to show perspective as to size, shape, and relationship of parts early in the lesson?	❏	◯
If displaying tools or equipment with which the students will work on the job, did you show them an over-the-shoulder view as they will see and work with them on job?	❏	◯
Are they simple?	❏	◯
Did you use a horizontal format?	❏	◯
Are the planned graphics simple and clear?	❏	◯
Did you consider visual legibility? (See the legibility formulas in Chapter 8, "Rules of Thumb for Visuals.")	❏	◯
Did you limit each visual to one topic or idea?	❏	◯
If necessary, did you use two simple visuals rather than one complex one?	❏	◯
Did you avoid busy, distracting visuals? (Apply the "double 7" rule. Limit visuals to 6 or 7 lines of 6 or 7 words per line.)	❏	◯
Are all the visuals necessary?	❏	◯
Have you checked your visuals with an expert on the subject matter to confirm accuracy?	❏	◯
Have you considered students' age, sex, cultural values, etc. in visual content?	❏	◯

E. **Order visuals from your institutional studio laboratory or photographic supply house.** Check to be sure the following information is specified on the original order.

	Yes	No
Are slides to be duplicated from existing masters instead of other duplicates?	❏	◯

If slides will be made from existing clip-art or other
readily available materials, was it noted on the order?   ❏   O

Were local arrangements made for slides to be shot
on location?   ❏   O

Is the horizontal format stipulated on the order?   ❏   O

Did you plan for sufficient lead time for slides requiring
original artwork? (Preparation of artwork requires a longer
production time and will be handled individually.)
Again, specify horizontal format.   ❏   O

Have you arranged to maintain contact with the supplier
to resolve problems arising in legibility, cost, or redesign
of lesson materials?   ❏   O

    **F. After receiving slide materials, complete the following checklist. All
answers should be YES.**

	Yes	No
Do all visuals meet the 6W formula for legibility? (See "Rules of Thumb for Visuals" in Chapter 8.)	❏	O
Have you reviewed, sequenced, and numbered the master set of slides? (See suggestions for organization and storage in the following section.)	❏	O
Has a subject matter expert checked the visuals for accuracy?	❏	O
Have you maintained a horizontal format?	❏	O
Have you filed the original slides with all essential data, including the name of the course, for storage as the master for duplication? (See suggestions on the following page.)	❏	O

Suggestions for Organizing and Storing Slides

    To set up, sequence, and number master copies of slides, always start
with a *black* slide as number 1. (With more recent model projectors this
step may be unnecessary as light will not be projected with empty slide.)
To number slides for viewing:

    1. Set up slides on lighted viewer, arranged in lesson sequence. Place a
       small dot on the lower left-hand corner of the slide as viewed
       correctly. (See Fig. 9.1, view A.)

2. Turn slide upside down—the dot will be in the upper right-hand corner—and write the slide number at the location of the dot as shown in view. B.

3. When assembling the slides in the tray, the number on the slide should be in the upper *right*-hand corner, over the number on the slide tray base

Figure 9.1
Slide Organization

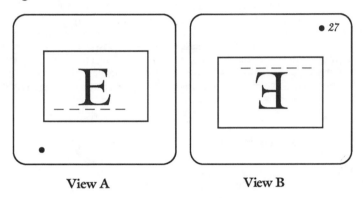

View A　　　　View B

4. Store master copies of slides in a safe, cool place. To avoid handling lesson slides, store them in the slide tray or carrousel in which they will be used.

5. Use slides mounted in plastic or glass in 80-slide trays only. Use of 140-slide trays is not encouraged because slides may easily jam in the projector.

6. Project on a proper sized screen to check legibility. Remember, the 6W formula calls for 1 foot of screen width for each 6 feet of viewing distance from the screen.

7. When ordering copies of slide sets, specify in your order whether you want the duplicates collated and numbered.

8. If word slides are requested, avoid water-colored negative slides when many copies will be necessary.

Filmstrips

Filmstrips are becoming a rarity. Many filmstrips still exist, but few new ones are prepared. Today, other media are most often selected to serve the same purpose. There are many similarities between filmstrips and slides in production and application. The principal differences between between these media are the mode of packaging and the equipment for utilization. Both are made with 35mm motion picture type film. Filmstrips, however, use the film in continuous strips with each visual composed in a single, horizontal frame. This technique of using the format of 35mm motion picture film provides one of the advantages of filmstrips, because continuous processing in high-speed printing and developing equipment makes duplication of multiple copies economical and rapid. The other advantage of filmstrips in comparison with slides, which must be packaged individually, is that filmstrips provide many pictures on one field of film that is light in weight, easy to mail, and requires little storage space.

Slides may be re-sequenced or changed quite simply. Editing 35mm filmstrips requires time and professional processing. Careful thought must be given to the integrity of the visual content and possible need for revision before committing to filmstrips as a delivery system. The potential savings gained in the reproduction, distribution, and storage of filmstrips could be offset by the need for expensive editing and redistribution of materials.

Relating Filmstrips to Instructional Objectives

Class of media, characteristics, application to cognitive, psychomotor, and affective learning are all the same as for slides.

Unique Advantages and Disadvantages of Filmstrips

Advantages:

+ Filmstrips can be used as either an instructional aid *or* an instructional medium.
+ There are many existing filmstrips for various subjects that are easily obtained by educational centers and school districts.
+ Filmstrips are easily repaired with clear tape if cut or ripped.

+ As an instructional medium (when used in combination with audio or print), filmstrips provide locked-in visual content and sequence, which ensures both lesson integrity and against visuals being lost, reversed, or out of sequence.
+ The compact size of the visuals accommodates the production and distribution of individualized lesson material.
+ They are easily reproducible in large quantities.
+ They are small, which permits compact packaging and storage, ease of distribution, and convenient transportation for use in various locations.
+ Reproduction of filmstrips in large quantities is generally more economical than slides in cost per projected visual.

+ Since filmstrips with sound are packaged with audio accompaniment on discs, tapes, or (usually) cassettes, alternative sound tracks for different audiences are easily provided, such as in various foreign languages of for technical and non-technical audiences.

Disadvantages:

− Because of the locked-in sequence of visuals on a strip of 35mm film, editing and updating of filmstrip materials may become more time consuming and expensive than slides.
− Because filmstrip processing requires copy stand and laboratory processing, the time required for the preparation of release prints is often longer than processing slides.

Suggestions for Using Filmstrips

• Store films in a cool, dry place.
• Avoid touching the film with your fingers. If film becomes smudged or
• Label film holders clearly to avoid excess handling of film.
• Never release master copies or work prints for use other than duplicating.

✔✔✔
Checklist of Unique Considerations for Selecting and Developing Filmstrips for Instruction

(Consider adapting these checklists to fit your own situation)

Instructions. Use this series of questions to help you confirm or reevaluate your decision to use filmstrips as a visual medium. Use the checklist for slides, earlier in this chapter, to help plan the development of your lesson material and guide you in your contacts with production personnel.

Analyze lesson content and objectives to determine if this medium is best suited to your needs. All answers should be YES.

	Yes	No
Is it desirable for the visual display to be locked-in, prohibiting re-sequencing or editing of visual content?	❏	○

Is the lesson content stable, requiring little updating or
editing in the near future?   ❏   ○

Will it be necessary to duplicate and ship many copies
of the lesson, which includes visuals?   ❏   ○

CHAPTER 10

Motion Visuals

For many years, film and video were treated as competitive and unique systems. Production experiences in motion pictures for entertainment, news, and education have resulted in a blending. TV and film are clearly becoming interlocked as coordinate systems. Finished productions are made from under-cutting of film and video. Productions are made on video systems and transferred to film for distribution. Production techniques in both media are becoming less distinctive. Only the most experienced observers can identify the effects and treatment of content peculiar to each. From the viewpoint of the user, the student simply learns or is informed by motion visuals.

It is possible to make long lists of likenesses and differences between film and television. However, we wish to accommodate the average course developer's responsibility level. Therefore, we will focus on those comparisons, advantages, and disadvantages that relate directly to the problems of selection and development of motion visuals for communicating instructional content. This will involve some issues such as distribution plans. You can comfortably leave the more technical differences between film and video (not relevant to your problems of planning for production, distribution, and use) to the engineers and craft specialists.

One common use of motion visuals is to affect attitude changes—at least temporarily. Well done products can have considerable impact on their viewers. However, we can only gain these results through careful audience analysis, planning, and (usually) considerable expense. There are plentiful sources of films and video tapes available for rent or purchase (see the Selected Readings listing at the end of this book). It is wise to check these resources before committing to an original product. If used, however, BE SURE TO GET COPYRIGHT RELEASE BEFORE COPYING.

Another useful application of motion visuals is modeling wanted behaviors to students, displaying examples of human interaction, and presenting situational problems for students to solve. These are most often presented in short vignette form after which students discuss their reactions and solutions or answer test items. A good rule of thumb for producing these materials is to keep them short (preferably one concept at a time). Allow as much student response time as possible.

In recent years, video has become increasingly popular as a medium for conducting individualized instruction. Advancements in both video and computer technology have allowed these systems to take many forms. Remote control pads allow students to control their programs. "Refresher" systems have made the use of video tape for still frames economical. Videodiscs (often used in combination with computer systems) can control student response and progress through the learning process.

Videodisc technology was not successful as a home entertainment medium. However, it is still available for home use. It is in the training room that videodisc found its home. Yet, it is still very time-consuming and costly to produce for most training situations. This condition will undoubtedly change with advancements in the technology and with standardization and mass distribution of disc materials.

An important factor in the choice of video production by many organizations is the availability of in-house production facilities. Possibly because of this factor alone, institutions ordinarily produce films through commercial studios. Because of this situation, we place our emphasis on video. However, most of the developmental steps suggested in the checklists will be the same for film as for video.

The most important event in training use of video is the widespread home use of $\frac{1}{2}$ inch VHS video technology. It has made inexpensive video widely available. The common availability extended to the training department. It was really needed in training for "watch yourself" processes like training the trainer and role play reviews. This transfer of technology from the home to the training room helps speed the adaptation of emerging technologies.

Video is not limited to "live" video (actual people, places, things). Graphic video is an excellent means for presenting concepts we cannot present as "live" motion. For example: movement of the solar system, how a television receives signals and displays images, and physics principles.

Some Rules of Thumb for Producing Motion Visuals

Whether working with video or film, here are some rules of thumb. Keep them in mind when considering motion visuals for production:

- These media are designed to show motion, not still pictures.
- Motion visuals are excellent for affective (attitude-changing) presentations, if they are well done.

- For instructional purposes motion visuals are best-used on a one-to-one relationship. Regardless of audience size, you should aim scripts at a student as an individual.
- The sound track must be relevant to the visuals and should be in the active voice.
- The narration should not tell what is happening on the screen, unless interpretation or clarification is necessary, or you must stress a critical point.
- All motion visual media have an exact content. You should edit and validate them before presentation. Before releasing, check the materials with a subject matter expert and with small, representative groups of students.
- Since both video and motion film are essentially visual media, develop the narration from a carefully designed visual script. The writer must think in visuals.
- Remember, you don't really have a captive audience; the audience can mentally turn you off. Your script plan must include consideration of the attitudes of the viewers, based on their cultures, age, sex, expectations, etc.
- Change views periodically to fit the audiences' attention span. Keep running time to the minimum.
- Production of motion visual materials is a complex operation, requiring the participation of people from varied disciplines and technical skills. Functioning by approval of a committee only adds to expense, frustration, and confusion. The responsibility for approval at various stages of production and for the acceptance of the final product should rest with one person. Designate whoever has that final responsibility as the producer and be available for coordinating with the various production groups.

These rules are not by any means a comprehensive statement of all the pitfalls or the benefits of motion visual media. They may not even be applicable in every case.

We do not intend to help perpetuate the controversy of film versus video when considered as competitive media. The guidelines and checklists are simply to provide you with a basic and organized approach to the pre-production stages of instruction using motion visual media to help increase the likelihood of a successful product.

VIDEO

Relating Video To Instructional Objectives

Class of Media: Instructional medium.

Characteristics: Motion visual, audio, or silent.

Application to types of learning:

Cognitive objectives. Video can be used to:
   Teach recognition and discrimination of relevant motion stimuli. For example: relative speed of moving objects, deviations in movement, and interactions of objects and real things. It is possible (but not often economical) to display a series of relevant still visuals with or without audio stimuli, as would be done with slides, photographs, and filmstrips.

   • Teach rules and principles. It is possible (but not economical) to display series of words (verbal abstractions) as with other still visuals or print.
   • Model performance, especially in situations requiring human interaction.
   • Provide immediate feedback to students about their performance, as they display their skills and their ability to apply rules and principles.

Psychomotor objectives. Video is:
   Useful to model motion skills. It can exaggerate motion (slow or fast) to teach mind-body coordination. For example: techniques in manipulating tools, climbing, or swimming.

   Useful to provide immediate visual feedback to students on their ability to perform motion skills.

Affective objectives. Video most useful to create attitudes and emotions by various techniques and effects. It is an excellent tool for displaying affective information through optical effects and associated visual imagery.

Advantages and Disadvantages of Video

Advantages:

   + Motion (with or without sound) can be reproduced to display both relevant stimuli and desired student responses called for by the instruction. One example of this use is displaying vignettes that show the interaction of people, to show the student what should (or should not) be done.
   + Instant replays provide an opportunity to critique or rate the performance of students, by taping selected actions for use in courses on how to develop interpersonal skills (for example: interviewing techniques, conducting meetings, and giving presentations). Instructors or speakers can use it for guidance in editing material before final presentation.

   + Visual effects can be produced to enhance either the learning process or entertainment value of the presentation. Depending on the writer's intent and ability to visualize effects (and the production staff), many effects can be produced on video tape. Examples are:

- compression or extension of time or illusion of activities happening simultaneously,
- split or multiple screen images for a variety of visual cues,
- a smooth flow of visual changes from one scene to the next, and
- the exaggeration of motion through various speeds from slow to fast.

+ Lock in content and sequencing of the training used interactively with workbooks, guides, texts, tools, or other items used on the job.
+ Present the same information simultaneously to various sized audiences in different locations by having monitors in various classrooms.
+ Present self-paced instruction (often in combination with computer based, or printed material) for individualized study.
+ Video production and dissemination are easier and less costly because the camcorder produces quality video at consumer prices.
+ VCRs provide an inexpensive means for displaying video.
+ Multiple VCRs, when interconnected, offer some simple editing capabilities.
+ Video editing can be done with a personal computer.

Disadvantages:

- Implementing materials requires video equipment to be locally available and compatible with the distributed video tape (in size and format).
- Video script writing is difficult for inexperienced writers and can be time-consuming.
- Production costs are high, and talented production teams expensive.
- Visual quality may be poor when transferred to film.
- Small monitor screens limit audience size unless part of a multiple monitor display or video projection system.
- Lettering on graphics for video limited to about one-half that of (higher resolution) film or still visuals.
- Changes in technology make obsolescence of video systems a continuing fact of life.

✔✔✔
Checklist of Considerations for Selecting and Developing Video for Instruction

(Consider adapting these checklists to fit your own situation.)

Preparing video training materials can be both expensive and complex. To anticipate all the problems and contingencies the course writer should be aware of during this process would be impossible. These guidelines, therefore, do not represent an all-inclusive list of considerations that will guarantee success. This is a set of mind-joggers for use with some suggested production guidelines at the end of this section. Segment A is to help you reconsider your choice of medium while segments B through M will help in the planning and development of materials.

A. Reevaluate your media selection. Analyze lesson objectives, content, and distribution considerations to determine if video is the best choice of medium. All answers should be YES.

	Yes	No
Is motion critical to the lesson? (Caution: We often assume motion is critical when it is not. To answer yes to this question, at least one of the following criteria should apply to your lesson content.)	❏	O
Is it necessary to display motion in an exaggerated form?		
• Motion is necessary to show psychomotor skills needed to manipulate objects or perform physical activities.	❏	O
• Motion is necessary to display changing visual cues used by people interacting with each other (for example: changes in facial expression and body movement associated with verbal communications).	❏	O
• Motion is necessary to display special effects or to develop an emotion or an attitude because the lesson content is primarily affective.	❏	O
• Immediate visual feedback is necessary to display students' physical and verbal performance.	❏	O
Are a locked-in content and sequence desirable?	❏	O
Does the lesson require exact reproduction?	❏	O
Will you display the lesson to small groups (instead of large audiences), and is video equipment available for display?	❏	O
Does the life of the course (or some other factor) justify the expense of video?	❏	O
Is this medium compatible with your student populations' backgrounds?	❏	O

B. Check for availability of an existing videotape suitable for your topic that you can rent or buy. (See the list of sources in the Selected Readings section.)

C. Briefly outline the lesson content in a logical order of presentation. Review the "Rules of Thumb for Visuals" in Chapter 8 and suggestions in Chapter 3, "Developmental Testing."

D. Prepare a storyboard outline for visual presentation in either rough sketch or verbal form. Check the following items. All answers should be YES.

	Yes	No
Have you reviewed the section on developmental testing in Chapter 3?	❏	○
Are visual scenes simple and direct?	❏	○
Have you planned to give the students perspective about the size and shape of objects or items with which they are unfamiliar?	❏	○
Will students see tools, equipment, or work locations as they will see them on the job?	❏	○
Have you avoided displaying a series of still visuals that you could show less expensively by another medium?	❏	○
Have you avoided needless use of humor or shock for effect?	❏	○

E. Review the planned visuals and rough narrative with a subject matter expert. All answers to the following should be YES.

	Yes	No
Does the sequence of events displayed match the real job?	❏	○
Have accurate working conditions, practices, and rules followed in the visuals?	❏	○
Is the narrative kept to a minimum? Does the narrative describe the job accurately?	❏	○

F. Rough draft the visual scenes down the left-hand side of note paper, then insert the supporting narrative alongside the visual part. We have provided a suggested script format for video materials at the end of this section.

G. Revise the rough draft of the script until satisfied with the initial draft. Check the following. All answers should be YES.

	Yes	No
Have you kept the narrative lean? (Video is primarily a visual medium.)	❏	O
Have you avoided repeating verbally what is shown on the screen?	❏	O
Have you used colloquial speech and avoided jargon and technical terms when possible? (See suggestions for audio scripts written to support visuals in Chapter 7, "Audio," to guide you in checking the audio portion of your script.)	❏	O
Have you avoided expensive location shots when possible?	❏	O
Have you avoided using only a talking face for long periods?	❏	O
Have you planned for a lesson directed to one student instead of a large audience? (Television is best displayed on a one-to-one basis.)	❏	O
Have you used the active voice in the audio part of the script?	❏	O
Have you avoided using long series of still visuals?	❏	O

H. **Review the section "Video Graphics" on the following page.** Then revise the initial script again to add visual and sound directions for the script. Note special effects and graphic requirements.

I. **Edit initial script again. Note all directions, such as visuals, camera shots, and special effects.** Consider the following. All answers should be YES.

	Yes	No
Have you avoided the talking face or excessive still visuals supported by narration?	❏	O
Does your script have an opening, a body, and a closing?	❏	O
If displaying someone doing something, have you planned to edit the activity, so you don't have one camera showing the entire scene? (Watching an event on the screen seems much longer than seeing it in real life.)	❏	O
Have you considered what special effects will be needed to enhance and clarify the presentation?	❏	O
Have you made note of them in the script?	❏	O

J. Have the script printed double spaced as shown in the video script example in this section. Edit again, if necessary, to be sure that the visual display has continuity and is accurate. Be sure the audio narration supports the visuals and is written to be heard—not read! When you use video interactively with workbooks, direct the students to workbook or worksheet pages with the video display. Bring them back to the video by print instructions.

K. Review the script with a subject matter expert to ensure accuracy of content and credibility with target population. Edit where necessary.

L. Complete the developmental testing of the material with representative students until satisfied that the instruction and media work.

M. Complete the pre-production notes for use by local production groups. (See suggested model in this section.)

N. Arrange with local or outside video production personnel for taping. (A suggested request form is included at the end of this section.)

Video Graphics

- Illustrations for use in video productions may include: photographs, slides, transparencies, motion pictures, graphics, poster boards, chalkboard displays, and easel and flip chart displays.
- The TV format ratio is 3:4 Use artwork proportions compatible with this ratio, for example: 6 x 8, 9 x 12, 12 x 16.
- Allow for a loss of margin in artwork and slides because of variations in adjustment of television receivers.
- When using 35mm slides for TV, use a horizontal format. Compensate for the ratio difference by allowing extra margin on each side of the viewing area.
- Because the video legibility formula is 12W, you must use bold graphics free from unnecessary details. Limit printed outlines or lists to not more than 5-7 lines, and no more than 3-5 words per line. Visuals must be legibility "proofed" as described in Chapter 8, "Guidelines for Visuals."
- Motion picture film may reproduce satisfactorily on video tape. Film clips may be available from which you can use portions to improve the quality of the program lesson. BE CAREFUL NOT TO BREAK COPYRIGHT LAWS. Be sure you have the right to copy.
- Avoid graphics of questionable visual quality. When possible use the original or master copy.
- Review Chapter 8, "Guidelines for Visuals," for help in planning the legibility and format of video graphics.

FILM

The course developer who chooses to work in this medium is faced with a dilemma. Doing film right can be costly. It would not be wise to create such a low cost production that the students may turn the message off due to boredom or poor production quality. Nevertheless, you may reach the decision to use film as an instructional medium. However, consideration must be given to the problems of availability of production and display facilities, pre-production plans, and expense approval. These issues must be resolved early in the lesson development process.

Because of the many similarities between film and video, there will necessarily be some overlap in characteristics, advantages, and disadvantages. Yet, some differences, primarily in distribution, and processing time, do exist and course developers must consider them.

Recently developed colorization techniques can add color to original black and white film. It is extremely unlikely that you will find economic justification to consider that technology for a training production.

Relating Film to Instructional Objectives

Class of media, characteristics, application to cognitive, psychomotor, and affective learning are all the same as for video.

Unique Advantages and Disadvantages of Film

Advantages:

+ The long history of films has developed large resources of available films in libraries.
+ The variety of available film sizes and types can provide visual displays for use with large audiences (unlike video) and small groups or for individual viewing.
+ Film can be used with both front and rear screen projection.
+ In some (even remote) locations, film projectors are more readily available than video equipment.
+ The quality of visual and sound when transferred to video tape is generally better than that of transfer of video to film.
+ Standardized film sizes (unlike video) allow use on an international basis ensuring viewing when needed.

Disadvantages:

− Production costs are high and talented production teams are scarce.
− Film processing requires time for development. There are no instant feedback capabilities.

- Most training and education institutions do not have low-cost, in-house facilities for producing quality sound films.
- Film stock cannot be erased and reused.
- Care must be taken in the handling of films to prevent breakage or deterioration.
- Films must be cleaned regularly.

✔✔✔

Checklist of Considerations for Selecting and Developing Film for Instruction

Because of the many similarities in the development processes required for film and video, the following information is brief. The *video checklist* should be used for development purposes. However, keep the following points in mind when preparing instruction on motion film.

- When reconsidering your choice of media in step A of the video checklist, keep in mind that film is used *primarily* for viewing by large audiences. Also, in-house film production and editing facilities may be limited, and initial introduction costs for film may be higher than video.

- When reviewing the "Rules of Thumb for Visuals," remember that film graphics are based on the 6W formula, film format is a horizontal 3 to 4 ratio. You should order duplicate copies from the original internegative.

- You should consult your local production personnel about your plans as early as possible.

- Some suggested formats for scripting and production requests are included at the end of this section. The formats are designed to be used for either video or film.

SAMPLE SCRIPT

Location: Local Office

Scene 1

VISUAL	NARRATION
Title: Step 1 Preparation (2 sec)	
Fade to: Bert writing letter at desk. Art walks up and leans over.	ART: Hey Bert / Got a problem / Could I see you?
(MS working in as close as possible.)	BERT: Sure Art / What's the problem?
	ART: Chuck Lewis pulled the 8:30 to 5:30 shift and Wally got the 8 to 5 all next week.
Bert: Quizzical look.	BERT: That's right / Did Chuck come to see you?
	ART: Uh huh / You <u>know</u> Wally has less seniority.
	BERT: Yes, but let me check the schedule and we can get together on this later this afternoon / Say right after lunch.
Bert turns to clerk on pause.	BERT: Just a second // Jane / Is the conference room available this afternoon?
Cut to Jane. Jane picks up schedule, looks through to page.	JANE: Just a // Yes / free all afternoon.
	BERT: <u>Good</u> / I'll be there with Art / Let's meet there after lunch / I'll bring the new schedule and the previous one too / OK?
On pause, Bert turns to Art. Art smiles, turns, and leaves. Bert gets out schedules and copy of contract.	
(Zoom to CU)	ART: OK / See you there.

Sample of Preproduction Notes: Union Grievance Procedure

Setting:

Narrator sitting at (or on) desk. Easel sheets slightly off stage. Union contract book for narrator to hold.

Vignettes shot in studio. Props require two office desks for office scenes; one table and setting of chairs for conference room scene. Door visible in both scenes.

Special Effects:

Superimposed graphics (35mm word slides).
One split screen.
Fades between scenes.
Filtered voice on "thinking" shot.
Filtered voice on phone.

Location:

All scenes should be shot in studio with sufficient quality to provide optical transfer to 16mm at a future date.

Talent:

Professional talent narrator (male) with good presence and relaxed manner. Bert and Art *may* be professional; Art is younger. Manager and clerk can be of local talent.

Costumes:

Bert should be wearing sports jacket and tie, Art in shirt sleeves (no tie). Manager (Wally) in suit and tie. No make-up.

Shooting Sequence:

Suggest narrators' scenes be shot at one time. Vignette scenes edited in later.
Suggest the two vignettes be shot at same time with fades between each scene. For rerun of the "good" vignette, fades can be shortened to provide visual continuity.

Sample Video/Film Production Request

Video _____ Film _____   Date _____

Production Format   Producer/writer: _____

Tape size _____   _____

Open reel _____ Cassette_____   _____

Film size _____   Company: _____

Internegative Yes_____ No_____   _____

Copyright needed Yes _____No_____   Program Title: _____

                                        _____

                                        Deadline—when must master

                                        be ready?_____

                                        _____

TARGET AUDIENCE: For whom is the program intended? _____
_____

_____

TALENT: Who will arrange for talent personnel?

Writer _____

Production Group _____

What talent will be used?   Professional _____

                              Nonprofessional _____

Name(s) and Telephone Number(s) of local talent used:_____
_____
_____
_____
_____

Are preproduction notes completed and attached? Yes_____ No _____

Are at least three copies of script attached?   Yes_____ No _____

List visuals needed for production (include title and logo if used):

1. _____ 6. _____

2. _____ 7. _____

3. _____ 8 _____

4. _____ 9. _____

5. _____ 10. _____

Note type of visual needed: slides, chart, easel, etc. (Show additional visuals on reverse side of this form.)

APPROVAL: Name of person who has authority to approve expenditures and accept product: _____

DISTRIBUTION: How many copies will be required? _____

FORMAT NEEDED:
    Tape: Reel _____   Size _____
                 Cassette _____   Size _____

    Film: Reel _____   Size _____
                 Cassette _____   Size _____

Sample List of Video Production Personnel

The list below is an example of *some* of the personnel you might meet when dealing with a large video or film studio. A brief description of each staff member's responsibilities is included as general information. In a small in-house production group, the staff is obviously smaller, and several responsibilities or functions may be assumed by one person.

Producer
Responsible for creation and production of a single show. Passes approval during various stages of production and accepts final responsibility for the end product.

Production Assistant
Handles such details as clearing music rights, copyrights, delivery of graphics, etc.

Unit Manager
Acts as business manager in seeing that costs are kept within production budget.

Director
Determines the creative aspects of the show and directs the camera during taping.

Assistant Director
Responsible for the timing of the show, cues in special effects and music, and prepares camera shots.

Floor or Stage Manager
Directs the activities on the floor of the studio, and cues performers and stage hands.

Technical Director
In charge of all technical personnel and runs the console during taping.

Audio (or Sound) Director
Responsible for all audio in the production.

Video Director
Handles master video recorder during the production.

Director of Photography or Cinematographer
In charge of lighting and camera crew.

Script Supervisor
Works with director keeping records of what scenes were shot, camera angles, costume details, etc.

CHAPTER 11

Technology-Based Learning

Today, technology evolves rapidly—sophistication increases exponentially. Training is a busy area, often using the same "tried and true" techniques that have worked for years. The problem with such techniques is that sometimes they don't solve today's problem as well as they did yesterday's. Today, training often must deal with a new environment of the systems and tools used with increasing frequency to boost productivity in various organizations. A well designed and executed "lecture" cannot deliver immediate feedback, varying examples appropriate to each individual present, and cease when the student reaches mastery.

Technology for learning has been around for three decades.[1] Today, it is no longer an experiment. We are beginning to see many important projects using technology for learning in all sectors. It is the practical use of computer technology for learning—and it works! Further, there is a trend to integrate technology into production and delivery of what we had previously considered "conventional" media.

Raymond Fox, President, Society for Applied Learning Technology, wrote:

---

[1]This timing is based on the late-1950s National Science Foundation grants for computer-based education projects at the University of Illinois and Brigham Young University.

"There is an ever advancing body of knowledge pertaining to more effective technologies for development of interactive instruction systems. Coincident with this are technologies advances in available hardware and software to support development of these instruction systems. The challenge for designing a course for communicating specific ideas or information is to understand how these new technologies can assist in that task and what changes to existing strategies and design must take place to capitalize on the benefits these technologies offer. "[2]

The environment may be right for your situation, *and it may not*. The important point is that, when technology can help, it usually can help in a big way. Often, the toughest problems are the ones it solves best. It is a prospect worth considering. ■

Technology-based Learning in General

Technology brings significant capabilities. Among them are to:

- interact rapidly with individuals,
- store and process vast amounts of information in a variety of forms, and
- combine with other media to display a broad range of audiovisual stimuli.

These features give it potential to become dominant in instruction. It is rapidly becoming more common to use computers in a variety of instructional activities. Some of these include the production of graphic and other audiovisual media, and the development, delivery, and management of instructional materials.

Why Technology . . . Not Computers?

Technology has a basis in computers. Today, there is a small computer chip in nearly all electrical equipment. It is becoming more difficult to separate the "computerness" of objects we use. Are your fuel injection system, FAX, VCR, or video game computers? It really doesn't matter. These items incorporate more processing power. We don't really care if the technology we use to improve our instruction is a "computer" or not.

Technology offers several advantages for producing audiovisual media. We can produce statistically accurate graphs and charts for a variety of visual media. Some computer-generated graphic systems can rapidly produce different views of three dimensional objects offering a choice of images to the user. We produce attractive title slides, word slides, and graphic

---

[2]This text first appeared in an article "Letter from the President" by Raymond G. Fox, President of the Society for Applied Learning Technology, in the *Society for Applied Learning Technology Newsletter*, Summer 1989, p. 1.

slides by computer systems rapidly at comparatively low-cost. We use computers for precise editing and assembly of video and film productions. Today, computer-based word processing systems are commonplace in producing most print media.

Problems

The rapid advances in technology and more wide spread application to instruction have not left this field without some problems. Some vexing issues facing instructional personnel contemplating a technology-based approach are:

- Rapid obsolescence of costly hardware and software. The rapidly changing technology creates a high likelihood that equipment bought today will be obsolete the year after next.
- Few generally understood administrative guidelines. We still debate questions (for example: how much computer knowledge an instructional technologist needs or how best to interface computer and instructional specialists).
- A literature composed, primarily, of professional and trade journal articles. Some of this literature is technical, written from a computer science viewpoint and confusing to most instructional designers. It is no longer true that *all* the literature is primarily written from a computer science viewpoint. There are many technology-based multimedia trade journals that present CAI development from a trainer or ISD viewpoint. These sources include *Instructional Delivery System, Journal of Computer-Based Instruction,* and *CBT Directions.*

Hardware, Software, and Courseware

We often hear the terms hardware, software, and courseware during a discussion of technology-based learning. "Hardware" is a straight-forward term. It describes the actual, visible, physical items involved. Hardware includes the learning station, drives of all kinds, printers, keyboards, cables, mice, and any other physical item.

"Software" is the programs written in computer languages that makes the computer parts of a system work as they should. We may never see evidence of the "software" beyond the system working properly.

Confusion can arise between the terms "software" and "courseware." In technical terms, some courseware is software. We learning specialists do not need such technical (data processing) precision. The technology and non-technology elements that support learning are courseware. Courseware includes the computer delivered CAI lessons and CMI tests, and the associated video, audio, texts, and other learning resources. The result of these distinctions is that learning specialists rarely refer to software. Our business is with the courseware.

Forms of Delivery Systems

The marketplace offers a splendid variety of computers available for instructional purposes. Some systems are very simple and offer the least number of options. Other, more costly, systems offer a large range of attributes and options. Many computers and associated computers are available for purchase. Leasing is possible, depending the client's needs and budget.

When the Second Edition of this book appeared, the major decision was whether to deliver instruction with stand-alone computers or on a large-computer-based network. Today a question is whether to deliver instruction with stand-alone computers or on a small-computer based network (LAN).

Despite the brand or model, we can classify instructional computer systems into two general groups: networked and stand alone.

Network System: Typically this system has student learning stations connected to a larger computer by a cabling system These are local area networks (LAN). The computer (and system) may be a regular part of the work site. It may be a dedicated instructional system. The student stations may number in the hundreds and be of varying configurations. Alternatively, the student learning stations may be dispersed. It is possible to connect with a LAN or even to connect several LANs in a wide area network (WAN).

Stand-alone System: This hardly needs a description. Almost any PC can serve as a stand alone learning station. It is a self contained unit. Each unit is totally independent from others providing maximum flexibility of curriculum

Advantages and Disadvantages of Networks

Advantages:

+ If the students will be working with computers on the job, the computer used for training is usually similar, needing little transfer of learning.
+ The ability of the instructor to concentrate on instructor-related tasks, allowing them to attend specifically to those students who may be having problems.
+ Excellent means for simulation situations that call for individualized yet coordinated task performance. For example, CAI networked crew coordination training allows each station to represent a specific flight task requirement where the host system monitors the coordination of the stations and provides appropriate response.
+ Quick updating of course materials and records. Developers and instructors may access the processor from a learning station and revise materials rapidly.
+ Learning stations can often interact with each other, even at long distances. This allows students or authors to communicate and leave messages for each other or to question an instructor about course material.

+ Versions of software and courseware will be the same for all users. It is simpler to maintain current versions of the software than when separate software exists on each computer.
+ The possibility of software piracy is reduced.

Disadvantages:

- Dedicated instructional systems may be difficult to justify on a cost-effectiveness basis.
- Any breakdowns in the file server will affect every student on the network. Breakdowns elsewhere within the network *may* also affect all network users.
- Breakdowns in isolated parts of the network can cause delays in the instructional program.
- Network versions of software and courseware often required at higher cost.
- Expense of network cabling and software itself is an additional cost.
- Network user interface may be somewhat different from what the user will experience with a PC.
- Network software requires extra steps to learn.

Advantages and Disadvantages of Stand-Alone Systems

Advantages:

+ Normally, least expensive system to buy.
+ Since there is no network, a breakdown of one PC will not affect all the students and one student's PC cannot affect others.
+ Response time may be faster than network systems.
+ A wide variety of commercially produced courseware available for purchase.
+ Network versions of software and courseware not needed.
+ Individual PCs economically better for a small number of users.

Disadvantages:

- No centralized location for gathering receiving. and updating data .
- Must distribute revisions in software materials to each student.
- Gathering test results and other management functions can be cumbersome and time-consuming.
- No communication links between students, developers, and instructors.
- No ability to share resources, such as a printer.
- Differences in individual computers or software installed can absorb considerable instructor time.

People in Technology-based Instructional Development

The courseware development people consist of the different members of the instructional development team. Of course, in smaller organizations there may not be a team of six of more people. These are really roles—not people. One person often performs one or more roles. One person can perform all the roles when working alone. The six roles involved are shown in Figure 11.1.

Each of these courseware development process personnel and roles is described at the end of this chapter.

Figure 11.1
Technology-based Courseware Development Roles

```
• analyst

  • designer

  • developer

• media specialist

  • programmer/data entry person

  • subject matter expert (SME)
```

Courseware Authoring

A friend once described the inventor of the piano as an individual who felt that he had achieved a tremendous accomplishment and thereby secured his place in history. Contrary to his expectations, it is the accomplishments of Brahms, Beethoven, Bach, and scores of other composers which command historical notice. Few can identify the inventor of the instrument itself. As an analogy, there have been astonishing developments in the field of the technological components which constitute instruction delivery systems: the personal computer, the videodisc, CD-ROM as well as others. However, to realize the potential of this technology, the fame must accrue to the developers of interactive instructions materials. Achievement of this end is not without its challenges....[3]

---

[3] Fox, R. "Letter from the President" in *Society for Applied Learning Technology Newsletter*, Summer 1989, p. 1.

Smile!

Photography is an omnipresent part of our society. You may not realize that it endured in the United States with no popular appeal for about fifty years. The camera was easy to handle. The problem lay in the developing process. It was too complicated, time-consuming, and costly for most people. Only when George Eastman developed a simplified, cost-effective way to produce a finished product for the public did photography come into popular use.

Today, there is a like situation with technology-based learning. That is, there are two ways to get courseware. You can buy it off-the-shelf (generic) or have it custom-made. Generic software is ordinarily not available for most local training needs. Therefore, it is not a choice for most training needs.

You can build courseware locally in two ways. You can write it yourself with an authoring system or general purpose programming language. Or, you can pay to have it prepared by a courseware development organization. Contracting for customized courseware is an added expense. Courseware authoring, like the early photo developing process, has been a difficult, time-consuming, and expensive task. Given this situation, it is not difficult to understand why technology-based learning is not a more widely-used method.

Vendors have devoted impressive amounts of time and money to writing courses for general use. Whether the specific course you want is already available depends on your area of interest. If you are working with specialized skills and technologies, you will probably have to produce your own courseware.

Author Languages

We thought we were past this stage already. However, while preparing the current edition of this book, we found a major 1990 project where CAI courseware was written in general purpose computer languages. Agghhh, *again*! Hardly anyone would try to calculate the shape of a new airfoil with a programing language intended for generating business reports. Even so, one organization did use COBOL to program courseware. Strange as it may appear to those who haven't fallen into that trap, you can find people behaving similarly in technology-based learning. We call this the "Hammer Syndrome." Abraham Maslow is attributed with saying that, if all you have is a hammer, everything will look like a nail. If all you know is the BASIC computer language, you will try to use it for everything. It should be no surprise that no one language is well-suited for everything. Languages are suited specifically for many purposes. Decades ago, people figured this out and created author languages. The author language, to be suitable for un-reserved recommendation to any organization, must have the following characteristics:

- high level,
- specifically designed for instructional computing, and
- user oriented.

It should be obvious that it must be a language specifically designed for instructional applications.

Programming is analogous to developing the film. Some people will always want to do it. Most don't. We have to get rid of the *need* for programming! Organizations that use appropriate authoring languages for their courseware may move to "programmerless systems" and reduce the requirement for use of the author language.

Author Systems

Some authoring systems include a high level, user oriented learning-specific author language. This shows their development into a system from a language. There are a growing number of author systems for courseware development. The widespread use of such systems has significantly reduced the cost of lesson development. These useful author systems should also aid in the path to higher quality courseware.

Documentation

Since the ability to update materials is an advantage of technology-based learning, the importance of documentation is great. This problem is widely recognized. Unfortunately, learning specialists sometimes do not create or retain documentation of the process used to develop their instructional materials. This can make future revisions difficult.

Documents that should be retained include: course specifications; learning maps; grouped and sequenced instructional objectives; test items; learning activity descriptions; lesson designs; and assessment, evaluation, and transfer of learning system plans. Among the most important documents are programmer-ready materials—those that guide programming.

Starting Out

It is as difficult to create good technology-based lessons as conventional ones. As vendors develop continually more robust authoring systems, anyone will be able to create courseware. In practical terms it depends more on whether your organization formally carries out all the development steps when developing training.

An organization with a strong instructional development capability could consider their first course being contractor-developed. They should participate in the process. You can diminish dependence on consultants in developing courseware gradually, until the organization is self-sufficient in selected areas. Your staff can develop the skill needed to develop good courseware. If the organization is of adequate size, with a continuing need for new courseware, you can develop an internal courseware development organization.

The Display Screen

How little text you can put on one display may surprise you. We use the flipchart, chalkboard, and handouts regularly. These are large format when compared to a computer display. The information we can put on them won't fit on the screen. The display screen is a *finite* area. To offset this limitation, designers must adopt several new techniques.[4]

- Repeat key concepts and ideas often.
- Present information with space-saving graphics, icons, and symbols in place of lengthy explanations or repetitions.
- Use windows—small ones are best—to display material to which the learner must refer often.

Following these procedures, you break all instruction down to very small modules. If the screen is inflexible, our programs become a series of small, discrete, self-contained modules. We assemble them to produce a coherent lesson. An interaction lies at the core of each module to assure that the learner understands its content.

Graphical User Interface

In the first known study of its kind, Zenith Data Systems (ZDS) and Microsoft Corporation compared the performance of two different user interfaces. They compared character-based CUI (character user interface) and graphical user interfaces (GUI) with novice and experienced users.[5]

Research results show that GUI provides benefits over CUI in office environments. Specifically, the research supports seven benefits of the GUI. GUI users:

- work faster ,
- work better (complete more of their tasks accurately),
- have higher productivity than CUI users,
- express lower frustration,
- express lower fatigue after working with PCs,
- are better able than CUI users to self-teach and explore, and
- learn more capabilities within applications.

These findings support three conclusions. GUI generates:

- higher output per work hour through higher productivity,
- higher output per employee because of lower frustration and fatigue levels, and
- greater return on the technology investment because GUI users master more capabilities and need less training and support.

Many of these benefits are linked to the "navigation theory." It holds that the intuitive icons and menus embodied by GUIs help exploration, use, and retention of applications' functions—making users more productive, self-sufficient, and confident in their computing. The navigation theory

---

[4]Suggested by Hal Christianson.

[5]The study was developed and administered by Temple, Barker, & Sloane Inc., an independent research firm.

suggests that GUI is superior to CUI for all corporate microcomputer users: clerical, professional, and managerial.[6]

Human Factors and Ergonomics

We are rightfully concerned about the people who learn from our technology-based systems. Sometimes people direct this concern to possible harmful effects of working at a computer. There is a trend to deter harmful effects of studying or working with video displays. It is usual to hear some very legitimate questions about safety from the new technology-based learning users. These center on the use of the display. There is a concern that exposure to the video display terminal (VDT) might be harmful to users. Extensive research into the effects of exposure to VDTs in several countries did not identify harmful effects. Some unions have negotiated provisions in their contracts that allow VDT users an immediate transfer if they become pregnant. More recently, concerns have turned to magnetic fields. These are called very low-frequency (VLF) and extremely low-frequency (ELF) electromagnetic fields. Some research shows that magnetic fields are harmful to humans. Manufacturers have turned to reducing the magnetic fields generated by their products. VLF shields are incorporated in most new monitor designs.

Some workers have incurred disabilities from their improper posture while working at computers.[7] We can avoid this problem. We can expect improvements to continue, and to improve the physical aspects of tech-

---

[6]Research Summary from a Zenith Data Systems news release, dated May 15, 1990.

(1) Work Faster—On average, novice GUI users completed 42% more tasks than novice CUI users in the same time. Experienced GUI users completed 35% more tasks than CUI users.

(2) Work Better—Experienced GUI users correctly completed a higher proportion of attempted exercises: 91% vs. 74%. And 69% of experienced GUI users completed all tasks correctly vs. 17% for CUI users.

(3) More Productive—Both experienced and novice GUI users accomplished 58% more correct work in the same time than CUI users.

(4) Lower Frustration and (5) Lower Fatigue—After two days learning to use microcomputers and applications, GUI novices rated their frustration at 2.7 (out of 10), whereas CUI novices rated their frustration at 5.3. Experienced users' fatigue was rated at 4.3 for GUI and 5.8 for CUI.

(6) Better Ability to Self Teach and Explore—GUI novices felt greater confidence than CUI novices in their abilities to explore an application's advanced features: 5.0 vs. 2.4 before a test, and 7.5 vs. 5.8 after.

(7) Learn More Capabilities—GUI novices attempted 23% more new tasks than CUI novices

[7]Typewriters were almost always placed on typewriter stands. Computers were placed on higher desks. The carpal tunnel syndrome, and other repetitive strain injuries (RSI) were not a familiar business term until the advent of computers.

nology-based learning. Surely, learners can feel more, or less, comfortable while studying. Stress is probably the most ubiquitous office problem, and the hardest to pinpoint. It's unclear if the stress comes from working at a VDT or from the tighter deadlines and stricter monitoring of using computers. Whatever the reason, the stress is real. The National Institute for Occupational Safety and Health found that clerical workers, working with VDT's in the insurance industry had the highest stress level of any group it had studied. Their stress was higher than Air Traffic Controllers. An antidote for some stress is simply getting up and walking around. Thus, taking breaks is an effective cure for a case of the VDT's.

Based on their human comfort research, Northern Telecom recommended the following specifications. See Figure 11.2.

Figure 11.2.
Specifications for Human Comfort

• eye to screen distance	18-28"
• keyboard height off floor	27.5"
• seat height off floor	16"
• screen centerline height off floor	39"
• screen tilt	15°
(to reduce glare)	

Results of studies will receive publicity as they become available.[8] For now, here are some easy tips on how to stay healthy at the VDT:

- Be sure that your chair is not too high. Dangling feet reduce blood flow that can lead to swollen ankles. The chair should have an adjustable seat and back height, armrests, and swivel.
- Avoid any glare around the screen. Avoid direct light, whether from the sun or bright overhead. Light from a window, or from normal office lighting can make eyes strain to see the dimly lit screen.
- Place written material near the screen. Constant re-focusing from a VDT to paper can cause extreme eye strain. There are many document holders on the market that let you put papers wherever you want; the best place is near the screen.
- The keyboard and mouse should allow forearms to be horizontal. A keyboard that forces arms or wrists to work at extreme angles can lead to strained and even pinched nerves. Look for an adjustable height and distance set-up, with a wrist rest.
- The screen should tilt and swivel. It should be at or below eye level, and no more than 20 degrees below the line of sight. The more the head has to bend down, the greater the strain on the neck and back.

---

[8]Watch for OSHA's national office to develop and release general industry ergonomic standards, including mandatory guidelines for computer use and workplace design.

It should have a radiation shield or be a low emission design. Some users prefer a screen filter.

Other considerations in establishing a technology-based learning environment include:

- carpeting, low static (contributes to good acoustics)
- lighting, indirect (to reduce glare)
- acoustic ceiling
- administrative area separate
- audio delivered to learners by headphones
- air conditioning (for human comfort, not equipment)
- electrical power, stable (equipment must be protected against voltage surge)

Courseware Ergonomics

There is a wide variation in the "learner friendliness" of courseware. Well-designed courseware has built-in consistency. This eases learning. Learners benefit from consistency in the courseware "infrastructure." *Little things mean a lot.* The learner will have planned support available, with the use of certain keys. "Help" will be available, to provide planned instructions. A help function provides the learner with predetermined information on how to proceed. As technology-based learning becomes more widely used, you and I will demand courseware design that promotes ease of use.

Advantages and Disadvantages of Technology-Based Learning

Advantages:

- + Interaction with the system usually allows trainees to complete the instruction in less time than with traditional methods.
- + Stimulating multimedia presentations with high interaction can make learning less painful.
- + Instruction can be delivered when and where most convenient.
- + Scheduling can be flexible.
- + Students can show mastery of objectives at the outset, so an employee does not spend time studying already-familiar material.[9]
- + Prevents a trainee from proceeding to more advanced materials until all prerequisites are thoroughly understood.
- + Frees instructors from the lecture environment. They then have more time to counsel individual trainees. They also have more time to maintain (update) the curriculum and keep it relevant to the requirements of the organization.

---

[9]John Buchanan, then United Airlines training manager, said; "No amount of time or money can teach someone what they already know!"

+ Automated record keeping precisely measures student progress. Courses presented in an orderly, logical progression. With accurate records, instructors can easily track where students are in their training paths.
+ Reduced loss of productive time away from the job, or earlier readiness for a new job.
+ Can lead to more accurate job performance by learners, with benefits to productivity.
+ The savings realized should exceed the cost of the project within a reasonable time, such as five years.

Disadvantages:

− Initial cost of technology-based learning development is high, compared to the cost of designing and developing a lecture-based course.
− Development may require skills not now available.
− Equipping equal numbers of simultaneous learners costs more for technology-based learning.

CBL in General

Computer-based learning resources do not teach, nor do they manage the instruction. They do make learning easier, more appropriate, or more fun. The components of CBL include: computer supported learning resources, computer managed instruction, and computer assisted instruction. The Computer-Based Learning Model is shown in Figure 11.3.

University research pioneered the use of computers for learning. This origin led to use of the term computer-based *education*, or "CBE." When industrial organizations began to use the so-called computer-based education, they substituted the more comfortable term "training" for the academically oriented "education." The result was CBT. Some organizations chose to use "instruction," resulting in CBI.

Still, others who prefer thinking in learner-oriented terms prefer CBL. The authors' bias is clear from the title of this section. This sort of proliferation of terms does not cause confusion among experienced users, because they know the terms just mentioned are synonymous. Variations in meaning can make terms confusing. Unfortunately, that has happened with one term specifically. A closer look at what the major CBL-related terms mean will help. This is the "umbrella" term. It includes the activities described by the other terms. A personal favorite is the definition given by a man called the "father of CBE," Donald Bitzer, of the University of Illinois. Bitzer said that CBE is "anytime a person and a computer get together . . . and one of them learns something."

CBE, CBT, CBI, and CBL are really synonyms. The term Computer-based Learning is becoming increasingly popular, reflecting today's emphasis on learner centered thinking. It is also appropriate to all settings: academic, business, industrial and even the home. We will use CBL.

Figure 11.3
Computer-based Learning Model

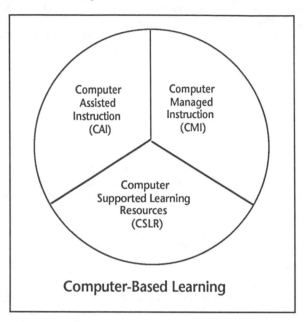

Terminology

Ron Anderson said that CBL has a "lexicon replete with jargon and acronyms apparently designed to baffle all but the initiated."[10] He was right. The terms can be confusing. Here is a simplified list to help with this chapter. Complete definitions appear in the glossary.

> CBL = Computer-based Learning
> CBL = CBE (Computer-based Education)
> CBL = CBT (Computer-based Training)
> CBL = CBI (Computer-based Instruction)
> Components of CBL =   Computer Assisted Instruction (CAI)
>   Computer Managed Instruction (CMI)
>   Computer Supported Learning Resources (CSLR)

It is variations in meaning that can make terms confusing. Some HRD practitioners use "CAI" instead of CBL (or CBE or CBT) as the general descriptive term. Usually, the person using "CAI" is unaware that such casual use can cause confusion. The main reason for the too broad use of

---

[10]In the Second Edition of this book.

"CAI" is that many people think that CAI is the whole field. Usually, they are completely unaware of the full range of technology-based instruction!

Components of CBL

Each component of CBL is the subject of a separate chapter of this book. Briefly, they are as follows:

Computer Assisted Instruction

CAI is the use of a computer in the actual instructional process. The various forms which CAI can take are modes. The modes of CAI are:

- Tutorial
- Drill and Practice
- Instructional Game
- Modeling
- Simulation
- Problem Solving

CAI includes the combination of computer and video called "interactive video." It is not a separate mode, since it does the function of one of the existing modes.

Computer Managed Instruction

CMI is the management of instruction by computer. CAI always directly involves learning. CMI does not. The modes of CMI are:

- Testing
- Prescription Generation
- Record Keeping

CMI is a potent technique. A smaller investment of resources in CMI can often produce a bigger result for the organization than CAI. Often, CMI may be the best way to begin use of CBL in an organization.

Computer Supported Learning Resources

CSLR provides access to information that we can use to learn. For example: a *library* is a non-computer learning resource. We use CSLR like a library. The difference is that a computer program supports a CSLR. CSLRs ease communication, retrieval, examination, and manipulation of the data. The modes of CSLR are:

- Data Bases
- Telecommunications
- Expert Systems
- Hypermedia

Relating CBL to Instructional Objectives

Class of Media: Instructional medium

Characteristics: Computers may combine with other media to provide individualized instruction. Students may be shown or placed in highly simulated environments by combining computer capabilities with other media or equipment for instruction or testing.

Application to types of learning:

Cognitive objectives. Computers can control interactive self-instruction to teach concepts, rules, principles, steps and processes, and complex calculations. Combined with other media, computers can teach recognition or discrimination of applicable visual stimuli and audio stimuli.

Psychomotor objectives. Computer terminals are an excellent "real world" device for teaching skills when students will work with terminals on the job. When combined with simulated equipment, or facilities from the job environment, computers are an excellent tool to create real world conditions.

Affective objectives. Very useful when used as described in Psychomotor Objectives.

Advantages and Disadvantages of CBL

Advantages:

+ Improved human performance possible.
+ Potential inclusion of human and physical resources formerly inaccessible to learners.
+ Sophisticated access, processing, viewing, and storage of resources possible.
+ Cost can be reasonable—based on the component used.

Disadvantages:

− Instructional success still depends on the quality of the instructional materials.
− May lead to an expense if not related to technology in current use.

✔✔✔
Checklist of Considerations for CBL

Instructions. The following checklist is intended as a "memory-jogger" when contemplating investing in a computer based learning system. Because of the many complex issues involved, the list cannot be comprehensive. The questions present only the most frequent or common issues you should consider when planning to develop a computer-based system. Therefore, you must edit (or add items to) the list, based on *known* local conditions.

It would be unusual to answer the questions with all yes's or no's. Use your own judgment in weighing the merits, or weight, of each question when tallying results of the lists.

Review decision to use CBL. Considering curriculum, task analysis, and instructional needs, weigh the value of your combination of answers to the following questions.

	Yes	No
Is individualized instruction desirable to serve most of your curriculum needs? (There are little or no advantages to student interaction or instructor intervention in classroom situation.)	❏	○
Are there skilled developers available to prepare the instruction?	❏	○
Will course content allow ample development time needed for quality materials?	❏	○
Are there existing course materials that meet your instructional needs available to lease or purchase?	❏	○
Have you determined what forms of media are needed to provide audio and visual stimuli required for the curriculum?	❏	○
Is upper management committed to supporting CBL?	❏	○
Has money been budgeted to allow maintenance of the system after installed?	❏	○
Is there a need for controlling student progress through course materials? For example: Is there a need for blocking unauthorized students from taking certain materials?	❏	○
Have you determined specifically what analysis and report data will be needed? (Too much data to struggle with can be as bad as not enough.)	❏	○
Are frequent or rapid updates of course materials necessary?	❏	○

Is centralized storage of data desirable or necessary?   ❏   ○

Must a large student population, spread over a wide
geographic area, be served?   ❏   ○

Must large amounts of data from student—scores
and results of analysis—be processed?   ❏   ○

Sample List of
Technology-Based Learning Development Personnel

Analyst

The analyst does the analysis—the first, most crucial (and sometimes neglected) step in the courseware development process. The analyst identifies the learning requirement and determines the nature and scope of the needed instruction.

Designer

The designer is responsible for the instructional plan and methods. The designer maintains close relations with other members of the team, especially the developers and subject matter experts.

Developer

The developer produces courseware based on the design. Developers may also write text, generate graphics, etc. Without a separate media specialist, they do those functions.

Media Specialist

Multimedia courseware obviously needs additional media, for which we consult specialists include text, video (tape or disc), and slides. The aid of a media specialist may be the only way for your organization to do a first-rate job. The media specialist often is an outside contractor.

Programmer/Data Entry Person

The programmer uses the author system (or the learning specific computer language) and development tools to create the courseware, including all modes of CMI, CAI, and CSLR.

The data entry person is a clerical level position. This person uses only courseware author systems.

Subject Matter Expert (SME)

The subject matter expert is usually not a permanent team member. The SME is intimately familiar with the subject matter.

CHAPTER 12

Computer Assisted Instruction

CAI IS THE USE OF A COMPUTER TO INTERACT DIRECTLY WITH the student for presenting lesson content. Because of the flexibility and capability of a computer to provide branching instruction, it can assume the role of an infinitely patient tutor. Computers may also control other media and provide students with necessary reference materials, performance aids, and clerical services, and simulate environmental or laboratory facilities, depending on the course.

CAI has produced some remarkable success stories and some dismal failures. However, most of the failures were caused by a lack of analysis and planning resulting in a mismatch between instructional needs and computer system capabilities. The checklist at the end of this chapter presents some considerations and activities that you should take into account before investing in CAI.

We used to debate whether computers were effective in presenting instruction. New organizations faced the question of whether they should use CAI. Many staged experiments to determine whether it really "worked" (long after that question had really been put to rest). Finally, research ended all this wasted activity.[1]

---

[1] Kulik, J., Kulik, C., and Cohen, P. (1980) "Effectiveness of Computer-based College Teaching: A Meta-analysis of Findings" in *Review of Educational Research*, Vol. 50, pp. 525-544.

CAI continues its increasing impact in all areas of instruction. Whether this impact is positive depends on the amount of analysis given an organization's real instructional needs. Ignoring this analysis can often lead to energy wasted. We have seen people trying to distort the world to fit it, somehow, into a computer for the sake of producing instruction. Effort devoted to determine the *proper* delivery system is well rewarded—no matter what that system is. ■

Computer Assisted Instruction in General

This term is the principal source of confusion and difficulty. CAI is the use of a computer in the actual instructional process. Some people, who should know better, generate confusion when they use "CAI" instead of CBL as the general descriptive term. Usually, the person using "CAI" in that way is unaware of the distinction.

For us, CAI is a medium of instruction. It applies in appropriate learning situations. Film, videotape, and textbooks are other media. CBL, CMI, and CBLR (all covered in other chapters) are not media.

The various forms in which we can apply CAI are modes. When you use CAI as a medium of instruction, it will be in one of these six modes. The modes of CAI are: tutorial, drill and practice, instructional games, modeling, simulation, and problem solving.

Figure 12.1
Modes of CAI

```
┌─────────────────────────────┐
│                             │
│   • Tutorial                │
│   • Drilll and Practice     │
│   • Instructional Game      │
│   • Modeling                │
│   • Simulation              │
│   • Problem Solving         │
│                             │
└─────────────────────────────┘
```

Tutorial

This is the mode most familiar to those new to the field. In a tutorial, the learner interacts one-on-one with the "program." The process in a good tutorial advances as the finest tutor would personally undertake the process.[2] A typical tutorial lesson presents some information—and then checks the learner's understanding. This process repeats throughout the lesson. Based on the learner's understanding, the learner's path continues to another point. If the learner did not understand, the tutorial presents the

---

[2]Illustrations describing the method used by Socrates are often used to explain the structure of a tutorial.

first point in a new way. The reinforcement process provides corrective comments to the learner.

A good tutorial uses "branching." It keeps the learner actively involved in the learning process. Figure 12.2 shows the general pattern of a lesson with branching. Its interactivity involves the student in the lesson. Learning cannot be passive.

Figure 12.2
Branching CAI

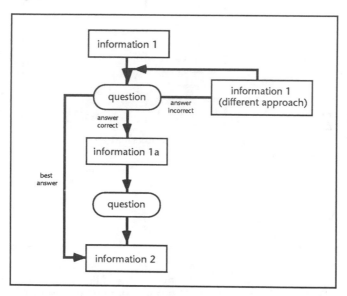

Poor tutorials are "linear." They are (derisively) called "page turners." Figure 12.3 shows the general pattern of a linear lesson. It has little interactivity. The contrast with a branching lesson is obvious. You may wonder why, if one is better, use the less effective design? The answer lies in the effort required to produce the branching lesson. It is greater. When CAI must be created "for a price" the result is often less interactivity.

Drill and Practice

Drill and practice is also a very familiar mode of CAI. One reason is that it takes less effort to produce than the other modes. This does not mean that it is not a valuable tool. It is. A well-developed concept of drill and practice existed well before there was anything called a computer. Drill and practice has repetitive presentation of problems to the learner. A drill and practice example is one in which presents the learner a problem such as, "How much is two and three?" When the learner answers the question another follows, such as "how much is three plus four?" After a given number of problems, the system informs the learner of the total number of questions presented, number right . . . and wrong. The series of addition problems is a simple example of the drill and practice technique. It is not the only form of drill and practice. The drill and practice mode of CAI is successful with far more complex subject matter. Drill and practice is a good choice for learning terminology or the steps in a procedure.

Figure 12.3
Linear CAI

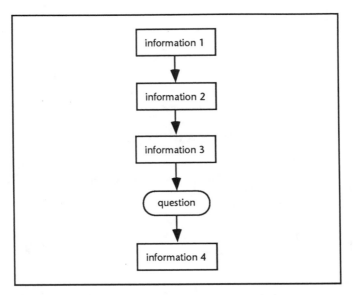

The series of addition problems is a simple example of the drill and practice technique. It is not the only form of drill and practice. The drill and practice mode of CAI is successful with far more complex subject matter. Drill and practice is a good choice for learning terminology or the steps in a procedure.

Figure 12.4
Drill and Practice

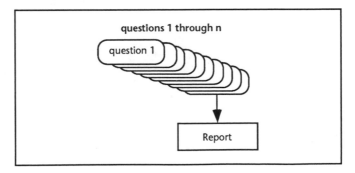

Sometimes, what appears to be a simulation is set up to provide drill and practice for a specific procedure. The "simulation" cannot actually simulate anything beyond the procedure to be learned. The learner repeats the lesson until the desired level of performance is reached. Another possibility is to use a real full simulator to repeatedly practice one limited procedure

Instructional Games

The term "game" does not mean frivolous activity. In CAI an instructional game is not always recognizable as a "game." The idea that they are "games" instead of instruction created a problem in their use. They are the problem child of CAI. It should be no surprise that instructional games often do contain an element of entertainment. In a CAI game, the computer looks up the tables, calculates, and keeps score. The learners can concentrate on the events of the game. Unfortunately, the dividing line between amusement and learning is not always easily discernible. It probably is unneeded anyway. Our point is that learning while "playing" is, nevertheless, learning.

Instructional games are a completely valid and "professional" way to stimulate learning. Formerly, some individuals have had difficulty believing that learners who enjoy the learning could be having a worthwhile experience.

Because of this prejudice, this mode of CAI is not used in all organizations. In fact, the use of games struck a mortal blow to some projects. Selection of games calls for discretion. Games probably should not grace the first phase of an organization's entry into CBL. There remains a real danger of project cancellation because of what may be seen as a "trivial" use of the organization's resources.

Models form the basis for many instructional games. The models used in games have varying degrees of validity. An instructional game has goals, scoring (usually), and an element of competition—that may be self-competition.

Modeling

The use of the CBL system to represent another system or process is modeling. The learner can change values and see the effects of the change on the model. A model is a non-realistic representation of the system (or representation may be unachievable). An example is a population model. The learner can change demographic variables such as birth rate, infant mortality, or death rate in the model. The learner sees the results such changes would create, if they actually took place. They may be displayed in a table or a graph. The learner can see the effects on the population over time. We can model population accurately, but it does not lend itself to realistic representation.

Simulation

Simulation involves a representation of a situation or device, with some degree of realism. The computer simulates the item of equipment, device, system, or sub-system. Simulation enables the learner to experience operating that equipment. A strength of simulation is that the learning can happen without destruction of the equipment or harm to the learner or others. Simulation can be manual, in "hybrid" form using both manual and computer support, and solely with computer power. CBL simulation con-trasts with the most familiar examples of simulation—simulators.

Simulation and simulators deserve expanded coverage. They are the subject of Chapter 16.

Problem Solving

Problem solving was the mode of CAI seen least in industrial HRD (and other learning situations). That has changed. In problem solving, the student uses the computer itself as a tool to solve a (work-related) prob-lem. Any software may be used. It depends on what skill the learner needs. Problem solving has always had good application in math and science in-struction. The opportunities for appropriate use in typical learning situa-tions grow as more employees use computers to do their work.

Relating CAI to Instructional Objectives

Class of Media: Instructional medium.

Characteristics: CAI may use a variety of different learning stations or combine with other media to provide individualized instruction. By com-bining computer capabilities with other media or equipment students experience highly simulated environments.

Application to types of learning:

Cognitive objectives. CAI can control interactive self-instruction to teach concepts, rules, principles, steps and processes, and complex calcu-lations. Combined with other media, computers can teach recognition or discrimination of proper visual stimuli and audio stimuli.

Psychomotor objectives. Computers are an excellent "real world" device for teaching skills when students will work with terminals on the job. When combined with simulated equipment, or facilities from the job environment, computers are an excellent tool to create real world conditions. Some typical examples are: simulated landing of aircraft, docking a ship, or emergency drills.

Affective objectives. Very useful when used as described in Psychomotor objectives or to control film or video materials.

Advantages and Disadvantages of CAI

Advantages:

+ Individual instruction is the norm.
+ Self-paced instruction is the norm.

+ Normal classroom size groups can be accommodated.
+ Employees can use their own work station PC as a learning station.
+ Can be combined with CMI for instructional efficiency.
+ Instructor/student ratio can be higher than for instructor-based instruction.
+ The ability of instructors to concentrate on instructor-related tasks, allows them to attend specifically to those students who may be having problems.
+ Excellent means for simulation situations which call for individualized yet coordinated task performance. For example, CAI networked crew coordination training allows each station to represent a specific flight task requirement where the host system monitors the coordination of the stations and provides appropriate feedback. See Chapter 16.

Disadvantages:

– Development of high quality lessons requires significant effort.
– Generic CAI lessons may not be available to meet your needs.
– Learning stations may have greater hardware requirements than workstations.

✔✔✔
Checklist of Considerations for CAI

Instructions. The following checklist is a "memory-jogger" for contemplating use of simulators and simulations. Because of the many complex issues involved, the list cannot be comprehensive. The questions present only the most frequent or common issues for consideration. Edit the list (or add items) based on local conditions. It would be unusual to answer the questions with all yes's or no's. Use judgment in weighing the merits, or weight, of each question when tallying results of the lists.

Review decision to use CAI. Considering curriculum, task analysis and instructional needs, weigh the value of your combination of answers to the following:

A. Consider these general questions.

	Yes	No
Are qualified instructors for the content hard to find?	❏	O
Is CAI necessary to serve most of your curriculum needs?	❏	O

B. Consider these questions related to the subject matter:

	Yes	No
Can knowledge and conceptual subjects of the objectives be represented by words, symbols, or computer graphics?	❏	○
Do the training objectives require computer or computer-related behaviors.	❏	○
Does reaching the objective *not* need a large attitude change by the student.	❏	○
Does reaching the objective *not* require complex audio feedback to the learner?	❏	○
Is standardized training important?	❏	○
Is the subject matter conceptual?	❏	○
Is the subject matter intended for "beginning" learners in the chosen content?	❏	○
Is the subject matter proprietary?	❏	○
Is the subject matter reasonably stable?	❏	○

C. Consider these questions related to the learners:

	Yes	No
Are there considerable variations in student background and experience?	❏	○
Does the organization have limited money for travel and accommodations?	❏	○
Is decentralized training important?	❏	○
Is the student population geographically dispersed?	❏	○
Must the large numbers of students be trained in a limited time?	❏	○
Will large numbers of people be trained eventually?	❏	○

CHAPTER 13

Computer Managed Instruction

CMI PROVIDES A METHOD TO BE SURE THAT EACH STUDENT'S interaction is appropriate to ability. CMI carefully tracks each student, assessing progress and learning resource effectiveness, and carrying out these functions with reduced clerical effort. CMI can be a robust and extensive learning management tool. Central system CMI evolved exceptional sophistication in the past. On the principal systems, it was the most heavily used capability. Personal computers have lacked the processing power and storage to make CMI practical. Current models have the needed sufficiency.

Computer Managed Instruction originally entered instruction as a device to help instructors cope with growing clerical actions. As interest in self-paced instruction grew, so did demands on time and effort to score grades, maintain individual records, and summarize student and class results. These functions were often incremented existing computer systems used for administrative and summary reports. Your CMI system should feature all three modes of CMI. These are: testing, prescription generation, and record keeping.

Now the role of CMI has expanded. Added roles include supplying help in test building, assuring security of course materials, guiding students through lesson materials, and helping in analysis of both student results and segments of course content.

Possibly because CMI received less fanfare and funding than CAI, less attention focused on its successes and failures. It grew slowly and steadily

169

while staying in the background. CMI can serve independently in support of instruction. However, it is often thought of only as a support system for CAI. Since the two systems are compatible, they are usually used in tandem.

You break the instructional materials into content areas related to learning objectives (the rigorous objectives popularized by Robert Mager). Within each of these areas, the student alternates between the activities of testing, reviewing test results, selecting study materials assigned by the instructional prescription process, and studying. The computer managed instruction program directs the learner to learning experiences. They may be on the computer system, by a media device other than the computer terminal, or both. The system automatically records the student's progress and maintains extensive records. The instructor's may use them in helping the student to learn and for administrative purposes. The CMI system allows the learner to progress at one's own pace. It eases the management and control of the educational process for the instructor. It also provides feedback to both the learner and the facilitator about progress (or lack of it) and retention of knowledge.

CMI is as strong as it sounds. Several years ago United Airlines proved very effective use of CBL solely through use of CMI. CMI, as carried out on small computers, continues to grow in sophistication. It will soon approach the power of the best central versions. There are two problems delaying this. One is the capacity of the smaller systems. The other is the big lead in the effort necessary to develop a sophisticated learning management system.

An important consideration is the economy of effort typical with CMI use. A given amount of human or financial resources, if dedicated to CMI, can often affect a larger HRD effort than CAI. For example, if you have an entire videotape course that is satisfactory coverage for a given subject, you can make it even better with CMI. By relating the videotapes to objectives, and creating the appropriate learning management structure, you can make the course accountable (the students will learn what you expect). You also reduce individual student effort. Comparable effort devoted to producing CAI lessons might only replace a single videotape. The benefits and potential of important savings possible through CMI will justify that extra effort and attention directed toward effective incorporation in the organization's CBL project. ■

CMI in General

It should come as no surprise that CMI is *truly* the management of instruction by computer. The term is not as familiar as CAI to many course developers. This surely does is not reflect its inherent worth, or its frequency of use. It may reflect less romance in managing instruction well than in teaching with an "exotic" technology. The distinction is that CAI always directly involves learning, and CMI does not.

Anyhow, CMI has hidden in the shadow of CAI, at least for those not using CBL. This is a self-correcting condition. Since CMI offers the necessary power to apply considerable efficiency to learning, it will receive increasing recognition as more organizations begin to use the testing, prescription generation, and record keeping modes. These modes are listed in Figure 13.1.

Figure 13.1
Modes of CMI

> • testing
> • prescription generation
> • record keeping

Testing

CMI testing is the CBL function to measure the learner's knowledge of specified objectives. Sometimes CAI includes quizzes called progress checks to determine the state of learning in progress. These may branch the learner to various parts of the lesson. They are different from CMI. CMI testing offers learning efficiency by verifying the learner's mastery of the objectives. This determination is the foundation of CMI, since it accurately provides the information needed to prescribe learning activities.

Prescription Generation

In prescription generation, the CMI system generates an instructional prescription for each unmastered learning objective. Each separate learner receives an individual prescription. So, as you and I approach a new subject we bring different backgrounds and experiences. Each of us may know parts of the subject, but not all of it.

The test will show which different parts each of us does not know. Refer to Figure 13.2 to see a diagram of the prescription generation process. Then we will each receive different prescriptions. You determine the prescriptions during the design of the instruction. Since individuals master different objectives, each will only study the materials needed. CMI directs each learner only to those learning resources that support the unmastered objective(s). This shortens the time each learner must study. The selectivity results in reduced time spent in instruction. This is the basis for instructional efficiencies associated with CBL.

Record Keeping

The CMI system continuously generates and stores records of individual and group progress. An important feature is automatic generation of these records. They are then available to the learning specialist, as needed, on demand. You are free from statistics and records you really do not need to see. There is also no need to keep a closet with shelves piled high with old records and reports. We can see them when, and if, wanted. Certain records, such as the individual grade book, are usually accessible to the learner.

CMI is a compelling technique. It is usual that a smaller investment of resources can produce a bigger result for the organization with CMI than with CAI. An exclusively CMI solution can often successfully solve a given organization, project, or performance problem. It is also usual for CMI to be the best way for an organization to start use of computers in training. In the practical world of learning, the use of CMI can often produce a concrete financial saving compared with traditional methods.

Figure 13.2
Computer Managed Instruction Model

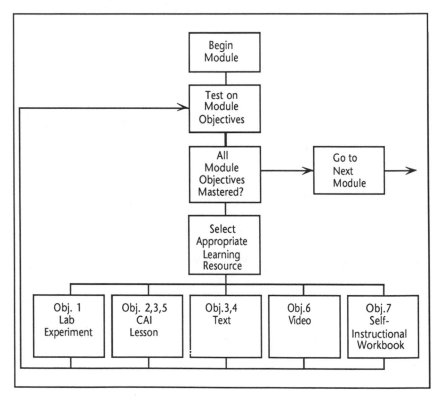

Relating CMI to Instructional Objectives

Class of Media: Instructional support system.

Characteristics: Using computers to manage instruction is a proven tool. Organizations have founds that management of instruction can be important even if the instructional delivery itself is not computer-based.

Application to types of learning:

Cognitive objectives. Not applicable.

Psychomotor objectives. Not applicable.

Affective objectives. Not applicable.

CMI and Media

CMI is the natural friend of all media prescription generation mode can assign the learner to audio, text, videotapes, or disc. This suggests that CMI is a component of paramount importance in any computer-based learning system.

Advantages and Disadvantages of CMI

Advantages:

+ Normally, least costly computer support for instruction.
+ Should a breakdown of the CMI system happen, the study materials remain available to students.
+ Automatic gathering of test results.
+ Sophisticated collection processing and automatic storage of instructional results.
+ Extensive analysis of instructional success possible.

Disadvantages:

− Does not teach or instruct directly.
− Instructional success still depends on the quality of the instructional materials (not a part of CMI).

✔✔✔
Checklist of Considerations for CMI

Instructions. The following checklist is a "memory-jogger" for contemplating use of CMI. Because of the many complex issues involved, the list cannot be comprehensive. The questions present only the most frequent or common issues for consideration. Edit the list (or add items) based on your local conditions.

Consider relevance of for CMI applications to instructional process. It would be unusual to answer the questions with all yes's or no's. Use judgment in weighing the merits, or weight, of each question when tallying results of the lists.

	Yes	No
Is the recording of student performance important?	❑	O
Is there a need to score or summarize many student tests?	❑	O
Is there a need for controlling student progress through course materials? For example:		
• To control pre- and post-lesson tests, preventing students from taking lessons out of sequence?	❑	O
• To end punishing testing? (Stop tests after student misses a set number of questions.)	❑	O
• To route students to remedial lessons or automatically provide drill and practice?	❑	O
• To fix a series of lessons or units through a course?	❑	O
Is there a need for course security (blocking unauthorized students from taking certain materials)?	❑	O
Is there a need for storing large amounts of course development data (for example: task analysis, student population analysis, or student performance data by objective)?	❑	O
Is there a need for cross-referencing capabilities of course data such as tasks, sub tasks, etc.?	❑	O
Is there a need to provide students with job aids or reference tools such as calculator facilities, log tables, references and directories?	❑	O
Have you determined specifically what analysis and report data you need? (Too much data can be as bad as not enough.)	❑	O

CHAPTER 14

Computer Supported Learning Resources

CSLR IS THE LEAST OFTEN SEEN COMPONENT OF COMPUTER-based learning. You may be comfortable with the term "data base." The oldest form of CSLR is a data base. It is a good exemplar of the type. A data base is a pool of information, useful to a learner, but does not (itself) teach. It only provides information that we can use to learn. For example: a library is a non-computer learning resource. We use a CSLR in the same way as a library, except a useful CSLR is always supported by a computer program. The computer program expedites the retrieval, examination. and manipulation of the data.

A possible point of confusion might exist between Computer Supported Learning Resources (CSLR) and the learning resources which CMI prescribes. CSLR is a completely separate part of CBL. A learning resource prescribed by CMI is anything predetermined to teach its associated learning objective. The learning resource prescribed by CMI may be a CAI lesson, videotape, textbook, audiotape, lecture, or any other learning experience. CSLR resources help the learner, but do not teach directly (like the library).

Another mode of CSLR is communications. Communications can take many forms. We can record comments and notes for later use. Files can help information sharing among users with like interests. Individuals and groups can exchange notes among themselves. Instantaneous communication is possible among users of a network of any size. Learning specialists use this capability to exchange information. The learner and a (remote) subject matter expert can also communicate. Computers and communication networks also ease distance learning as video teleconferencing and computer conferencing.

A newer mode of CSLR is hypermedia. Hypermedia is what data bases have been waiting for! It provides a friendly front end to permit the user to use the data based on individual interest—as opposed to CAI's predetermined way. The computer program smoothes sophisticated retrieval, examination, and manipulation of the data.

Another mode of CSLR is expert systems. Expert systems are a CSLR because they are computer-based and don't teach. They are simply electronic job aids.

Thus far, CSLR has not come into its own. There are several factors that prevent more extensive use. Some need existing data bases. There were not the "development tools" (as there are for CAI and CMI) to make their implementation easier. They most often require more access to, and a bigger share of, the computer power, memory, and storage. They cannot promise direct realization of learning objectives (like the library). Their less clearly defined results make them a less sure investment for the organization. ■

CSLR in General

Computer supported learning resources do not teach, nor do they manage the instruction. They do make learning easier, more appropriate, or more fun. The modes of CSLR include: data bases, telecommunications, expert systems, and hypermedia. They are listed in Figure 14.1.

Figure 14.1
Modes of CSLR

> • Data bases
> • Telecommunications
> • Expert Systems
> • Hypermedia

Relating CSLR to Instructional Objectives

Class of Media: Instructional support system.

Characteristics: Using computers to support instruction is a tool that only began to emerge in the 1990's.

Application to types of learning:

Cognitive objectives. Not applicable.

Psychomotor objectives. Not applicable.

Affective objectives. Not applicable.

CSLR and Media

CSLR can support, or associated with, any media. Since its elements are relatively untried, new ways of using them will evolve. We can consider them a complement to any existing computer-based learning system.

Advantages and Disadvantages of CSLR

Advantages:

+ Improved human performance possible.
+ Should a breakdown of the one CSLR component happen; other study materials remain available to students.
+ Potential inclusion of human and physical resources formerly inaccessible to learners.
+ Sophisticated access, processing, viewing, and storage of resources possible.
+ Cost can be reasonable—depending on the mode used.

Disadvantages:

– Does not teach or instruct.
– Instructional success still depends on the quality of the instructional materials (not a part of CSLR).
– Leads to a new expense, if not related to technology in current use.

✔✔✔
Checklist of Considerations for CSLR

Not applicable. See considerations for each mode of CSLR.

Data Bases in General

Most academic institutions have access to 75 or more data bases. As our ability to access data bases improves, there will be still more of them. The key one for HRD is the organization's own data bases. They have the data that can provide significant and realistic learning for some employees.

Also, some data bases are becoming available on CD-ROM. This permits examination without the attendant telecommunications cost and possible inconvenience.

Relating Data Bases to Instructional Objectives

Class of Media: Instructional support system.

Characteristics: Using computers to support instruction is a tool that only began to emerge in the 1990's.

Application to types of learning:

Cognitive objectives. Not applicable.

Psychomotor objectives. Not applicable.

Affective objectives. Not applicable.

Data Bases and Media

Data Bases can contain or reference media.

Advantages and Disadvantages of Data Bases

Advantages:

+ Sophisticated access, processing, viewing, and storage of resources possible.
+ Wide ranging content.
+ Access to distant data bases possible.
+ Access to the organization's own data bases permits manipulation of realistic data (need not actually change data in the organization's data bases by student manipulation).
+ Sophisticated access, processing, viewing, and storage of resources possible.

Disadvantages:

- Does not teach or instruct.
- Sometimes not directly tied to particular learning objectives.
- Student access depends on student's motivation and may depend on ability to use the data base.
- May lead to a new expense if not related to technology in current use.

✔✔✔
Checklist of Considerations for Data Bases

Instructions. The following checklist is intended as a "memory-jogger" when contemplating use of data bases. The questions present only the most frequent or common issues for consideration. Edit the list (or add items) based on your local conditions.

Consider the requirement for data bases to the instructional process It would be unusual to answer the questions with all yes's or no's. You must use judgment in weighing the merits, or weight, of each question when tallying results of the lists.

	Yes	No
Do data bases exist in the organization?	❏	◯
Do learners ordinarily access data bases at work?	❏	◯
Do data bases that exist contain information applicable to instruction?	❏	◯
Does the organization have current access to remote data bases?	❏	◯
Does the organization have data bases on CD-ROM?	❏	◯

Distance Learning

Distance learning is a growing way of supplying instruction to learners who are dispersed over a wide geographic area. It can allow for specialists who wish to study advanced subjects for whom a reasonable-size group could not form in their own vicinity. It also enables learners to take part in learning activities day or night, weekday, or weekend. Generally, there are two distinct ways of delivering instruction. Either of them will use other media appropriately to support parts of the instruction. In this section we will focus exclusively on the distance learning part of the instruction. We can organize distant learners either as:

- individuals (located in many places)
- group(s) (Large group may include separate small groups. Usually, there is a group at any sub-site)

Group distant learners all study simultaneously. Individual learners may study in one or both of two timing varieties. They are:

- synchronous (all simultaneously)
- asynchronous (at different times—usually of their own choosing)

Each of these methods offers different advantages to the learners and to the organization delivering the instruction. In practice, organizations implement distance learning programs using one of two strategies. The strategy selected depends on whether the learners are groups or individuals, and whether the individual study at the same time or different times. These strategies include the following:

- video-teleconferencing (group synchronous)
- computer conferencing (individual asynchronous)

These possibilities are represented in the Distance Learning Model shown in Figure 14.2.

Figure 14.2
Distance Learning Model

	Synchronous	Asynchronous
Group	Video Teleconferencing	Computer Conferencing
Individual	Computer Conferencing (unusual)	Computer Conferencing (little used)

Either methodology includes certain advantages, and should be selected based on the factors that best suit the instructional plan.

Distance Learning—Video Teleconferencing

An excellent representative of video teleconferencing is the National Technology University (NTU). It is a coordinated, national delivery system that provides advanced education for engineers and scientists. NTU had 29 participating universities in the early 1990s. Modern telecommunications provide the delivery system.

NTU broadcasts courses taught on the university campuses over its Satellite Network. Over one-third of the broadcasts are live-interactive. Courses are broadcast from the 28 universities with uplinks or broadcast stations. Direct phone lines from the receiving sites to the campus classroom provide for faculty-student interaction. Electronic mail, computer conferencing, and telephone office hours supplement this interaction. Enrollees reported that the courses were challenging and applicable to their work environment.

An internal training-type representative of this class of instruction is the corporate training center of NEC Corporation. The center is in a suburb of Tokyo. Regular classes are conducted routinely at the Tokyo site. They are "attended" by corporate students located in distant company offices in Hokkaido and Kyushu, hundreds of miles north and south of Tokyo. In this case, the linked classrooms feature live, full motion video, telephone (FAX), and computer.

Video teleconferencing is also used for live interactive meetings of various kinds. Briefing or updating distant groups is a common use of this technology. In most of these uses, organized learning is not usually expected, and almost never measured or verified.

Distance Learning—Computer Conferencing

An excellent representative of computer conferencing is the courses offered by New York Institute of Technology (NYIT). The computer conferencing courses serve a population constituted differently than video teleconferencing. Single learners study from any location. The instructor may also be anywhere. For example, one instructor lives in Oregon. Her learners lived throughout New York State. Since the premise is that classes do not meet, it does not matter that instructor and student work in widely separated cities.[1]

The model for most video teleconferencing courses is the regular classroom. The instruction is quite normal, except that at least a part of the class is in another location. Computer conferencing uses a new paradigm. Students use a computer with modem to communicate with a central computer that hosts the conferencing system's software. The instructor introduces a topic that results in student input related to the topic. Other students comment on the input of their peers. Instructors, or even

---

[1] Realistically, they cannot meet. Distances are too great. Students, who rave about the advantages of distance learning by computer conferencing, count the inability to meet the other students as their greatest regret.

students, may create side conferences to follow-up on a particularly interesting issue. More nearly multimedia, students may complete assignments using textbook, videotape, magazine article reprint, or handout. Far more pre-instructional organization is necessary. Students must have all materials well before of the need for them. The principal difference is that, unlike classroom instruction, it is not satisfactory merely to sit and watch the instructor and other students. One *must* take part.[2]

Relating Distance Learning to Instructional Objectives

Class of Media: Instructional method.

Characteristics: Learners are isolated from the primary instructional site. They may be collocated or separated from one another. Video or computer media provide the instruction. Instruction often includes other media.

Application to types of learning:

Cognitive objectives. Distance learning methods are suitable for cognitive learning.

Psychomotor objectives. Difficulties showing motion in distant video makes it less desirable, but not impossible. Computer conferencing is unsuited to teach psychomotor objectives.

Affective objectives. All the potential of video is present in video-based distance learning. It is a strong method for affective objectives. The intense individual participation of students in a computer conferencing mode makes affective objectives suitable.

Distance Learning and Media

Distance Learning often uses media for support. These include textbook, audio cassette, videotape, magazine article reprint, or handout.

Advantages and Disadvantages of Distance Learning

Advantages:

+ Possible to learn at one's own geographic location.
+ Possible to study topics that would not justify normal group instruction.
+ Access to distant expert instructors is possible.

---

[2]Learners claim this difference is a primary attraction of the method.

+ In computer conferencing, learners can access the system at times of their own choosing (nights, early morning, etc.).

Disadvantages:

- No personal (first hand) contact.
- No support from other learners when participating alone at one's site.
- Support from central site may be less convenient to access.
- Equipment needed may be unfamiliar to the individual learner.
- May lead to a new expense if not related to technology in current use.

✔✔✔
Checklist of Considerations for Distance Learning

Instructions. The following checklist is a "memory-jogger" for contemplating use of distance learning. The questions present only the most frequent or common issues for consideration. Edit the list (or add items) based on your local conditions. It would be unusual to answer the questions with all yes's or no's. Use judgment in weighing the merits, or weight, of each question when tallying results of the lists.

	Yes	No
Is necessary equipment already installed?	❏	○
Does distance learning potential justify installation?	❏	○
Is it possible to share needed equipment?	❏	○
Do topics justify normal group instruction?	❏	○
Access to local expert instructors is possible?	❏	○
Would learning participation at times of the learner's own choosing be important?	❏	○
Is personal (first hand) contact needed for the topic?	❏	○
Can you provide needed support to learners?	❏	○
Does top management support the distance learning project?	❏	○

Hypertext in General

Hypertext offers training developers important new capabilities.[3] This potent new tool has excited many trainers. However, before we can go very far, we must distinguish between product names and the general terms that training professionals *should* use. HyperCard is one particular product's name. The term "hypermedia" refers to all such products. We also must know about "hypertext."

Hypertext

Just after World War II, Vanevar Bush, the noted atomic scientist, described the idea behind hypertext. Hypertext software links textual information.

Using a personal computer, we can rapidly and accurately browse through documents. Picking a word or phrase in the text leads us directly to linked documents, cross-references, annotations, and footnotes. We *could* do this manually. Now the personal computer makes it possible to use the text information we want in any sequence we wish—with blinding speed.

Hypermedia

Hypermedia is a more inclusive term. It incorporates everything hypertext can do and extends the concept beyond mere text. Words can link directly to a wide variety of media. Visuals include still or motion video, graphs, illustrations, diagrams, computer-generated graphics, and animation. Hypermedia links can also connect directly to audio sources to provide voice, music, and other sounds. Even if your particular organization's application uses text links alone, we refer to it as hypermedia instead of hypertext. This is because of the software's potential capability to add the other media links.

Terminology

Unfortunately, the companies that make hypermedia software have chosen *not* to use common terminology. Here are some definitions.
- hypermedia programs = stacks
- pages (screens) within a stack = cards
- potentially active spots on the screen that begin a link when chosen = buttons. (Buttons may look like actual physical buttons or take the shape of a familiar object.)
- buttons that look like objects = icons. (They may be visible or invisible—hiding behind a machine part that we want make active. When we try to "touch" the part with our mouse, we touch the invisible button and see what the designer intended.)

---

[3]The U.S. Hypermedia software market is forecasted to grow more than 800 percent, to over 13 million shipments by 1997. Source Market Intelligence Research Corporation.

Hypermedia is not CAI.

These two computer-based technologies are not alike. They can be used together in a complementary way.

Hypermedia provides the user rapid access to information at will. The user's path through the information is unstructured and self-directed. Hypermedia is a terrific way for a motivated learner to study. Computer assisted instruction is fundamentally different.

The CAI designer carefully plans how the information will unfold to the learner. Normally, the learner follows a completely structured and controlled path through the information. The structure is necessary. It guarantees achievement of the planned learning objectives.

The hypermedia stack is a compelling supplement to training. Because of its "library-like" characteristics, hypermedia can serve as a resource accessible from within a CAI lesson. Hypermedia can continue as a job aid after training ends. One way to separate the two technologies is to think of *hypermedia user* and *CAI learner*. It can provide the interface between the user and software that would otherwise be hard to use. Both MS/DOS and Macintosh computers have hypermedia products available.

**Figure 12.3 Example HyperCard Stack
(Shown Reduced Size)**

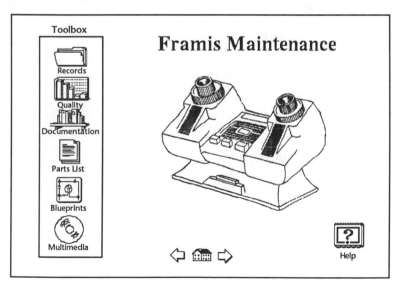

The sample card helps the user get information about maintaining the Framis. The user touches one of the icon buttons with a mouse. Blueprints, schedules, records, or even a videodisc demonstration of a maintenance procedure appear as desired. The card is useful to learn new procedures. Users can also easily access information such as maintenance records, or to calculate or analyze quality control data. The framis maintenance card of our widget activator stack won't just fly into existence because we want it. First, like other training-related items, we must plan carefully to be confident of the usefulness of the finished stack.

Then we create the stack through a form of programming. A "script" controls a button's action on the linked relationship between cards, and even stacks. The simplicity that has enabled "non-techies" to create their own stacks is the basis for the success of hypermedia. Scripts use regular English words such as "print this card" or "turn video on."

Hypermedia software makes an excellent "front end" for many user applications. Normally it is easy to learn and use. In practice, this means that hypermedia may be part of a single user interface that includes embedded animation, CAI, and expert systems modules.

Relating Hypertext to Instructional Objectives

Class of Media: Instructional support.

Characteristics: Hypertext does not teach. It provides learner controlled access to other media and resources.

Application to types of learning:

Cognitive objectives. Hypertext is suitable to support cognitive learning objectives.

Psychomotor objectives. Hypertext can access sequences on video media. It can indirectly support psychomotor objectives.

Affective objectives. All the potential of video display is supported by hypertext. It would be a strong support for affective objectives.

Hypertext and Media

Like CMI, hypertext is the natural ally of other media. Its nature is to provide user-friendly access to other media for support of learning or performance.

Advantages and Disadvantages of Hypertext

Advantages:

+ Possible to directly support on-job performance.
+ Possible to access a variety of media and other resources easily.
+ Possible to access information as wanted by the learner.

+ Access to data base, spreadsheet, still or motion video information is possible.
+ Easier to program than most computer languages.

Disadvantages:

- Does not teach or instruct.
- May not tie directly to particular learning objectives.
- Generic stacks probably not available for your need.
- Creation of useful stacks require programming.
- Uncontrolled student access to the information depends on the student's interest and motivation.

✔✔✔
Checklist of Considerations for Hypertext

Instructions. The following checklist is intended as a "memory-jogger" when contemplating use of hypertext. The questions present only the most frequent or common issues for consideration. Edit the list (or add items) based on your local conditions.

Consider need for data bases to the instructional process It would be unusual to answer the questions with all yes's or no's. You must use judgment in weighing the merits, or weight, of each question when tallying results of the lists.

	Yes	No
Does necessary equipment exist?	❏	◯
Are staff available with enough skill to program the hypermedia?	❏	◯
Do topics lend themselves to access as desired by the learner?	❏	◯
Does this approach meet organizational instructional goals?	❏	◯
Does this approach meet the organization's performance objectives?	❏	◯
Are student sufficiently motivated to benefit from the planned hypertext application?	❏	◯

Expert Systems in General

Not so long ago, the usual response was "What is an expert system?" Expert systems are computer programs that capture the knowledge of human experts. They are the only form of artificial intelligence that has a significant impact on learning.

Job aids help an employee to do some job-related activity. If we use a job aid, it is probably because the task is difficult to remember or too complex to train the employee reliably to do dependably. The classic job aid is the pilot's checklist. All job aids can reduce the amount of, or even replace, some training. Usually, it is because the time needed to train the employee to "expertise" called for would not be practical, necessary, or desirable. It is perfectly adequate, and not misleading, to think of an expert system as an electronic job aid. It is an application of artificial intelligence, programmed in a "special" way, but the result works like a job aid.

Expert systems are only job aids in electronic clothing. This software produces big paybacks today for many firms engaged in the finance, manufacturing, service, and other sectors. We create the programs by capturing the logical thought patterns *experts* use in solving problems. The systems tell users the best solution to a problem. They can also ask why it is best.

Creating these systems is where instructional technologists come in. We have an important role to play in that process—typically called *knowledge engineering*. That term might not have been intentionally designed to put off trainers, but it always does. The difference between an instructional analyst and a knowledge engineer is slight. The knowledge engineer already knows what form the product of the analysis must take to program into an expert system. We can teach this to a training analyst in a few hours.

In practice, the expert system may be one part of a single user interface. The user may have access to a package that includes embedded animation, CAI, and hypermedia modules.

We use these systems in a variety of applications. The expected uses of such systems are potentially very large. Corporations report big success with expert systems. For example, American Express estimates that its expert systems increase the efficiency of credit authorizers about 50 percent. Texas Instruments expects its capital-proposal package to reduce cost overruns and preparation expenses by average of $2 million annually. Digital Equipment saves $70 million a year from its 10 major expert systems. E.I. du Pont de Nemours & Co. claims a return on investment in expert systems of 1,500 percent. Savings total about $10 million. ■

Reduced Training

Expert systems replace training. That is *always* true. All job aids reduce training because they enable a person to do tasks reliably, accurately, and promptly. They lessen training needed to achieve the same standards. If we define our job as "running sessions" this is a problem. If, on the other hand, we define our job as solving human performance related problems to make our organizations work better—the problem becomes an opportunity.

Characteristics for Expert Systems

We can identify characteristics of appropriate task domain for expert systems. Such domains:

- need human expertise
- can be solved with knowledge
- do not need common sense
- have a narrow focus
- have a minimum number of solutions
- are moderately difficult
- have a high payoff

Resources for Expert Systems

The personnel, hardware, and schedule resources available for expert system development must be determined. We can verify them according to the following checklist: [4]

- Is a domain expert available for consultation?
- Is a competent knowledge engineer available to transfer information into a comprehensive knowledge base?
- Is an expert system programmer available?
- Is hardware available for expert system development?
- Are the development and delivery environment compatible (same system)?
- Is enough time available for expert system development?
- Have you identified the maintenance organization for the system?

Expert Systems and Media

Expert systems may work from within or "called" from any other computer application. Therefore, a CAI lesson may have an expert system available to the learner in the same was as a glossary of terms. The expert system would provide information that the learner has not, or will not, learned to obtain or produce.

Relating Expert Systems to Instructional Objectives

Class of Media: Instructional support.

Characteristics: Expert Systems do not teach. They are electronic job aids.

---

[4] *Checklist developed by Kim Stevenson, Grumman Corporation.*

Application to types of learning:

Cognitive objectives. Not applicable.

Psychomotor objectives. Not applicable.

Affective objectives. Not applicable.

Advantages and Disadvantages of Expert Systems

Advantages:

+ Possible to support on-job performance without (costly, long, difficult) training.
+ Possible to access data base or spreadsheet resources if needed.
+ Less costly to the organization than training.
+ Easier to program than most computer languages.

Disadvantages:

– Does not teach or instruct.
– May not be directly tied to particular learning objectives.
– User access to the information depends on the user's motivation.

✔✔✔
Checklist of Considerations for Expert Systems

Instructions. The following checklist is a "memory-jogger" for contemplating use of hypertext. The questions present only the most frequent or common issues for consideration. Edit the list (or add items) based on your local conditions. It would be unusual to answer the questions with all yes's or no's. Use judgment in weighing the merits, or weight, of each question when tallying results of the lists.

(Consider adapting these checklists to fit the local situation.)

A. Determine where expert systems will apply to the tasks or activities. A YES answer must apply to at least one of the following questions. If all answers are NO, the task should probably be re-designed, eliminated, or if necessary, trained to recall level.

	Yes	No
Is the task dangerous enough to need a job aid because of safety factors?	❏	⭕

Will performance errors lead to costly damage of either
equipment or property? ❑ ○

Is the task very complicated? Should it be entrusted
to memory? ❑ ○

Is the task only done infrequently? Might a performer forget
the steps or procedures? ❑ ○

Can less qualified people, with guidance, do a task normally
done on the job from memory? ❑ ○

Would having less qualified people do the job negatively affect
the productivity of others? ❑ ○

Are there frequent changes in details or steps of the task? ❑ ○

B. Consider applying the expert system to the work situations. All
answers should be YES. (Any NO answers indicate it may be practical to
re-design the job or train for at least part of the task.)

	Yes	No
Will the use of an expert system reduce the likelihood of error?	❑	○
Will the expert system be practical in the job environment (for example, will it obstruct or slow up either the performer or other workers)?	❑	○
Will the expert system be safe to use within the work situation (not interfere with physical activities especially those requiring quick reaction)?	❑	○
Will the working environment support the use of an expert system? (Is space available, enough light, etc.?)	❑	○
Will the performer be able to use the expert system without disturbing the confidence of others? (If dealing with the public, the performer will not appear inept or incapable.)	❑	○

C. Plan development of the expert system. (All answers should be
YES.)

	Yes	No
Have you got all information about the prescribed method of performance (for example: practices, work rules, and published methods)?	❑	○
Have you examined the work environment and noted physical characteristics that may support an expert system (for example, working surfaces, lighting, cleanliness)?	❑	○

Have you observed the task performance in actual work locations? (If possible you should also try to do the task yourself.) ❏ ◯

Have you observed and noted how competent performers do the task? ❏ ◯

If differences exist between prescribed performance and good performance on the job, have you resolved which is the best way to do the task? ❏ ◯

D. Design the initial expert system for developmental testing. (All answers should be YES.)

	Yes	No
Have you considered the physical characteristics of the working location? (Accessibility of job aid, portability, cleanliness of working area, and lighting.)	❏	◯
Have you checked to determine that another expert system does not include some procedures in this task?	❏	◯
If another expert system includes some steps in this task, have you tried to combine them into one?	❏	◯
Have you developed your expert system based on the proper sequence of events?	❏	◯

E. Developmentally test the expert system. (All answers should be YES.)

	Yes	No
Have you picked new workers (workers who do not already know how to do the task reliably) for testing the expert system?	❏	◯
Have you observed their performance without rushing to help them when they faltered?	❏	◯
Have you noted where they appeared to have difficulty or made errors?	❏	◯
Have you discussed their opinion of the expert system with them? Did you ask about the times they appeared to have problems?	❏	◯
Did you, if possible, test the expert system yourself in real working conditions?	❏	◯

Is the expert system compatible with the working conditions? (If used in a confined working area, does it take up valuable space, etc.)   ❏   ○

If used with other expert system, does it complement them?   ❏   ○

Have you used terms and phrases on the expert system familiar to the performer?   ❏   ○

    F. Repeat developmental testing until satisfied with the content and the basic design.

    G. Produce and distribute the expert system. (All answers should be YES.)

                                                       Yes   No

Have you checked the expert system for completeness and accuracy?   ❏   ○

Have you considered durability of the expert system when used in the work location? (Will it be resistant to environmental hazards?)   ❏   ○

Will the expert system be easily legible?   ❏   ○

If you must revise the expert system often, have you compensated for this factor in the design?   ❏   ○

CHAPTER 15

Interactive Multimedia

THE REAL POWER OF INTERACTIVE MULTIMEDIA IS *NOT* THE often glitzy graphics shown, but the method "behind the scenes." It is the computer program that controls the graphics. It is the result of the coming together of two major technologies. Industrial grade videodisc units can present simple programs entirely without any computer. Sometimes we use a small programming device to enter the program. Embry Riddle Aeronautical University of Daytona Beach, Florida, used this approach for much of their instruction.

Educators and trainers have exploited this new entity quite effectively. Video specialists in education and training have been willing to put video under computer control because individualized interaction becomes possible this way. On the other hand, our computer specialists perceive that the realism of video enhances the capabilities of computer-assisted learning. The result has been a dazzling technology that places moving and still pictures under computer control with computer text and graphics. It combines them both with audio in a new form of dynamic presentation never known before. The basic product of this technology is the laser-read, interactive videodisc (IVD).

Technically, IVD and interactive multimedia (IM) are only CAI. They receive separate attention in the public mind because of the different talent needed to create them and marketing efforts to "sell something new."

These advanced systems provide the same degree of control capability for auxiliary devices. The devices include random access audio, random access videotape, and videodisc. Use of these standard, or other unique, accessory devices begins to approach the full potential of the technology-based learning system.

195

Videodisc, the best-known optical disk, is simply a storage medium much like a floppy disc. It stores video, similar to a videotape. The computer software controls the videodisc player. Videotape is a linear format meant to play from beginning to end. Videodisc yields random access to any of the frames of video stored on one side. Interactive simply means that the user's responses determine the sequence of the presentation. This medium supports motion visuals and accurate, repeatable instruction.

The capabilities of the basic videodisc technology are:

- Analog video and audio. This means that editing changes are severely limited
- Twelve inch platter. Holds about 30 minutes of linear play video on each side. It has synchronized dual channels of audio or 54,000 still pictures with very limited audio per frame.
- Three "levels" of interactive video. Level one IVD provides control through a manual keypad. Level two IVD uses a built-in microprocessor. It permits limited programing and resident memory. Level three IVD interfaces in real time with a PC. This greatly improves programming possibilities and adds huge quantities of memory.
- Input devices. These include keypad, keyboard, joy stlck, mouse, trackball, touch panel, or light pen.
- Read-only technology. This results from a permanently recorded impression on the disc. No change is possible after the disc is mastered.
- Interactive learning programs. The programs use moving and still pictures coupled with audio and computer text and graphics.
- Authoring systems. They reduced (but did not end) the complexity of instructional design and development.

The three levels of interactive videodisc are shown in Figure 15.1

Figure 15.1

Levels of Interactive Videodisc

- level 1 - manually operated controls
- level 2 - built-in microprocessor
- level 3 - interface for PC

The capabilities of the classical videodisc proved to be its limitations. These attributes governed the videodisc as it emerged in the late 1970's. Over time, however, learning needs prompted new capability development. The most important of these were:

- Overlay of analog video images with computer generated text and graphics. This called for more costly hardware and a growth in the power of authoring systems.
- Sound-over-still through computer hard disks.
- The coming of CD-ROM with its vast memory capacities. The memory greatly increased audio possible for each frame. This feature cut the costs of instructional program development. It made it possible to create interactive videodisc programs based increasingly on (less expensive) still photography instead of costly motion visuals. A single disc, combined with paper-based materials, can support many hours of instruction.

The interactive videodisc equipment has been an ideal medium to use with self-teaching instruction. Interactive multimedia is CAI carried to its logical end. ■

Interactive Multimedia in General[1]

A Rose is a Rose...
Everything true of CAI is true of interactive multimedia.

Hypermedia
Hypermedia has the power to "front end" other computer-based technologies. Hypermedia is described in Chapter 14 as a Computer Supported Learning Resource. This strength makes them the obvious choice to provide access to CDI or DVI programs. Hypermedia and interactive multimedia are synergistic—but are not the same. In practice, the interactive multimedia may be one part of a single user interface. The user may have access to a package that includes an expert system. embedded animation, CAI, and hypermedia modules.

Two Kinds of Media—Many Flavors
IVD and IM use optical disc video storage technologies. Both analog and digital optical disc media are in use. The analog-based laser media is interactive videodisc (IVD) — 54,000 frames. The digital-based laser media include CD-ROM or WORM data storage media. CD-ROM has 270,000 pages. In the case of an encyclopedia, 9 million words, 15,000 illustrations in black and white and color, and 60 minutes of sound were combined with 6,5000 dictionary entries on a single disc. WORM technology (write once read many) can be applied to any of the small discs

Compact Disc
With the success of the 12-inch videodisc and the coming of the compact disc, efforts to "downsize" the technology to the smaller platter were

---

[1]John Eldridge provided valuable help in preparation of the Interactive Multimedia section.

inevitable. Two products have emerged: digital video interactive (DVI) and compact disc interactive (CDI). DVI is an American system offered to the market by Intel Corporation. CDI is a Philips corporation product. It capitalizes on that company's sponsorship of the CD-ROM and CD Audio standards.

There are significant technical differences between 12-inch IVD and compact disc. To understand the capabilities, a trainer or a manager need only think of the interactive videodisc. Like their larger counterpart, both DVI and CDI will deliver:

- motion, and
- still video, mixed with
- computer text, and
- graphics, and
- audio under computer guidance for interactive learning materials.

While the older videodisc technology also delivered the same assortment of learning tools, in the all-digital compact disc newer flexibility and capabilities emerge. They are:

- About 550 megabytes of digital information. It can be text, images, graphics, sound, and computer programs. All are integrated in a package created by an authoring system. Then they are used under the command of a computer.
- Hardware and software compression of this digital information to make gargantuan storage possible. This is possible with rapid reading and use.
- On-the-fly editing of the information, reducing preproduction costs significantly. For example: a wipe or dissolve is achieved by computer code that modifies the image at the instant it appears in the digital stream for processing and display.
- Four levels of audio in mixtures of audio at a range of fidelities. The range is from 18-20 hours of AM radio quality to 72 minutes of CD-Audiodisc quality sound under the control of the computer program.
- Seven thousand still images.
- Up to one hour of full motion video, depending on the pixel density, display resolution, and number of colors.
- Digital still and motion images, sound, computer text and graphics are all mixed and matched by the computer into an instructional program. It is not possible to store them all to maximum capacity on one disc. That is, there cannot be 7,000 stills and one hour of video stored on one disc. Everything (pictures, text, graphics, audio, and computer program) must be stored together and brought into the computer using a single-bit stream. That it works at all is a triumph of electronics and computer programming.

While both of the two product lines are based on the same basic technology, the two companies have radically different approaches to somewhat different commercial target audiences. The result is two *incompatible* and significantly different systems. DVI is a computer peripheral: you buy a board and insert it into your old computer. Or, you buy a new computer with the necessary DVI chips on the systems board. CDI is a separate box with its own built-in computer. DVI aims primarily at the professional, business, and organizational market. CDI is aimed at the mass consumer market. Philips hopes to attract the CD audiophile to interactive multimedia. In both cases we, in the education and training world, benefit. Although the two products are completely incompatible, the success of both will lead to better products and lower prices to education and training.

Because of the inherent advantages of the smaller disc, eventually these systems will replace the larger and more costly 12 inch videodisc.

Tactile Input Required

Today, computer systems do not make most learners feel threatened. However, some user groups appear to dislike typing. They respond much better to the use of the screen for input. Examples of such groups include: managers, physicians, and aviators. Typing has nothing to do with most subjects learned on an IM system. We can conduct serious and successful instruction without such tactile input. We can use the screen for access to the computer in several ways. The most common in IM use today are the light pen, touch-panel screen, and mouse. Using any of these access methods can help avoid the need for typing. Today, there is little question that an organization's system should provide such a capability. This is, again, a question of using the right tool for the job.

Cost

In 1990, a simple, custom-made IVD program can cost at least $30,000; a comparable generic videodisc's price is around $10,000. Many practitioners look at the real advantage of the technology—the ability to train for specific tasks—and wonder whether generic videodiscs can ever fit the bill for corporate use. Careful needs assessment to determine whether a generic videodisc can accomplish training objectives will help answer the "make or buy" question. The chairperson of Phillips Petroleum, in talking about the company's 14 year old internal corporate video department, said "Ten years ago, video was the stepchild to other ways to communicate—print and public speaking. These days, it's a regular part of our communications, and it's an essential part of most of our management, training, and sales jobs."[2]

For training managers, organizations can buy (DVI or CDI) videodisc systems in a smaller size with consequent savings in storage and handling at lower costs. The major disadvantage is that these new systems reside on hardware and software that is different and incompatible with the older technology.

CDI products for a viewing system only are about $1,000. Authoring capabilities add another $2,500 to the costs. Today, authoring systems have not reached a firm figure but promise to be several thousand dollars. DVI proposes to charge about $2,500 for the basic chip set with added costs for specialized hardware. Whether existing authoring systems can be tailored to the requirements of a real-time operating system is unclear

---

[2]According to *Corporate Video Decisions* (October 1988).

Relating Interactive Multimedia to Instructional Objectives

Class of Media: Instructional medium

Characteristics: Typically presents a highly simulated environment by combining computer capabilities with video for instruction.

Application to types of learning:

Cognitive objectives. Used to teach recognition or discrimination of applicable visual stimuli and audio stimuli.

Psychomotor objectives. An excellent tool to re-create real world conditions.

Affective objectives. Interactive multimedia is very useful in the affective domain. The strength of detailed portrayal of situations and interactive participation of the learner increases its usefulness for affective domain objectives

Advantages and Disadvantages of Interactive Multimedia

Advantages:

+ Possible to directly support on-job performance.
+ Possible to access a variety of media and other resources easily.
+ Possible to access information as wanted by the learner.
+ Individual, self-paced instruction for individual students.
+ The ability of the instructor to concentrate on instructor-related tasks, allowing them to attend specifically to those students who may be having problems.
+ Excellent means for simulation situations that need individualized, yet coordinated, task performance. For example, networked crew coordination training allows each station to represent a specific flight task requirement where the host system monitors the coordination of the stations and provides appropriate feedback.
+ Hardware may be same as for home use, with low cost.

Disadvantages:

− Does not teach or instruct.
− May not tie directly to particular learning objectives.
− Uncontrolled student access to the information depends on the student's interest and motivation.

- Development of lessons requires skills that may not be available.
- Development of high quality lessons requires extensive effort.
- Generic IM lessons may not be available to meet your needs.

✔✔✔
Checklist of Considerations for Selecting and Using Interactive Multimedia for Instruction

(Consider adapting these checklists to fit the local situation.)

Instructions. The following checklist is a "memory-jogger" for contemplating use of interactive multimedia. Because of the many complex issues involved, the list cannot be comprehensive. The questions present only the most frequent or common issues for consideration. Edit the list (or add items) based on local conditions. It would be unusual to answer the questions with all yes's or no's. Use judgment in weighing the merits, or weight, of each question when tallying results of the lists.

Review decision to use interactive multimedia. Considering curriculum, task analysis, and instructional needs, weigh the value of your combination of answers to the following:

A. Consider these general issues:

	Yes	No
Are qualified instructors for the content hard to find?	❏	○
Are staff available with enough skill to program the lessons?	❏	○
Are students sufficiently motivated to benefit from the planned multimedia application?	❏	○
Does necessary equipment exist?	❏	○
Does this approach meet organizational instructional goals?	❏	○
Is standardized training important?	❏	○

B. Consider these subject matter-related issues:

	Yes	No
Are there considerable variations in student background and experience?	❏	○
Do topics lend themselves to access as desired by the learner?	❏	○
Is IM necessary to serve most of your curriculum needs?	❏	○

Is the subject matter proprietary? ❏ ○

Is the subject matter reasonably stable? ❏ ○

Must the large numbers of students be trained in
a limited time? ❏ ○

Will large numbers of people be trained eventually? ❏ ○

C. Consider these location-related issues:

	Yes	No

Does the organization have limited money for travel
and accommodations? ❏ ○

Is decentralized training important? ❏ ○

Is the student population geographically dispersed? ❏ ○

CHAPTER 16

Simulation and Simulators

N EXT TO ON-THE-JOB TRAINING, MANY EXPERTS AGREE simulation is the most powerful means of transferring skills and knowledge to learners. The aviation and power industries use massive, complex, costly, and highly realistic simulators to provide instruction in a variety of critical occupations. However, these simulators are only the tip of the simulation iceberg. Rarely is simulation considered for most organization's training problems. Many learning specialists never stop to consider that several different levels of fidelity in simulation are possible.

In this chapter we will distinguish between *simulation* and *simulators*. Simulation is a strategy. We can achieve simulation using a variety of equipment. Simulators are hardware. They are special purpose devices that provide simulation exclusively. There is a broad range of simulation possible that does not come so readily to mind. Non-computer simulation is also a useful media. Personal computers, so widely available, can support hybrid simulations. And, more especially because they are progressively robust, the chance to use personal computer-based simulation is increasingly within your grasp.

Simulation allows students to practice with equipment in a way that would be costly and dangerous on the real one. Practice with a real item will tie up costly equipment and run the risk of damage in the process. Simulation techniques are extremely desirable for training in subjects where students must assess information and begin correct action within a short time. This is a characteristic of many high technology occupations.

While most of our organizations don't have two million in the budget for a simulator this year, the concept of simulation can easily be applied to nearly any training program. The ever-increasing power of personal com-

203

puters can transform your classroom desk-top into an effective platform for simulation.

The combination of the hardware and software features makes the PC an excellent choice for complex simulations. The graphics capability, combined with the tactile input, permit the student's computer to function as though it were an item of other specific equipment. The resulting learning experiences approximate the benefits of "hands on" practice with the actual equipment. "This often provides greater insight into the cause and effect relationship depicted. The special control features and feedback mechanisms can sometimes provide the student the opportunity to see and understand complex electrical, mechanical and thermal phenomena. Learners can then see phenomenon not viewable in either an actual operating unit or in the normal training simulator. Only meters, indication lights, and control switches are available there for student interaction. All this combines to enhance the training experience and results in a better retention and overall knowledge of the subject material."[1]

In many technical occupational fields, some sort of practice before using the actual equipment is extremely helpful, and important. Classic examples are aircraft flight crew and nuclear power reactor operators. Both industries use very costly special, and specific, simulators. One computer learning terminal can be used to integrate other learning experiences with the equipment simulation, and can simulate an "automatic pilot"—and a moment later provide another learner with a nuclear power reactor control panel. The CBL terminal is obviously more flexible and less expensive than the special simulators for either.

The computer learning station does not replace the specialized simulator. Its typical and proper role is to supplement it. The combination of simulation capability with a properly developed training program, can increase the quality of training in the classroom, and during full scale simulator sessions. The training technique illustrated here is important. The airlines recognized and developed the advantage of the dual simulation-simulator method. Training on a learning station before the simulator session enables the simulator to put the trainee's knowledge to the test in a realistic way. The more costly special simulator then does not simply teach or provide experience. It tests the learner's real knowledge of the equipment. It does it in a way that other means cannot. Software programs are available off-the-shelf for many generic job applications. Where budget allows, many consultants are standing by to customize an interactive, computer based simulation to fit your training needs. ■

Computer Simulations and Simulators in General

Simulation is the representation of a situation or device, with a degree of fidelity. It allows learners to see and practice a wanted performance. Simulation provides practice in a way that, if done in the real world, would

---

[1]David C. Paquin, of Niagara Mohawk Power.

be costly, inconvenient, impractical, foolish, unwise, dangerous, impossible, or "all of the above."

Methods of Simulation
Methods of simulation include:

- computer,
- hybrid (combined manual and computer), and
- manual.

With today's advancements, computer simulation comes much closer to hands-on training. More typical organizations don't need the complexity associated with the aircraft and nuclear power industries. By taking advantage of inexpensive, desk-top computers, training groups can provide realistic simulation to their learners. Simulation done exclusively, or nearly exclusively, by PCs and other electronic devices, is called "computer" simulation.

Often, the advantages of computer simulation, such as instant re-configuration control and automatic record keeping, will be combined with manual simulation. Desk-top computers communicate with mechanically built simulators through simple electronic converters to insert faults or change system line-ups at the press of a button. This combination of computer and manual simulation is "hybrid" simulation.

Of course, simulation can be done without a computer. The instructor could choose to build a model of the system to be learned using smaller or partial components as compared to the real equipment. For example, we could mount pressure switches, gauges, a tank, and a pump on a roll-around cart to simulate the operation of a large system. This type of simulation, without computer, is considered "manual" simulation. Manual simulation offers the advantage of learners getting "hands-on" real hardware, even if it is scaled down or incomplete. On the contrary, it is often the very same components found at the work site.

Fidelity of Simulation
We can rank simulation fidelity as:

- low,
- medium, or
- high.

Simulation "fidelity" is a description of its realness or degree of accuracy. This is called fidelity. Increased fidelity usually improves the rate at which advanced learners internalize new material. It may, however, impede learning in certain situations. Often, complex is *not* better, just more confusing. High fidelity training environments usually have associated prerequisites, such as basic skills in a particular discipline. The appropriate fidelity level may depend upon the stage in which the learner exists in the overall training program. Low fidelity could be better for new learners while high fidelity would be more suited for advanced learners.

Categories of Simulation

The categories of simulation are either:

- part-task, or
- whole-task.

Simulators will provide a learning experience as either whole-task or part-task. A whole-task simulation is one in which training is provided for the complete task to be performed, instead of providing the learning experience in stages. The massive simulators used in nuclear power tend to be whole-task as the operator crews complete all or most of their training in this environment. The aircraft industry, on the other hand, uses smaller computer-based simulation to complement its full scale flight simulators. These are part-task simulators.

The Simulation Model[2]

Each of the qualities just presented; methods, categories, and fidelity combine to define any simulation. Figure 16.1 shows the methods.

Figure 16.1
Part-Whole Simulation

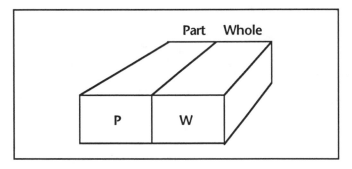

Figure 16.2 and 16.3 show the components of simulation buildup to the complete simulation model. There are 12 combinations in all.

The model illustrates the relationships of the combination of methods, fidelity, and categories. The model is used to illustrate to full range of simulation possible: from part task—manual—low fidelity to whole task—computer-based—high fidelity. For most learning specialists, it helps raise consciousness of the range available.

---

[2]The Simulation Model grew out of work done with Cheryl Samuels-Campbell. See Reynolds, A. and Samuels-Campbell, C. "Simulations: Time to Take Another Look!" *Performance and Instruction*. Vol. 24, No. 4, May 1985, pp. 15-17.

Figure 16.2
Part-Whole and Manual-Computer Simulation

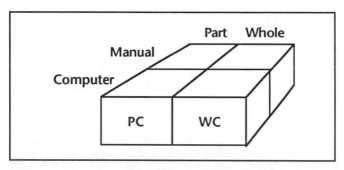

For example, the front lower right cell of the model is labeled WCH. WCH represents whole task/computer-based/high fidelity simulation. One WCH simulation is the aircraft-specific flight simulator. A more common example is PMH, part task/manual/high fidelity, represented by the in-basket exercise. PMH is not among the six labeled cells in the figure. It is among the six cell labels at the rear in this view. They represent the manual equivalents of the computer cells in front. For example, a whole task/manual simulation, available in all three fidelity levels is the mockup.

Figure 16.3
The Simulation Model

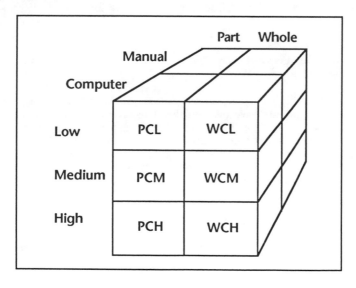

Smaller Could be Better

One could argue that bigger may be better. However, it is clear beyond any doubt that big is not always essential. Here are some arguments for less than majestic simulation:

- Manual simulation is important in more organizations than computerized ones.
- Low or medium fidelity is often adequate for the training at hand.
- Part task is completely adequate for meeting most training needs.

Psychomotor skills dominate our concept of simulations. Don't let that obscure the potential for other type activities such as in-basket exercises, role play, situation simulation, business games, or any other modest effort to simulate. The availability of computers is a boon to simulations for a wide variety of training. The imaginative usefulness of small computer to enhance simulations is still largely untapped

The level of fidelity, or degree of realism, will affect the rate of learning and the transfer of learning to the real equipment. How realistic does the simulated equipment need to be? Research has shown that high fidelity is not needed for learning procedural tasks. The reduced fidelity simulated environment is ideal for a beginning learner. The actual equipment may be quite intimidating. If so, it may also be significantly less conducive to learning. "Overload" is the intimidation factor caused by actual equipment or high fidelity simulation. Complexities and details of the real situation can overwhelm the learner. Too many new stimuli emerge for the learner to to get the desired content. In summarizing research into simulator fidelity requirements, reduced fidelity can improve learning for a novice because:

- High fidelity means higher complexity that taxes memory and other cognitive abilities.
- Proven instructional techniques that improve initial learning tend to reduce fidelity.[3]

Remember, high fidelity, or maximum job/task simulation, is only appropriate if students have prerequisite skills. For example, it would be a waste of money and time if a novice pilot began in a simulator without having the basic skill requirements. A simulator simulates the real flying conditions. This could create a stressful learning atmosphere and deter learning if the pilot is not ready for this degree of fidelity. In this case, more (fidelity) is not necessarily better!

Simulation—the Mode

Simulation is one of the modes of CAI. However, it is linked so closely to the system and method chosen it deserves separate consideration. The combination of the hardware and software features make computer simulation an excellent choice for complex simulations. Graphics capability, combined with the tactile input screen, permit the student's learning

---

[3] See Alessi, M., and Trollip, S. *Computer-Based Instruction: Methods and Development.* Englewood Cliffs, NJ: Prentice Hall, 1985.

station to function as though it was the specific equipment item. The learning experiences that result approximate the benefits of a "hands on" practice session with the actual equipment.

Simulation can increase insight into the cause-effect relationship illustrated. The computer learning station can use special control features and feedback. This will provide the learner the opportunity to see and understand complex electronic and mechanical (or other) phenomena in a unique way.

Simulation in the Airlines

Major airlines were quick to recognize the value of computer-based learning to solve their training problems. Extensive use of graphics and animation are common in aviation simulations. The rapid display of complex flight panels is essential to represent accurately an operation on the aircraft. The use of an interactive computer learning system provides the student input by touching the screen. The success enjoyed by the airlines prompted them to make major use of computer simulation in the training the next time an entirely new series of aircraft came into service. The next series of aircraft delivered, the Boeing 767, provided the first opportunity to design a complete computer-based training system for an aircraft. The aircraft's flight management system, with seven computers that replaced electromechanical devices, almost suggested computer-based learning simulation.

Simulation in the Nuclear Power Plants

Nuclear utility companies recognize the value of full fidelity simulators to solve their training problems. Dozens of nuclear utility companies in the United States operate enormous simulators. Priced at over a million dollars each, these room-size simulators are replicas of the real reactor's control rooms. The displays are identical in placement and appearance to those located in the actual control room. The simulator responds identically to the actual reactor system. They are unique and specially programmed to create situations that have or could occur in the plant. Training is for the crews who will start up the (simulated) plant, recognize and correct plant problems, and safely shut it down several times over before operating the real thing. Why all the expense? For one, regulating agencies, always in search of the utmost in training, require simulator training. For another, imagine the incalculable costs associated with an accident the scope of the Three Mile Island event. All of this is exceptionally expensive to buy and use.[4]

Simulating Time

Computers allow us to easily simulate one of the essential elements of practice—time. Timing can be critical when the realistic timing of events is important. One of the most critical elements associated with modern-day training is timing. The nuclear plant operator must start and stop pumps in specific sequence. Technicians often are needed to perform steps not only

---

[4]The Nuclear Regulatory Commission requires plants to have access to simulators. They test and certify reactor operators on simulators.

sequentially, but within very short time periods. Computers can obviously time events with perfection. You may have considered the benefits of doing things in "real time." The accurate representation of time is important for some things, but it is not always the most important timing possibility.

One of the great advantages of simulators over using real equipment is their ability to compress or extend time. Changed time scale presents important opportunities for learning. Slowed time, stepping in small increments, permits examination of a process to understand a specific progression. Events that happen in microseconds can be frozen in time for close inspection. This is particularly useful to the beginning student, who can, without danger to personnel or equipment, cautiously weigh the alternatives before making a major decision. In some situations, you can ease learning by freezing time and events. This permits an examination of the simulated system in ways that would not be possible in the real world. It can freeze a speeding neutron as it blazes across a uranium core!

Accelerated time permits us to examine conditions that develop over hours, days, or even months. Obviously, the learner can't sit there waiting for things to develop over such a long time. This permits the learner to see the potential result of action or inaction over the organization's cycle.

A simulator can stop the world or make it spin like crazy! That is no small achievement.

Skill Types

It is important not to limit your thinking of simulator training to psychomotor skills. While this is the type of learning traditionally associated with many simulators, cognitive and even affective goals may also be met using simulation. Business games, situation simulation, and role play are examples of manual or hybrid simulation often used to achieve cognitive or affective objectives. Personal computers continue to become more interactive and increasingly ergonomic. As they do, their ability to deal one-on-one with the learner in affective and cognitive tasks is limited only by the imaginations of programmers and educators.

Relating Simulations to Instructional Objectives

Class of Media: Instructional medium.

Characteristics: Simulators resemble real equipment to a high degree. Simulations may use a variety of different learning stations or combine with other media to provide realistic instruction. Students experience highly simulated environments by combining computer capabilities with other media or equipment for instruction or testing.

Application to types of learning:

Cognitive objectives. Simulators and simulations can control interactive self-instruction to teach operation, steps, and processes.

Psychomotor objectives. Simulators and simulations are an excellent tool to create real world situations. Some typical examples are: simulated landing of aircraft, docking a ship, or emergency drills. Sometimes, models or mockups can be used to allow students to observe results.

Affective objectives. Very useful when used as described in Psychomotor objectives or when used to control film or video materials.

Advantages and Disadvantages of Simulations and Simulators

Advantages of Simulations:

+ Lower fidelity simulations available at reduced cost.
+ Possible to practice events that happen rarely.
+ Possible to practice events too dangerous or damaging for use on real equipment
+ Response time can be realistic, or faster or slower, as demanded by the instruction.
+ Simulations normally have greater capabilities than simulators, providing greater flexibility in instructional methods and curriculum.
+ Test results generated automatically.

Disadvantages of Simulations:

- Little commercially produced courseware available.
- Simulation is the most expensive CAI mode to develop.
- Skilled developers may not be available in the organization.
- Usually, one of the more costly computer configurations is required.

Advantages of Simulators:

+ Possible to practice events that happen rarely.
+ Possible to practice events too dangerous or damaging for use on real equipment
+ Provides the "highest quality" practice possible without real equipment..
+ Response time can be realistic, or faster or slower, as demanded by the instruction.
+ Simulators normally have greater capabilities than computer simulations.
+ Test results generated automatically.

Disadvantages of Simulators:

- A breakdown of the simulator will prevent all the students from practicing.
- No commercially produced courseware available.
- Normally, the most costly system to buy.

✔✔✔
Checklist of Considerations for Selecting and Using Computer Simulations for Instruction

Instructions. The following checklist is a "memory-jogger" for contemplating use of simulators and simulations. Because of the many complex issues involved, the list cannot be comprehensive. The questions present only the most frequent or common issues for consideration. Edit the list (or add items) based on your local conditions. It would be unusual to answer the questions with all yes's or no's. Review the decision to use simulators or simulations. Considering curriculum, task analysis, and instructional needs, weigh the value of your combination of answers to the following:

	Yes	No
Are simulators or simulations necessary to serve most of your curriculum needs?	❏	○
Is damage to equipment, environment, or personnel likely in training with actual equipment?	❏	○
Are there skilled developers available to prepare complex simulation programming needed?	❏	○
Does necessary equipment exist?	❏	○
Has money been budgeted to allow ample lead time for "trial and error" and for maintenance of the simulation after it is completed?	❏	○
Have you considered low cost non-computer simulations such as in-basket exercises, role plays, situation simulation, and business games?	❏	○
Have you determined what forms of simulation are needed to provide audio and visual stimuli called for in the curriculum?	❏	○
Have you foreseen needs for:		
• Frequency of revisions or updates of information?	❏	○
• The specific analysis or results data that will be needed?	❏	○
• Testing procedures (results gathering)?	❏	○
• Number of computer simulations and associated media equipment?	❏	○

- Geographic locations of the simulation workstations? ❏ ○

Is upper management committed to supporting simulation? ❏ ○

Will course content allow enough development time
needed for quality materials? ❏ ○

Will the equipment simulated have sufficient life to justify
the expense? (Costly materials shouldn't be obsolete
soon after their development.) ❏ ○

✔✔✔
Checklist of Considerations for Selecting and Using Simulators for Instruction

Instructions. The following checklist is a "memory-jogger" for contemplating use of simulators and simulations. Because of the many complex issues involved, the list cannot be comprehensive. The questions present only the most frequent or common issues for consideration. Edit the list (or add items) based on your local conditions. It would be unusual to answer the questions with all yes's or no's. Use judgment in weighing the merits, or weight, of each question when tallying results of the lists.

Review the decision to use simulators or simulations. Considering curriculum, task analysis, and instructional needs, weigh the value of your combination of answers to the following:

	Yes	No
Are simulators or simulations necessary to serve most of your curriculum needs?	❏	○
Is it unsafe or impractical to practice on the real equipment?	❏	○
Are there skilled operators available to run the complex simulations needed for learning?	❏	○
Has money been budgeted to allow ample lead time for "trial and error" and for maintenance of the simulator after it is installed?	❏	○
Have you considered part task computer simulations?	❏	○

Have you foreseen needs for:

- Frequency of revisions or updates of information? ❏ ○

- The specific analysis or results data that will be needed? ❏ ○

- Testing procedures (results gathering)? ❏ ○

Is upper management committed to supporting the simulator? ❏ ○

Will the equipment simulated have sufficient life to justify
the expense? (Costly materials shouldn't be obsolete
soon after their development.) ❏ ○

CHAPTER 17

Media in the New Millennium

O PEN . . . SESAME! WITH THESE MAGICAL WORDS, ALI BABA gained access to hidden treasure. Today, with the magical word "spreadsheet" you can see your personal computer respond by opening your spreadsheet software.[1] To say "Management Training," "Mark-7 Widget Operator Course," or "Sales Call Simulation" is only an additional step. Naturally, if you can call for the course by name, you can interact vocally as you study within it, as well.

There is no reason to think that the future will be like the present. Advances in technologies unheard of 20 years ago influence our life. This is true on a sliding scale (Any 20 year period in the 20th century ended with technologies in use that were unheard of at the start.)

George Orwell chose the year 1984 in the 1950's. He wanted to pick a time not too near, yet not too far in the future—when the world had changed greatly. Fortunately, the dreadful world he described in his book *1984* did not materialize. The one that did was both better and more advanced.

For about 30 years 1984 represented the future. Incredibly the future is behind us! We now look to the second millennium—the year 2000—as our future. Today society's access to technology, in industrialized countries,

---

[1]You may not have voice recognition at your site today, but it exists and is becoming more readily available at lower cost.

is growing at an exponential rate.[2] This is true in the instructional technology field as well. The rate is shown in Figure 17.1.

Figure 17.1
Growth Rate of Technology-based Instruction

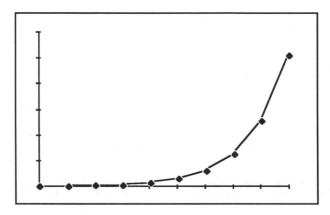

Training is a reflection of the society in which it exists. We live in a society that, as early as 1982, found the "computer" picked as the *Time* magazine "man [sic.] of the year." We carry out training in a society in which technology is both continually more powerful, and more accessible for the development and delivery of instruction. In the future human resource development will also reflect the society in which it exists. One cannot help wonder what that society will be like.

Our premise is that the basis for impact of technology on society is its progressive availability and sophistication. It happens that the accessibility of such ever more refined technology is entirely predictable. Access to more robust technology has been a benefit of greater miniaturization in computer chips. Future levels exist in today's development laboratories. Therefore, we can predict the power that will be available to society soon. Some abbreviated predictions of what society will be like are represented in Figure 17.2.

Even the realization of the fantastic implementations now foreseen for this century will not exhaust the cycle of increasing sophistication. ■

Instructional Media in the Future Workplace

Several interesting considerations emerge when we begin to think about learning in the future workplace. Two basic questions are:

• How will the work incorporate HRD?

---

[2]Obviously, it cannot maintain such a rate of growth indefinitely. However, it has for at least a decade. Measures of such growth charted in the 1970's showed the same rate of growth.

• What will the learning be like?

Figure 17.2
A Glimpse of Society in the Future

> **TODAY - up to 4 million transistors per chip**
> • automobiles use microprocessors for engine economy
> • up to 10% of homes have computers or terminals
> • computer aided diagnosis
> • robots significantly affect factory production
> • most schools have at least some computers
>
> **2000 - up to 100 million transistors per chip**
> • microelectronic body implants introduced
> • automobiles have diagnostic and
>   preventive maintenance chips
> • all banks interconnected
> • "smart" highways developed
> • most homes have computers
> • data communications exceeds voice in total volume
> • robots and automated systems produce up to half of
>   all manufactured goods
> • implant chips restore sight and hearing
> • computer assisted medicine accessed from the home
> • extensive computer use in schools

The first question will bring us to look at several areas. These include:

• instructional design and delivery tools,
• automated job aids,
• CBL incorporated in work,
• widespread personal computers on workers' desks,
• implications of location of that desk, and
• changes in learning opportunities.

Instructional Design and Delivery Tools

One thing is sure: Future work stations will not look exactly like today's PCs. (Today's automobiles don't look like the Model T.) The employee's individual work station will be a far more integrated work area. It could be an "active desktop." The work surface itself (now a desk) will be active, permitting input, and giving output, for graphic images and text. Input and output to the workstation system will be by voice. The employee will access a network including all necessary data bases, and other people who are useful resources. These data bases and people will be both within, and outside, the organization.

Design

Authoring Systems, Languages, and Environments. Today, more powerful, user friendly courseware generation tools have emerged. Anyone is be able to enter complex graphics or specify branching. The widespread use of such tools has significantly reduced the cost of lesson development. They even help those who have little course development experience to organize material into a coherent lesson. Other utilities that help directly in the design-development process will become available as well. Unfortunately, the danger of poor lessons will increase apace.

In the near future, even more powerful author tools will help in development of higher quality courseware. They will emerge more slowly. Flexible automated aids to aid in developing instruction using common strategies will become more common. The use of author languages (even high level ones) will draw to a close for ordinary developers. The combination of these tools will positively affect development efforts and eventually, end the use of the general author languages.

Eventually, they will be replaced by comprehensive author environments. These environments will surpass even the "authors workbench" envisioned by Richard Davis a decade ago. All the tools and capabilities to produce multimedia instruction will reside in a single author environment, along with artificially intelligent design tools. These tools will do much of the course development, and warn against poor design. The author will provide only the creative direction to the development.

Figure 17.3
Future Authoring

Past	Present	Future
author languages	author systems	author environments

Text. Today, most developers rely on word processing and computer graphics to produce text for instruction. The result has been a dramatic improvement in the quality of text materials used in training.

Figure 17.4
Future Text Preparation

Past	Present	Future
people physically cut and paste objects	people electronically cut and paste objects	people specify desired outcomes systems electronically assemble objects

Naturally, these advances were not created for instruction. They are simply the use of commercially common tools available in the workplace. Future text development will spring from the same source. Tools will permit writers to generate business documents with less direct work. Similar to author environments, these tools will permit the writer to specify the text, graphics, and style to be used. The document will be assembled automatically. The writer will furnish the creative spark for the document.

Flexibility In Instructional Strategy. The use of more powerful course-ware development tools will provide increased flexibility in selecting the "right" instructional approach for courseware. Until now, we tended to compromise on the "most doable" one. For example: using new develop-ment tools developers will be able to make games and simulations. Today these instructional strategies are underutilized because of difficulty of development. The increased instructional flexibility that results from many strategies will boost efforts to make learning enjoyable and practical.

Figure 17.5
Future Instructional Strategies

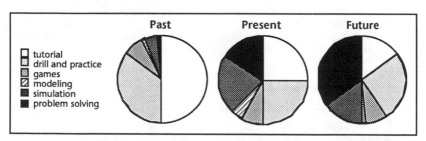

Future CAI will keep the classic modes: tutorial, drill and practice, games, modeling, simulation. We expect to see much more problem solving simply because many more workers use computers. Near-future training will feature more simulation. It was costly, impossible, or both for many organizations. We will also see greater flexibility in combining strategies.

Figure 17.6
Future Self Directed Learning

Past	Present	Future
non self-directed	rarely self-directed	commonly self-directed

The result will be commonly used learning activities that we would, in today's world, consider "highly creative." That is, to a greater degree, the learners will be in control of the HRD activities.[3] The direction of their study will be a result of their personal interest and initiative.

Delivery

Audio. The "open sesame" example focused on the direction of audio technology. Voice recognition and synthesis is another area that will open new potential for HRD. This means that the instructional system will both speak to the learner, and understand the reply.

Speech recognition and generation has defied earlier prophets. In the 1960s, the person doing the foremost research in computerized speech predicted little likelihood of any practical implementation before the year 2000. We can divide speech technology into two areas: generation (or synthesis) and recognition. Speech generation and recognition will become available as tools for instruction. In practice, we mean that the instructional system will be able to speak to the learner, and understand the reply—by 1995.

Since this technology is upon us, future developments will center on improvements. Today's implementations are limited in number of words remembered and quality of speech generated. Generation, particularly, is related to available memory. Future developments will make memory ever cheaper and more available. Speech will benefit directly. Artificially intelligent techniques may contribute to creation of entirely new "learning encounters" that we are hardly able to envision today.

Figure 17.7
Future Instructional Audio

Past	Present	Future
audio tape	digital audio (CD and DAT)	digital audio solid state (chips)
no speech recognition or generation	emergent speech recognition and generation	speech recognition and generation is the norm

Color Graphics Common. Instructional graphics will be created and distributed more readily in other media. Computer graphics for learner's materials will be printed on low cost, plain paper, using color printers. Overheads and slides will be generated locally from the same source. Color material from any of these sources will be readable by a computer peripheral for incorporation into computer-based instructional methods. We will

---

[3]Individuals directing their own HRD activities is theoretically sound. See Knowles, Malcomb. *The Adult Learner: A Neglected Species. Second Edition.* Houston, Texas: Gulf Publishing Company, 1979.

be able to use color wherever appropriate without extraordinary expense or effort.

Figure 17.8
Future Color in Media

Past	Present	Future
color from photographs	color from video display terminals	color directly from paper output devices
too expensive for most training uses	too expensive for many training uses	appropriate for most training uses

Communications. Communication among learners and with facilitators at other locations is one of the benefits of telecommunications. Future learners will also be able to access powerful, more useful central information data bases, and use micro resources for processing at their learning station.

Computer supported learning resources were not used extensively in the past. Eventually, elements that can be potentially supportive to learning will increase. There will be more data bases, with broader access. These compelling and plentiful resources will make greater flexibility of learner involvement in learning possible and common. As communications usage increases, future learners will deal with data bases more often in their work.

Technological advances will benefit the facilitator as well as the learner. The ever-increasing power and capacity available to all users will increase. Concurrently, the unit cost of a given level of capability will decrease. Improved human factor considerations in learning hardware and software will also evolve.

Figure 17.9
Future Instructional Communications

Past	Present	Future
one-to-one communications	organizaton initiated computer conferencing and video teleconferencing	learner initiated one-to-one and one-to-many communications

Video. Videotape will be replaced by optical discs. Even today, at major conference expositions, a trainer from Mars would have had to surmise from the percentage of exhibits that interactive video is the most commonly used instructional strategy. The newer digital optical discs will replace today's common analog laser disc, and multimedia will rule. The rate of these changes will be determined by acceptance of the consumer version of the new disc-based media. Upon consumer acceptance, disc technology will follow the lead of VHS. These are shown in Figure 17.10.

Figure 17.10
Future Video

Past	Present	Future
videotape analog videodisc	digital optical disc technologies	digital solid state (chips)

In the more distant future, interactive video and multimedia may not use discs. Discs are an interim technology. Projected advances in increased memory available will permit images to be stored in digital form, directly in the computer on a chip. Digital storage of video images directly in the computer will make "photographic" quality graphics available for direct use in instruction. We can do this today. But the cost is prohibitive. Future reductions in computer memory costs make us quite confident in predicting this development.

Delivery on Other Systems

We hope there be greater standardization among computers generally. Difficulties in courseware use caused by persistent multiple hardware types. The multiplicity of formats is the result of commercial competition. Sometimes one format dominates the marketplace resulting in de facto standardization. In other cases, the competing formats remain.

Standardization will bring more widespread transportability of courseware from one delivery system to another. Today, without such utilities, the effort required to make a lesson function on another type system is nearly as large an effort as the original. Courseware development utilities will provide improved capability to specify the particular delivery system before development. Then the tool automatically follows development parameters appropriate for the system(s) selected.

Figure 17.11
Future Media Compatibility

Past	Present	Future
competing delivery formats require separate development	competing delivery formats require conversion	competing delivery formats accommodated by versatile development tools

Creation of a version for a second or third system could be possible at low or no added cost. Courseware generation utilities will also ease development of versions of courseware for other cultures and languages. Primitive versions of these courseware development utilities exist today. The future will bring increased power, variety, and flexibility in these systems.

Administration. Automatic record handling will continue. Automatic posting of learner completion records to the organization's personnel systems will be common. These postings will update performance appraisal data automatically. Training needed by each employee will be identified at performance appraisal time. Agreement on the activities needed will generate automatic enrollment in the technology-delivered course needed.

Evolving Job Aids

Job aids have always been an important tool for improving human performance. The advent of electronic form for "packaging" job aids suggests that their use will grow. Expert systems are really just job aids. Today expert systems are usually separate programs that run on a PC. In the future they will be built into other software used at work. They may be available at the worker's request or appear whenever a performance seems questionable.

Figure 17.12
Future Job Aids

Past	Present	Future
packet cards printed checklists flow charts	expert systems on personal computers	expert systems integrated into workstations

Personal Computers on Workers' Desks

More workers will have VDTs at their desks, or will use one during their work. These VDTs are potential delivery devices for CBL courseware. At some point these work stations may not be simple VDTs. The work station may include a far more integrated work area. The work surface itself may become active, permitting input, and giving output, for graphic images and text. There will be more data bases, with broader access. These powerful and plentiful resources will make possible greater learner involvement in the design of the learning.

John Naisbitt says; "To be really successful, you will have to be trilingual: fluent in English, Spanish, and computer." Eventually, an increasing number of workers will have a terminal at their work site. At some point these work stations may not be simple VDTs. See an amplification of what possibilities exist later in this chapter. This placement of the necessary equipment for learning at an individual's work site will make delivery of HRD services in this manner the future norm.

Figure 17.13
Future Workstations

Past	Present	Future
lecture in classrooms	individual learning center	individual learning at the workstation

Learning Incorporated in Work

Here is the key! The work station is also the learning station. It has obvious potential for a range of sophisticated learning strategies, including use of a wide range of supporting resources. This couldn't happen in the past. Most workstations were then technically inadequate for the demands of instruction. Technology has caught up with needs. Today's computers can be configured with all the needed processing, displays, and storage capabilities.

We will use the computer-based learning technique as an interface or "front end" part or most of the time for non-educational, direct work functions. The difference between this application of instruction and job aids can blur. In practice, it is partly like a job aid, since it replaces training in involved tasks. The other side of the technique is to provide the needed training, either as a requirement or an option, right on the equipment. As other "intelligent" devices proliferate, use of technology-based learning for emulation and control of them will become a meaningful part of HRD.

In some occupations, it seems clear there is tremendous potential for HRD activities involving technology-based learning incorporated in the work itself. The classic example of a future possibility of this technique is a nuclear reactor operator. The operator, while at work, can "read" actual current reactor data. Then CBL lessons will ease the manipulation of the data. This will help to learn more of the internal dynamics of the actual reactor to understand how the reactor may behave in the immediate future. This study of "what if" using actual live data from the reactor in operation has enormous potential for facilitation of important learning. There is a strong contrast of internal dynamics of the actual on-site (as opposed to theoretical or "canned problem") reactor.

Figure 17.14
Future Timing of Learning

Past	Present	Future
block scheduled periodic classes in classrooms	individually scheduled individualized learning in learning centers	individually initiated individualized learning at own workstation

Workplace Location

More workers may work at home, with commercial-grade equipment (to use for HRD at hours of their convenience). The attractive term "electronic cottage" appears in Alvin Toffler's *The Third Wave*.

Figure 17.15
Future Media Development Work Locations

Past	Present	Future
almost all media development work performed in offices and factories	some media development work performed in home work-sites	much media development work performed in home and other off-site locations
full-time employer/employee relationship	full-time employer/employee relationship	part-time employer/ semi-employee relationship much job sharing

The cottage is the worker's own home. Angus Reynolds can personally testify to the beauty of this concept. He, by choice, worked for a major multinational corporation from his home for over five years (while working for the same organization for a longer period). His immediate manager's office was over 1,000 miles away! His productivity was greater in his "electronic cottage." The concept works because it offers advantages both to the employer and employee. It isn't right for all employees, all jobs, or all managers.[4]

---

[4]This ended when reorganization produced a new manager who was unable to handle the management of a distant employee.

Even today, with commercial-grade equipment, course development can be completed by the cottage employee at hours of personal convenience. Members of the courseware development group, will have very sophisticated courseware generators. The electronic cottage is workable even now for both course development and learning delivery. It is applicable to a vast percentage of the workforce. In the future, we expect it to become commonplace.

Changes in Learning Opportunities

The university is a concept. In the pure sense, it is not tied to a building. University resources linked to powerful learning tools offer the possibility of personal development at home, as a part of the organization's HRD.

Figure 17.16
Future Formal Learning Opportunities

Past	Present	Future
almost all formal learning	some formal learning	much formal learning
sponsored by institution of higher learning	sponsored by institution of higher learning	sponsored by employing organization
delivered by institution of higher learning	delivered by institution of higher learning	delivered by institution of higher learning
using conventional (lecture) delivery means	using conventional (lecture) and unconventional (distance learning) delivery means	using unconventional (distance learning) delivery means
on-site at institution of higher learning	on-site at work location	on-site at employee's home or other work location

Common access to these knowledge-based systems may contribute to greater synergy and sharing of resources between them. The powerful learning tools that will become widespread in the future can tap other sources for learning. Most organizations' HRD programs include formal learning situations involving universities through tuition assistance. The organization's learning tools will link to the university's resources. This offers the same options for personal development at work (and therefore in the electronic cottage), as a part of the organization's total employee development program. Such joint programs will call for new ways of working together. Presumably they will be compatible with the direction of university education.

What Does Learning Look Like?

The learner "George" is in a group that will benefit from a planned training program. George is assigned to a block of time when he and several other employees will use the CBL terminals and some lab equipment. He has his own copies of the organization's new colorful training manuals. He will be able to keep them after the program is over.

George reports to the organization's technology-based learning area on his scheduled day. There are more learners than learning stations. Learners will spend some time using other center resources such as the test equipment. It is an on-going program, so some other learners have completed parts of the program. As one completes the program, another learner is assigned and begins. This provides for an efficient use of resources. A learner only is in the program until the learning is complete. Therefore, many will return to productive work sooner than would be possible in a block instruction situation.

Hilda, the facilitator, greets George. She explains the program and shows him the various items that he will need. George received his copies of the manuals the previous week. He has already looked them over. He is motivated to learn. He is glad to have the chance to "keep up" with advances in the organization's latest technology. It looks as if he will qualify to work on the company's newest equipment. Hilda introduces him to the learning station, explains how he will proceed through the course, and answers his questions.

George starts with a test. The test shows which parts of the instruction he *really* needs. By identifying what in the course he already knows, he is not forced to waste training time.[5] The result of this test for the first module of instruction is a study assignment prescription. It is the learning activities uniquely suited to George's needs. George will turn to the lab equipment, manuals, audiovisual materials, instructor conference, or CAI activity to learn the information he needs to "master" the module. He will call on company experts distant from his learning site. The organization's training department has identified a "subject matter expert" to take calls from trainees enrolled in a complex subject. George may be able to get help directly on his learning station, if it is a part of a network.

When he has finished the learning activities, he will take another test. It measures his knowledge of those objectives that he did not master at first. This test is somewhat more detailed, since the objectives are already iden-

---

[5] A side issue related to this principle is that if we simply asked him which parts he knows, he would answer honestly. However, he may not realize there are certain points that he thinks he knows, but is mistaken. The system is much more precise in pinpointing needs.

tified as important to his knowledge of the subject. Ideally George will master the remaining objectives for the first module, and go on to the test for the second module. If he still does not master some objectives that he missed on the first test, he will receive another learning activities prescription. Hilda's attention will also be flagged automatically.

What Could Learning Look Like?

George could use his workstation for most studying. Many of the learning activities delivered on other media can be adopted for delivery on it. Possibly, the workstation-learning station may be on or near the factory floor where George is a member of the maintenance staff. Then he can leave the learning on a moment's notice to do essential repairs. When he comes back, he can begin again just where he left the lesson. The workstation may just as well be at his (remote) work location for a time while he and possibly other employees complete a planned program.

George is part of the maintenance staff. He could not work at a home work-site. Grace, an accountant in the same organization, could use the workstation as a learning station for courses appropriate to his needs. Hilda would be available by phone or electronic mail to help him identify needed learning resources.

Proceed With Confidence!

We have examined some characteristics of the inside of learning in the future. Now, let's take a look at the human side. It is important to know how well future learning fits the adult learning situation. Bob Mager did not intend to describe future training in his book *Troubleshooting the Troubleshooting Course*, just good training. Nevertheless, it provides the an excellent description of what training ought to be *anytime*.

> In short, state-of-the-art instruction derives its objectives from a real need (a job), creates instruction that is tightly related to the accomplishment of those objectives, and removes obstacles between the learners and the learning. It encourages and assists students to progress as rapidly as their growing competence will allow and makes their world a little brighter, rather than dimmer, when they demonstrate progress. It provides instruction and practice until each student can perform as desired, and then it stops.[6]

Today, to meet the higher needs and expectations of the world in which we live, we must effectively harness the power of advancing technologies. They become important, or even essential, "technological multipliers."

---

[6] Mager, R. *Troubleshooting the Troubleshooting Course*. Belmont, CA: Pitman Learning, Inc. 1982, p. 136.

These multipliers offer the promise of profound and beneficial impact on the delivery and application of knowledge in less industrialized countries.[7]

One of our favorite stories is about the (archetypical eccentric) computer-design genius Seymour Cray. The company where he worked forced him to make an input to a marketing document for a computer system that he was designing. His input was just three words: "proceed with confidence." Seymour Cray could foresee demand for more powerful computers. We in the instructional field should be able to foresee some of what learning will be like in the next two decades. The field is not standing still, but will move and evolve rapidly. We will be a major factor in this evolution.

It is easy to be a prophet! The problem of forecasting the training future is that it keeps catching up with you. Some things that I confidently predicted in 1980 (for realization by 1986) were already upon us in two years—others have not yet arrived. The predictions of implementation of technology in this chapter are conservative. The increased level of technology available in our societies will reflect in more powerful tools for learning. We will make increasing use of media in training programs of all kinds. Knowing this, it should be possible for each of us to prepare to function effectively in the evolving environment. The obvious advice is clear—proceed with confidence!

---

[7] Reynolds, A. Computer-based Learning: The Technological Multiplier. *Proceedings, Conference on Educational Technology to Improve International Education and Training.* Washington: Society for Applied Learning Technology. 1982.

Suggested Readings

THE REFERENCES HERE ARE SUGGESTED AS A WAY TO BEGIN exploring the areas covered in the book. A great many resources are available to anyone who wishes to pursue the topics of media, media selection, and instructional development in more depth. The following list represents only a small sample of these sources. The references are categorized somewhat arbitrarily, and they include brief descriptions of content to help readers locate topics of interest. Because some sources are broader in scope than others, they may be listed more than once. ■

Instruction—General

Allen, S. A Manager's Guide to Audiovisuals New York: McGraw-Hill, 1979.

American Society for Training and Development. *Training and Development Handbook: A Guide to Human Resource Development, Third Edition.* New York: McGraw-Hill, 1987. A comprehensive collection of writings and bibliography of texts available on Human Resource Development.

Bloom, B., et al. *Taxonomy of Educational Objectives: Book 1: Cognitive Domain.* White Plains, NY: Longman, 1977.

Brown, J., Lewis, R. and Harcleroad, F. *A V Instruction: Technology, Media. and Methods* Sixth edition. New York: McGraw-Hill, 1982. Though this is a text directed primarily toward using media in formal education at all levels, the principles and background information included can be readily applied to instruction for business, industry, government, and other types of agencies.

Davies, I. *Instructional Techniques.* New York: McGraw-Hill, 1981. A basic, no-frills, guide to instructional processes for managers, supervisors, or anyone required to plan, conduct, or evaluate training.

Gagne, R. *The Conditions of Learning, Third Edition*. New York: Holt, Rinehart, and Winston, 1977. A discussion of a variety of forms of learning, problem solving, and learning hierarchies. Eight distinguishable classes of performance change (learning) are described, as are corresponding sets of conditions for learning.

Haladyna, T., and Roid, G. H. "Reviewing Criterion-Referenced Test Items." *Educational Technology* (August 1983), pp. 35-38.

Heinich, R.,. Molenda, M.. and Russell. J. *Instructional Media and the New Technologies of Instruction, Third Edition*. New York: Macmillan, 1989. Text aimed principally at teachers of primary and secondary levels of education but applicable also to business and industry. Content attempts to establish a middle ground between "humanist" and "technological" traditions in field of learning. Applications of audio-visual methods of learning are also stressed in this text.

Krathwohl, D., et al. *Taxonomy of Educational Objectives: Handbook 2: Affective Domain*. White Plains, NY: Longman, 1969.

Kurfiss, J. "Linking Psychological Theory and Instructional Technology." *International Journal of Instructional Media* (1981-1982), pp. 3-10.

Mager, R. *Preparing Instructional Objectives. Revised Second Edition*. Belmont, CA: Pitman Learning, Inc., 1987. A self-instructional, programmed text on preparing behavioral objectives.

Mager. R. *Measuring Instructional Intent or Got a Match?* Belmont, CA: Pitman Learning, Inc., 1973. A text explaining why and how to construct tests matching learning objectives.

Mager, R. *Troubleshooting the Troubleshooting Course*. Belmont, CA: Pitman Learning, Inc. 1982.

Schramm, W. *Big Media, little media*. Beverly Hills, CA: Sage Publications, 1977.

Spector, A. Instructional Strategies: Media in Nadler, L., and Nadler, Z. eds. *The Handbook of Human Resource Development, Second Edition*. New York, Wiley, 1990.

Wilcox, J. "A Campus Tour of Corporate Colleges." *Training and Development Journal* (May 1987), pp. 51-56.

Instructional Systems Development

Butler, F. *Instructional Systems Development for Vocational and Technical Training*. Englewood Cliffs, NJ: Educational Technology Publications, 1972. A general textbook which may be useful.

Commission on Instructional Technology To Improve Learning. *A Report to the President and the Congress of the United States* (Washington, DC: U.S. Government Printing Office, 1970). p. 19.

Center for Educational Technology. *Interservice Procedures for Instructional Systems Development* (Contract No: N61339-73-C--0150). Tallahasee, FL: Florida State University, 1976. If you want to go to the "horse's mouth" this is that document. It is complete, but ponderous. The document's executive summary is a useful summarization of ISD.

Davies, I. *Competency Based Learning: Technology, Management and Design*. New York: McGraw Hill, 1973. A good book on competency based learning.

Ford Foundation. *An Inquiry Into the Uses of Instructional Technology*. , 1973.

Gagne, R. and Briggs, L. *Principles of Instructional Design.* New York: Holt, Rinehart and Winston, 1974. A theoretical book by Robert Gagne, who is the theoretician behind much of what educational technologists do.

Kemp, J. *The Instructional Design Process.* New York: Harper & Row, 1985.

Mager, R. *Developing Instructional Objectives.* Belmont, CA: Pitman Learning, 1977. A book, widely heralded as the best, about developing instructional objectives.

Mager, R. and Pipe, P. *Analyzing Performance Problems* (Belmont, CA: Frearon Publishers, 1984).

Nadler, L. *Designing Training Programs: The Critical Events Model.* Reading, MA: Addison-Wesley, 1982.

Reiser, R., and Gagne, M. *Selecting Media for Instruction.* Englewood Cliffs, NJ: Educational Technology Publications, 1983.

Rosmiszowski, A. *Designing Instructional Systems.* New York: Nichols, 1981.

Rosmiszowski, A. *Producing Instructional Systems.* New York: Nichols, 1986.

Rosmiszowski, A. *The Selection and Use of Instructional Media.* New York: Nichols, 1987. These three books are written for the public education sector.

Adult Learning

Knowles, M. *The Adult Learner: A Neglected Species.* Houston: Gulf Publishing, 1979. This is a classic in the field of adult learning and is responsible for drawing much of the attention that this important subject has received.

Lanese, L. "Applying Principles of Learning to Adult Training Programs." *Educational Technology* (March 1983), pp. 15-17.

Media and Instruction—General

Association for Educational Communications and Technology. *Educational Technology: A Glossary of Terms.* Washington, DC: Author, 1979. A comprehensive glossary defining terminology used in the field of instructional technology.

Joyce, et al. *Handbook for Job Performance Aid Developers.* Air Force Human Resources Laboratory, 1973.

Kemp, J. and Smellie, D. *Planning and Producing Audio Visual Materials. Sixth Edition* New York: Harper and Row, 1989. A practical, basic text for media specialists and training personnel in the procedures an processes for production of the major audio-visual media.

Reynolds, A. "The Computer-based Learning Center," in Tracey, W. R. ed. *Human Resource Management and Development Handbook,* New York: American Management Association, 1984. A coverage, not only of the learning center, but other aspects of getting started with technology-based learning in organizations.

Schmid, W. *Media Center Management: A Practical Guide.* New York: Hasting House, 1980. A guide or handbook for managers of media facilities; covering a broad range of topics including design of plant facilities. managing various functions, and monitoring operations.

Stolovich, H. *Audiovisual Training Modules.* Englewood Cliffs, NJ: Educational Technology Publications, 1978. Detailed text on development of slide-tape or filmstrip-tape lessons. Explanations of how to develop materials from task analysis, objectives, and tests to end products.

Sullivan, S., and Baker, B. *A Handbook of Operating Information and Simplified Maintenance Instructions for Commonly Used Audio-visual Equipment, Revised Edition.* Huntsville, TX: KBS, 1982.

The State of Knowledge Pertaining to Selection of Cost-Effective Training Methods and Media. Alexandria, VA: HUMRRO Technical Repo 73-13, 1973. A report on the research conducted by Human Resource Research Organization to provide the Army with a training manual for selecting the most cost-effective training methods and media for specific training tasks.

Wilshusen, J. "How to Prevent Equipment Failures." *Instructional Innovator* (March 1980), pp. 35-36.

Printed Materials

Burbank, L, and Pett, D. "Designing Printed Instructional Materials." *Performance and Instruction* (October 1986), pp. 5-9.

Craig, J., and Meyer, S. *Designing With Type: A Basic Course in Typography, Second Edition.* New York: Watson-Guptill, 1980. The text presents a course in the process of selecting, designing, and laying out printed materials. The text is designed to apply to a wide range of readers.

Tinker, M. *Legibility of Print.* Ames, IA: Iowa State University Press, 1963. A summary of studies conducted on the use of various standard formats of print and their relative readability.

Williams, R. *The Macintosh is Not A Typewriter.* Santa Rosa, CA: Performance Enhancement Products—The Press, 1990.

Audio

Bartlett, B. *Introduction to Professional Recording Techniques.* Indianapolis, IN: Sams, 1987.

Canale, L., ed. *Digital Audio's Guide to Compact Discs.* New York: Bantam, 1986.

Deidman, S. "What Instructional Medias Producers Should Know About Using Music." *Performance and Instruction* (March 1981) pp. 21-23.

Eastman Kodak Co. "The Power of Sound in AV Presentations." *Slide Tape Presentation V10-39,* Rochester, NY: Author, 1983.

Wadsworth, R. *Basics of Audio and Visual Systems Design.* Indianapolis, IN: Sams, 1983.

Visuals

Bloomer, C. *Principles of Visual Perception.* New York: Van Nostrand Reinhold, 1976.

Clark, J. "Filmstrips: Versatility and Visual Impact." *Media and Methods* (January-February 1988), pp. 20-21.

DeBloois, M. ed. *Videodisc/Microcomputer Courseware Design.* Englewood Cliffs, NJ: Prentice-Hall, 1982.

DeChenne, J. "Effective Utilization of Overhead Projectors." *Media and Methods* (January 1982), pp. 6-7.

Eastman Kodak Co. *Kodak Pamphlet L-5. 1981 Introduction to Kodak Information.* Rochester, New York: Author, 1981. Catalog of pamphlets available through Kodak on design, planning, and production of a broad spectrum of media including graphics, photography, film, video, and design of classroom.

Gayeski, D. *Corporate and Instructional Video Design and Production.* Englewood Cliffs, NJ: Prentice-Hall, 1983.

Geest, D. *CD-I: A Designer's Overview.* New York: McGraw Hill, 1988.

Green, L. *501 Ways to Use the Overhead Projector.* Littleton,CO: Libraries Unlimited, 1982.

Helgerson, L. "Optical Discs: New Storage Media for Education." *T.H.E. Journal* (March 1987), pp. 50-52.

Johnson, V. "Picture Perfect Presentations." *Training and Development Journal,* (May 1989), pp. n-n.

Kennedy, T. *Directing the Video Program.* White Plains, NY: Knowledge Industry, 1988.

Kenny, M. *Presenting Yourself: A Kodak How-to Book.* New York: Wiley, 1982.

Kueter, R., and Miller, J. *Slides.* Englewood Cliffs, NJ: Educational Technology Publications, 1981.

Lambert, S. and Sallis, J. eds. *CD-I and Interactive Videodisc Technology.* Indianapolis, IN: Sams, 1986..

McBride, D. *How to Make Visual Presentations.* New York: Art Direction Book Company, 1982.

Millerson, G. *Video Production Handbook.* Stoneham, MA: Focal, 1986.

Smith, W. *Basic Video.* Fairfax, VA: Development Associates, Inc., 1982. Entry-level text or manual on selection, set-up, operation, and maintenance of single camera video tape recording systems in all formats.

Schwier, R. *Interactive Video.* Englewood Cliffs, NJ: Educational Technology Publications, 1988.

Wershing, S., and Singer, P. *Computer Graphics and Animation for Corporate Video.* White Plains, NY: Knowledge Industry, 1988.

Computers in Instruction

Alessi, S., and Trollip, S. *Computer-Based Instruction: Methods and Development.* Englewood Cliffs, NJ: Prentice-Hall, 1985.

Bodner, G. "Instructional Media: Resisting Technological Overkill—35-mm Slides as an Alternative to Videotape/Videodisk" [Sic.]. *Journal of College Science Teaching* (February 1985), pp. 360-363.

Dean, C., and Whitlock, Q. *A Handbook of Computer Based Training.* New York: Nichols Publishing, 1983.

DeBlois, M. *Videodisc/Microcomputer Courseware Design.* Englewood Cliffs, N.J.: Educational Technology Publications, 1982.

Galite, W. *Handbook of Screen Format Design.* Wellesley, MA.: Q.E.D. Information Sciences, 1981.

Gery, G. "Evaluating the Emerging Market: A Resource Guide to Computer-Aided Instruction." *Data Training.* A hardware comparison of many of the systems in use today. Updated and published annually.

Gillespie, L., and Buck, J. *CBT Starter Kit.* Reston, VA: Longman-Crown, 1984.

Goodman, D. *The Complete HyperCard Handbook*. New York: Bantam Books, 1988.

Hannafin, M., and Peck, K. *The Design, Development, and Evaluation of Instructional Software*. New York: Macmillan, 1988.

Heines, J., *Screen Designs for Computer-Assisted Instruction*. Bedford, MA: Digital Press, 1984.

Hooper, J. and Hannafin, M. "Variables Affecting the Legibility of Computer-Generated Text." *Journal of Instructional Development*, (1986) p. 67.

Jensen, J. "A Taxonomy of Microcomputer Authoring Systems." *Performance and Instruction*, July/August 1982. A coverage of the different means of authoring.

Kearsley, G. "Authoring Systems in Computer Based Education." *Communications of ACM*, Vol. 25, No. 7, (July 1982). A scholarly treatment of automatic programming systems for CBL.

Kuhlic, J., Kuhlic, C., and Cohen, P. "Effectiveness of Computer-based College Teaching: A Meta Analysis of Findings." *Review of Educational Research*, (July 1980). A review of research through 1980. Also, Kuhlic, Kuhlic, and Cohen are widely quoted in support of the fact that computer assisted instruction was proven faster than conventional instruction. This was the research that finally convinces skeptics that CBE works.

Reynolds, A. "A Computer-Based Learning Glossary for Human Resource Development Professionals" in *Computer-Based Training Today: A guide to research, specialized terms and publications in the field*. Arlington, VA: American Society for Training and Development, 1987.

Reynolds, A. "Computer-based Learning: The Technological Multiplier." *Proceedings, Conference on Educational Technology to Improve International Education and Training*. Washington: Society for Applied Learning Technology, 1982.

Reynolds, A. "Computers and HRD" in Nadler, L., and Nadler, Z. eds. *The Handbook of Human Resource Development, Second Edition*. New York, Wiley, 1990.

Sniederman, B. *Software Psychology: Human Factors in Computer and Information Systems*. Cambridge, MA.: Winthrop Publishers, 1980.

Testerman, J., and Jackson, J. "A Comprehensive Annotated Bibliography on Computer-Assisted Instruction, Parts I and II," *Computing Reviews (ACM)*, Vol. 14, No.s 10-11, (Oct.-Nov., 1973). Those who want to look at the research that laid the foundation for the field can find an extensive bibliography up to 1972.

Expert Systems

Adams, D., and Hamm, M. "Artificial Intelligence and Instruction: Thinking Tools for Education." *T.H.E. Journal* (August 1987), pp. 59-62.

Comcowich, W. "Expert Systems: A New Era in Videodiscs." *E-ITV* (August 1987), pp. 23-25.

Martins, G. "The Overselling of Expert Systems." *Datamation*, (July 1982), p.76. There has been considerable interest in artificial intelligence and expert systems recently. The are expert systems. There are also other programs touted as expert systems that are not. This article places this field in perspective.

Sleeman, D., and Brown, J. S. *Intelligent Tutoring Systems*. New York: Academic Press, 1982.

Distance Learning

Dallmann, C. "Teletraining in a Corporate Environment: Implementing Training through Teleconferencing Technology." *Media and Adult Learning* (Fall 1986), pp. 3-5.

Daniel, J. "Independence and Interaction in Distance Education: New Technologies for Home Instruction." *Programmed Learning and Educational Technology* (August 1983), pp. 155-160.

Hilton, J., and Jacobi, P. *Straight Talk about Video Teleconferencing.* New York: Prentice Hall, 1986.

Hudspeth, D., and Brey, R. *Instructional Telecommunications.* Westport, CT: Greenwood Press, Praeger, 1985.

Jones, M. *See, Hear, Interact: Beginning Developments in Two Way Television.* Metuchen, NJ: Scarecrow Press, 1984.

Parker, L. *Teletraining Means Business.* Madison, WI.: Center for Interactive Programs, University of Wisconsin, 1984.

Robertson, B. "Audio Teleconferencing: Low-Cost Technology for External Studies Networking." *Distance Education* (March 1987), pp. 121-130.

Rosetti, D., and Surynt, T. "Video Teleconferencing and Performance." *Journal of Business Communication* (Fall 1985), pp. 25-31.

Stern, C. "Teaching the Distance Learner Using New Technology." *Journal of Educational Technology Systems* 15, no. 4 (1986-1987), pp. 407-419.

Williams, F. *The Communications Revolution, Revised Edition.* Beverly Hills, CA: Sage Publications, 1984 .

Zemke, R. "The Rediscovery of Video Teleconferencing." *Training* (September 1986), pp. 28-34.

Simulations and Simulators

Dormant, D. *Rolemaps.* Englewood Cliffs, NJ.: Educational Technology Publications, 1980.

Dukes, R., and Seidner, Constance J., eds . *Learning with Simulations and Games.* Beverly Hills, CA: Sage Publications, 1978.

Evans, D. Games and Simulations in *Literacy Training.* Amer-sham, Buckinghamshire, England: Hulton Educational Publications, 1979.

Greenblat, C., and Duke, R. *Principles and-Practices of Gaming/Simulation.* Beverly Hills, CA: Sage Publications, 1981.

Molloy, W. "Making Role Plays Pay Off in Training." *Training* (May 1981), pp. 59-63.

Reiser, R. "Increasing the Instructional Effectiveness of Simulation Games." *Instructional Innovator* (March 1981), pp. 36-37.

Reynolds, A. and Samuels-Campbell, C. "Simulations: Time to Take Another Look!" *Performance and Instruction.* Vol. 24, No. 4, May 1985, pp. 15-17.

Stolovitch, H., and Thiagarajan, S. *Frame Games.* Englewood Cliffs, NJ: Educational Technology Publications, 1980.

Taylor, J., and Walford, R. *Learning and the Simulation Game.* Beverly Hills, CA: Sage Publications, 1978.

Thiagarajan, S., and Stolovitch, H. *Instructional Simulation Games.* Englewood Cliffs, NJ: Educational Technology Publications, 1978.

Van Ments, M. *The Effective Use of Role-Play: A Handbook for Teachers and Trainers.* New York: Nichols, 1983.

Wohlking, W., and Gill, P. *Role Playing* Englewood Cliffs, NJ: Educational Technology Publications, 1980.

The Future of Instruction

World Future Society. *Communications Tomorrow: The Coming Information Society*. Bethesda, MD.: Author, 1982.

Licklider, J. "A Glimpse of Education in the 1990s." Unpublished Manuscript, Laboratory for Computer Science, Massachusetts Institute of Technology, Cambridge, MA. Many future scenarios have been written. This one, written a decade ago, is the best written of those that apply to education. The author was very careful to use examples built upon existing (if not implemented) technology. Nevertheless, it still describes what education will, hopefully, be in the 1990s.

Reynolds, A. "1984: The International Versions" in *International HRD Annual, Vol. 1.*, ed. Doktor, R. Washington, DC: American Society for Training and Development, 1985.

Glossary

JARGON IS THE VOCABULARY FROM ANOTHER PERSON'S FIELD.
Sometimes specialized words convey a meaning much better than
common English. In any case, when specialized words are in common
use, like it or not, it is necessary to learn their meaning to communicate
effectively with others who use them. This specialized glossary for
media in learning is intended to help you "get past" the strange words
and on to the points discussed. [1]

Other HRD terms are included to indicate the correct use within the
instructional development field. Definitions of terms may use or refer to
other terms that appear alphabetically. Cross references such as "Contrast
with...," "Compare to...," and "See..." appear for your convenience.

No matter what level of experience you have, you might simply skim over
the words in the glossary in sequence. Stop to read the unfamiliar words.
Don't try to master all the terms in the glossary; use a "need to know"
strategy to become familiar with those terms most appropriate for your
particular involvement. As your experience grows, you will probably find the
terms familiar.

---

[1]This glossary is primarily composed of definitions developed by Angus
Reynolds; copyright 1981, 1982, 1983, 1984, 1986, 1987, and 1989. They have
appeared elsewhere including as "A Computer-Based Learning Glossary for
Human Resource Development Professionals" in *Computer-Based Training
Today: A guide to research, specialized terms and publications in the field*
(1987). Arlington, VA: American Society for Training and Development. Used
there and here with the author's permission. All rights reserved.

andragogy
A concept of how adults learn. A contrast is usually made with pedagogy—teaching children. See adult learning.

acetate
Refers to the plastic sheet used for overhead projection (whether or not technically accurate).

access
Process by which information contained either in memory or mass storage is made available to another sub-unit of a computer or, ultimately, to the user. Also, refers to the authority or ability to communicate with a remote computer.

adult learning
The field of education about adults. Especially important since individualized instruction matches well with what is known about how adults learn. Adult learning also is a term to contrast with pedagogy—the techniques for teaching children.

affective domain
Refers to the area of human learning associated with attitudes, opinions, and values. Contrast with cognitive and psychomotor.

algorithm
Organization of an activity into a set of steps. The resulting "path" is called an algorithm. An algorithm can be used as the basis of a job aid. See job aid.

alphanumeric
Both letters and numerals, and usually other characters, except those used in drawing pictures. Compare with graphic.

analog
Continuously variable physical quantities such as electrical voltages or flow of water. Used to represent numbers in a calculation. Also, an abbreviated form for analog computer. Compare with digital.

analysis
A process of determining the scope and nature of instructional materials needed to satisfy a given set of training needs. In analysis, the training requirements and the instructional program are defined. Existing materials are surveyed, and the design and development effort are planned. One of the phases in the ISD process. The others are design, development, implementation, and evaluation.

animation
The apparent movement of objects on a video or computer display. Characters can be drawn, selectively erased, and repositioned to produce animation. Animation can aid understanding through illustrating, and helps aid recall by highlighting steps in processes. It is an essential element of an equipment simulation—for example, a needle of a gauge moving realistically. Also, see graphics.

application
See application program and computer application.

application program
Software that includes the instructions to a computer that solve a particular problem. Compare with operating system and computer language. See computer application.

artificial intelligence
Artificial intelligence has been defined by Marvin Minsky as "the science of making machines do things that would require intelligence if done by man." Artificial intelligence has several aspects. One of particular interest in human resource development is the expert system—a computer program that offers a human performer advice. See expert system and job aid.

aspect ratio
> Ratio of the width to the height of the image.

audiotape
> Regular audiotape as used for entertainment is one of the media that can support learning. Seen less often than it merits.

audio-tutorial
> Audiotape recording directs the learner to various activities in a planned instructional sequence. An inexpensive, but effective method.

author
> The person who creates computer-based learning course material. Compare with programmer.

author(ing) language
> A computer language used specifically for creating CAI courseware. For example: Tencore™, instead of FORTRAN.

authoring system (aid) (utility)
> Special type of program that eases the programming of CAI courseware by enabling a content expert to interact with the computer and have the coding done automatically. Unlike an authoring language, it does not need programming knowledge or skill. Contrast with author language.

auxiliary device
> A device connected to a CBL system and controlled by it. Examples include: oscilloscope, audiotape, videotape, and videodisc. A videodisc controlled by a computer for learning purposes is termed interactive video. In computer terminology these are called "peripheral devices."

BASIC
> Acronym for Beginner's All-purpose Symbolic Instruction Code, a general purpose, high-level language designed for teaching programming. BASIC is unsuited to CAI development in comparison with an authoring language.

baud
> Unit of measure for transmission rate. A term with origin in the era of telegraphy, baud is now used interchangeably with "bits per second." Information can be sent by the computer at speeds that typically range from 1200 - 9600 baud.

branching
> In computer-based learning, directing the learner to one of two or more paths through other material on the basis of replies to questions. Contrast with linear.

brightness
> Describes the amount of light emitted from a surface such as a screen. Brightness is measured in foot-lamberts, foot-candles or lux.

bus
> Portion of main circuit board in which component boards are installed so that they can obtain access to multiple power and communications channels. Modern computers have a single bus, which provides access to memory, controllers, and interfaces for each component board plugged into a slot on the bus. (Different brands use different bus standards. Computers sold by one company may not all use the same bus.)

buttons
> Potentially active spots on the screen that begin a link when chosen. (Buttons may look like actual physical buttons or take the shape of a familiar object.)

C
> A general purpose computer language. It is widespread because of its portability to a wide variety of computers. C is unsuited to CAI development in comparison with an authoring language.

CAI
　Abbreviation for Computer Assisted Instruction. The use of a computer to deliver instruction. The modes of CAI are drill and practice, modeling, tutorial and simulation. This is the preferred term. The same as CAT and CAL. CAI, along with CMI and CSLR, are the components of CBE. Compare with CMI and CSLR. Unfortunately, some users say "CAI" when they mean CBE. Compare with CBE.

CAL
　Abbreviation for Computer Assisted Learning. The meaning is identical to CAI. See CAI.

camcorder
　Video camera and recorder in a single unit.

camera ready
　Copy ready to be photographed for printing.

cards
　Pages (screens) within a Hypermedia stack

carosel
　Most popular type of 35mm slide tray. Refers to the circular shape and motion of the tray.

CAT
　Abbreviation for Computer Assisted Training. The meaning is identical to CAI. See CAI.

CBE
　Abbreviation for Computer-based Education. Since computer-based learning was originally developed in a university setting, the term naturally applied to it was education. Therefore, CBE is the oldest of the several synonymous terms in use. See CBL.

CBI
　Abbreviation for Computer-Based Instruction. The meaning is identical to CBE, but seems to be the term preferred by some users in industry. See CBL.

CBL
　Abbreviation for Computer-Based Learning. CBE is the umbrella term that includes all forms of use of computers in support of learning. The components of CBL are CAI, CMI, and CSLR. CBL has been defined as, "anytime a person and a computer come together and one of them learns something." The meaning is identical to CBE, CBI, CBHRD, and CBT, but preferred by users who focus on the learner, rather than the instructor. See CBE.

CBT
　Abbreviation for Computer-Based Training. The meaning is identical to CBE, but preferred by some users with a training instead of education focus. See CBL.

CD-I
　One competitive format for interactive multimedia.

CD-ROM
　Acronym for Compact Disk Read Only Memory. Optical disk storage providing about 550 megabytes of storage (approximately enough for five encyclopedias) on a 5 $F(1,4)$ inch disk. The disk is read by a laser.

centered (justification).
　Contrast with flush right or left, justification, and ragged.

character
　See alphanumeric, graphic.

character printer
> A category of printers that produces a letter from a single mechanical strike. Produces the "letter quality" to which NLQ and laser printers are compared. See printer. Contrast with laser printer and NLQ printer.

check disc
> Refers to the test videodisc produced from the master to verify contents and placement.

chip
> See IC.

CMI
> Abbreviation for Computer Managed Instruction. The aspect of CBE that includes testing, prescription generation, and record keeping. CMI, along with CAI and CSLR, are the components of CBE. Compare with CAI and CSLR.

CMT
> Abbreviation for Computer Managed Training. Same as CMI.

coding
> Category of programming that involves generating the computer language version of the solution to the computer application that emerged from analysis and design. Compare with analysis, testing, and implementation. Also used to refer to a means of preparing information for storage in a form that enhances later processing.

cognitive domain
> Refers to the area of human learning associated with intellectual skills. Contrast with affective and psychomotor domains.

cognitive mapping
> A technique of using an imaginary "map" of concepts related to examples, showing which concepts are relevant to each.

cognitive style
> A concept, based on research that indicates different individuals think and learn differently. CBL offers a way to accommodate these differences, if known. This is not a recent discovery, but realization is elusive. Today, this area remains in the research stage.

composite video
> Refers to the output of certain computers and video cassette players.

computer application
> Human endeavor (a manual task) that is susceptible to being automated by computer technology. Also, any technique for applying computer technology to the solution of a variety of information processing problems. The applications most commonly done using microcomputers are: word processing, spreadsheets, data bases, graphics, and communications. See application program.

computer assisted instruction
> See CAI.

computer assisted learning
> See CAL.

computer assisted training
> See CAT.

computer chip
> See IC.

computer language
> Category of software that includes collections of instructions used in programming. One of over 100 languages used to program computers. Compare with operating system and application program. Contrast with author language and authoring utility.

computer literacy
> Knowledge of the basic elements of computer use. (When personal computers were a new phenomenon, people thought computer literacy should be a knowledge of computer science.) Computer literacy is important for an adult to function in modern society.

computer managed instruction
> See CMI.

computer managed learning
> See CML.

computer managed training
> See CMT.

computer model
> See modeling.

computer program
> See programming.

computer supported learning resources
> See CSLR.

computer terminal
> See terminal.

computer-readable
> Pertains to the storage of information or programs in such form that they can be entered automatically. Today, the media that commonly permit such entry include diskettes, and removeable disks. Computer input is also possible by scanning printed or typed text on paper. Such text is not considered "computer-readable."

configuration
> Used to determine the type and number of such hardware components as CPU, memory, disk storage, printers, and other peripheral devices for any computer system from largest to smallest.

connector
> Microcomputer sense—an inlet or outlet on a computer or peripheral, consisting of a configuration of pins and matching holes that permits computers and peripherals to be connected, usually by a cable. There are standards for these connectors, for example, RS–232 and SCSI. This suggests the actual connection would be simple and standard. In practice, there is still almost no standardization. That is "a cable is not simply a cable." One must find or make the particular cable that will work.

contrast ratio
> Ratio of brightness of the brightest possible area to the darkest possible area of an image.

copyfitting
> Adjustment of text to fit a page.

copy stand
> A stand used to photograph flat objects.

cost/benefit analysis
> A way of determining whether a project will save an amount equal or greater than its cost. Determining return on investment (ROI) is important for any media use. It may be important to demonstrate the cost effectiveness of the results expected.

courseware
> Term used to describe those computer application programs, and other media such as texts and video, that support educational objectives. Computer courseware is a special form of "software," a term reserved in this field for the programs that simply make the computer "run." Contrast with software and hardware.

CPU
> Abbreviation for Central Processing Unit. The CPUs of large computers are sometimes called mainframes. The CPU of a personal computer is often designated by the CPU chip that it contains. For example: 486 or 68040.

criterion referenced learning (instruction)
> See mastery learning.

cropping
> Marking the edges of a photograph to indicate the area to be printed.

CRT
> Abbreviation for Cathode Ray Tube. CRT refers to the screen technology commonly used in oscilloscopes, television sets, and computer terminals. Compare with video monitor and VDT. Contrast with LCD and plasma panel. See VDT.

CSLR
> Abbreviation for Computer Supported Learning Resources. A computer supported learning resource is any form of computer support or function that supports learning other than those that teach (CAI) or test, prescribe, or keep records (CMI). The modes of CSLR are communications, data base, and hypermedia. CSLR, plus CAI and CMI, are the components of CBE. Compare with CAI and CMI.

cursor
> Movable indicator on a display. The cursor identifies the position at which the next character typed from the keyboard will be displayed.

cut
> Instantaneous change from one visual to another.

DAT
> Digital audiotape. A casette format for high quality audio recording and playback. Quality equal to CD audio.

data acquisition
> A process. Information derived from analytical instruments (usually in analog form) is captured, converted to digital form, if necessary, and held in computer readable form.

data base
> Collection of information, organized for retrieval. Generally, it is implied that this information is available in computer readable form for either on-line or off-line access. However, some data bases that have been generated by a computer exist only in hard-copy form. An example may be the individual personnel records formed into a personnel data base.

debugging
> Originally meant identifying and removing errors from computer programs. Today, the same term is used for error identification and correction in any courseware.

delivery
> The process of delivering the learning activities to learners. Also, called implementation. A phase in the ISD process. See implementation.

design
> Preparation of a detailed plan for the learning experiences. The information gathered in the analysis phase forms the basis of the design plan. Parts of the design process include completion of a task analysis, specification of instructional objectives, definition of entry behaviors, grouping and sequencing of objectives, specification of learning activities and assessment and evaluation systems, and selection of existing materials. One of the phases in the ISD process. The others are analysis, development, implementation, and evaluation.

designer
> The member of an instructional development group who specializes in design activities. In small groups this may be only one of the tasks performed by a single person.

desktop publishing
> Production of high quality text materials with PC; desktop publishing, graphic, and word processing software; and, laser printer.

developer
> The member of an instructional development group who specializes in development activities. In small groups this may be only one of the tasks performed by a single person.

development
> Production of instructional materials ready for trial use. Materials are produced as specified in the design phase and in accordance with the design and development strategy specified in earlier phases. One of the phases in the ISD process. The others are analysis, design, implementation, and evaluation.

diazo (process)
> One method used to produce overhead transparencies. Usually, found in the reproduction department of large organizations.

digital
> Pertains to the use of numbers and counting to accomplish calculations or information processing. Contrast with analog.

digitizer
> An input device to permit rapid input of graphics, normally on a tablet by use of a stylus. Can be used for authoring or student input. See tactile input. Contrast with plotter.

DIP Switch
> A micro-switch, often with four to eight small toggles. DIP switches are common on peripherals, and must often be set in particular combinations to get a desired effect or compatibility.

disk
> See hard disk.

diskette
> A small magnetic media disk, typically used for microcomputer information storage. There are several sizes and formats in common use.

display
> General term for the visual output of a computer. May use CRT, LCD, or plasma panel technology. See VDT.

dissolve
> 1. Video/film technique of fading from one image to another.
> 2. Coordination of two projectors so that the image from one is replaced by the other.

documentation
> Pertains to written information added to, or included in, computer programs to make it easier to understand how they were designed or how they are supposed to be implemented. Inattention to documentation makes later revision very difficult. Poor documentation is a major weakness of a considerable percent age of all courseware.

dolly
> Physical movement of video camera toward or away from the subject. Contrast with pan and zoom.

DOS
>Acronym for Disk Operating System. The operating system is the software that makes the computer and the disk behave properly and usefully. Rhymes with loss, not gross.

dubbing
>Transfer of information from one audio or visual unit to another.

dummy
>Final layout of page elements to guide pasteup .

Dvorak keyboard
>A keyboard with keys placed in ergonomic relationship. Most often used keys are struck by the strongest fingers. Can be learned quickly and capable of greater speed than the qwerty keyboard. The Dvorak keyboard has not been widely accepted. See qwerty keyboard.

editing
>Rearrangement of audio or visual elements in a medium for presentation.

EIDS
>Acronym for Electronic Information Delivery System. A particular form of interactive video developed by the U.S. Army, using a unique form of videodisc. Selection as a standard among some U.S. government agencies may increase its long term importance. See interaction, and interactive video.

electronic chalkboard
>A special device resembling a chalkboard. Text or images drawn on the device are transmitted to a video monitor usually located at a distance. One method of transmitting information in distance learning.

electronic publishing
>See desktop publishing.

electronic still camera
>Camera that records images on a 2"x2" disc for viewing on a video monitor. Often used to capture images for electronic publishing.

electrostatic copier
>Correct term for the xerographic process. Note it is not correct practice to call any electrostatic copier a "xerox" machine. That is a protected trademark of the Xerox Corporation.

ergonomics
>The science of humanizing "technology." See human factors.

evaluation
>Evaluation can be considered as two separate steps. The evaluation done using learners before general implementation of the materials, called formative evaluation. And the measure of the effectiveness of the materials in solving the training problem identified in the analysis phase, called summative evaluation. One of the phases in the ISD process. The others are analysis, design, development, and implementation.

expert system
>One of the aspects of artificial intelligence. Expert system technology is of particular interest in human resource development since it is a computer program that offers advice to a human performer. The human would need less training to perform at a high standard. Compare with artificial intelligence and job aid.

facilitator
>The term used to describe an instructor in an individualized instruction setting. The facilitator works individually with each learner, supplying the particular advice and help as needed by that person.

fade in (out)
>Optical effect where a subject appears gradually from a black image or disappears in the opposite manner. Compare with dissolve, pan, and zoom.

FAX (facsimile)
> A system that transmits images on paper from one FAX machine to another. Can be used to for instructional communications and in distance learning classrooms.

felt board
> A flannel display board that an instructor can use to display small placards. The placards are backed with sandpaper.

filmograph
> A sequence of still images on film or videotape.

filmstrip
> A media based on 35mm film. It displays a series of still frames one at a time. Audio can be coordinated with the film. This medium is disappearing.

flipchart
> A common training support device consisting of a large pad of paper. The pad is attached to a special stand called an easel. Both together are often called a flipchart. The flipchart paper may be plain, lined, or quadrille.

floppy disk
> An aging term for diskettes. Today, not all diskettes are "floppy." See diskette. Contrast with hard disk.

flush right (left),. (justification).
> Contrast with centered and ragged.

font
> A complete set of type (or letter for display) of a single size and style. Different fonts may be used to create effects such as emphasis.

format(ing) (discs or diskettes)
> Discs and diskettes must be formatted before use. Same as initializing.

formative evaluation
> See evaluation.

FORTRAN
> Acronym for FORmula TRANslator, a general purpose, high-level language that is especially useful for scientific computing. FORTRAN is unsuited to CAI development in comparison to an authoring language.

frame
> The amount of graphic and text material that appears on the viewing screen at any one time. In computer-based learning, the concept can become slightly more difficult because the screen (the basic frame) can change greatly while retaining the same general appearance and information.

freeze frame
> One frame of video displayed continuously on the monitor.

generation (of video)
> Level of removal from the original recording. Each generation degrades the quality of the image.

grade book
> One of the typical record keeping features of CMI systems. See CMI.

graphics
> Ability to plot points, draw lines, or otherwise create pictures either in hard copy or on the display screen of a computer or a terminal. Graphics aid student understanding of complex items or processes, and can make an important contribution to the learning process. Compare with alphanumeric. Also, see animation.

graphics pad
> See digitizer.

hard copy
> Piece of paper on which a computer device has written. This term makes a distinction between permanent records and information provided on a computer display that is not permanent unless the user makes a record of it.

hard disk (drive)
> Computer storage device that uses rotating platters coated with magnetic surface for information storage, generally the fastest of the mass storage devices. Contrast with diskette.

hardware
> Category of computer components that involves physical equipment. It excludes the instructions to the equipment called software and the instructional software and supporting physical materials called courseware. Typically, hardware is divided into two major types: the central processing unit (CPU) and peripheral devices. Contrast with software and courseware.

Hertz
> Hz. The frequency of a signal. Often in millions or MHz, pronounced Mega Hertz.

high angle
> A video shot from higher than the subject. Compare with pan and zoom.

high resolution
> 1. General sense—True high resolution (2400 x 2400) is used for computer-aided design (CAD) and is beyond the scope of computer-based learning.
> 2. CBL sense—Resolution greater than the best television screen. High resolution in the CBL sense (480 x 640 or 512 x 512) is desirable for industrial HRD. See resolution. Contrast with NTSC.

high-level language
> A computer language that permits an action which actually requires several steps inside the computer to be specified by a single command. An example is Tencore™. Contrast with authoring utility.

hook-and-loop (board)
> A display board using velcro technology. Similar in use to a feltboard.

HRD
> Abbreviation for Human Resource Development. A series of organized activities, conducted within a specified time and designed to produce the possibility of behavioral change.

HRD Activity
> HRD activities include training, education and development. See HRD.

human factors
> 1. General sense—the design of equipment based on the human body; so that, people are comfortable working. See ergonomics.
> 2. CBL sense—those aspects of terminal or CBL course material that were included to make it easy for people to use.

human resource development
> See HRD.

IC
> Abbreviation for Integrated Circuit. Electronic unit that combines a single miniaturized component that minimizes power requirements, heat production, and processing time while increasing reliability. Because of their very small size and construction, these units are sometimes called "chips."

icons
> Symbols that look like objects. (When we try to "touch" the icon with our mouse, we touch the invisible button and see what the designer intended.)

implementation
A phase in the ISD process. Delivering the learning activities to the target population of learners in the intended environment. All instructional materials are reproduced and distributed during the implementation phase. Also called delivery. See delivery.

individualized instruction
A form of instruction where the learner is only taught the material that is not already known, instead of everything in a specified curriculum as is true with traditional instruction. (As an inherently individually oriented device, CBL system has the power necessary to administer individualized instruction, and it is almost always conducted in that format.)

InfoWindow
Display system marketed by IBM commonly used for interactive video.

Initializing (diskettes)
Diskettes must be initialized before use. Same as formatting.

input
Originally a computer term. Today, a shorthand way of referring to any information, in whatever form that is presented for consideration and later processing. Compare with output.

instructional games
One of the modes of CAI. The others are drill and practice, modeling, simulation and tutorial. This is different as amusement that has been programmed, so that the computer does the necessary calculations. The dividing line between amusement and education is not always easily discernible since learning by playing is still learning. Despite the instructional legitimacy and value of instructional gaming, it has not been well-accepted by some organizations.

instructional resource
See learning resource.

instructional systems design
See ISD.

instructional technology
The field of education concerned with the teaching strategy and media.

instructional television (ITV)
Any use of video in any format for learning. Also called instructional video.

instructional video
See instructional television.

integrated circuit
See IC.

interaction
A reciprocal interchange between the learner and the instructional media. In CAI an interaction is never simply pressing a key to advance the display. The interactivity of courseware is sometimes judged by counting the frequency of interactions. See levels of interaction.

interactive multimedia
A somewhat redundant term that has grown in popularity primarily because of marketing efforts. See interactive video and multimedia.

interactive video
A combination of CAI and videodisc media. The computer controls the lesson's interface with the program. A question may be asked and depending on the answer; the learner may be shown any one of several video sequences. Sequences can be still, regular, slow, or fast motion. In many ways this technology offers the power of both media. See auxiliary device, EIDS, and multimedia

IPS
> Inches per second. The standard for measuring tape speed.

ISD
> An abbreviation for Instructional Systems Development. This is a term for some systems that organize developing instruction. ISD is based on general systems theory. The phases of ISD are: analysis, design, development, implementation, and evaluation. See analysis, design, development, implementation, or evaluation.

italic (type)
> Type slanted to the right similar to handwriting. Contrast with roman.

ITV
> See instructional television.

job aid
> A simple, or complex, device that an employee uses to perform reliably. Usually employed to increase the likelihood of high fidelity performance. In some cases the employee may depend completely on the job aid for correct performance. The person needs less training to perform reliably. The best-known of these is the pilot's checklist. Compare with expert system.

justification
> Description of type margins. See centered, flush right or left justified, and ragged.

K
> Abbreviation for Kilo or thousand (actually, 1,024, or 2 to the 10th power). Used in the designation of the size of memory and mass storage. For example, many diskettes store about 800 Kbytes.

keyboard
> Element of a computer terminal or console that enables alphanumeric information to be sent to the computer. Most computer keyboards are variants of the standard typewriter (qwerty) keyboard.

keystone (effect)
> Refers to the distortion of an image projected on a surface at an angle. The shape resembles a "keystone."

LAN
> Acronym for Local Area Network. A LAN is a very small computer network. In CBL it is typically in one location, such as a classroom. A number of microcomputers, which can be of lesser power, share the computing power and often the storage of another microcomputer called a "file server." Peripherals such as printers can also be shared. Compare with WAN.

landscape
> Orientation of a display that is oriented horizontally. Contrast with portrait.

language
> 1. CBL sense—See author language.
> 2. General sense—See computer language and high-level language.

laptop computer
> The preferred term to describe one of the smaller of today's microcomputers. See personal computer. Includes a subcategory called "notebook computer." Microcomputers somewhat larger than laptop are often called "totable" and "lugable."

laser printer
> A category of printers based on electrostatic-toner process. Laser Printers can produce an output at or near camera ready quality. See camera ready.

lavalier microphone
> A portable microphone worn around the neck..

LCD
> Abbreviation for Liquid Crystal Diode. LCD refers to the screen technology commonly used in wristwatches, calculators, and laptop computer terminals. It is used in projection devices generally used with an overhead projector. Contrast with CRT, VDT, and plasma panel.

learner
> The preferred term for students; widely used in adult CBL settings.

learning center
> A special location for learning. Often contains materials for individualized self-paced study.

learning resource
> Something from which a learner might learn. Learning resources may be in text, audio, video, film, or computer form.

learning station
> A location for a person to study. May feature a computer and any associated input or output devices, based on the particular learning need. Contrast with workstation.

levels of interaction
> Term used to emphasize hierarchies of instructions to the computer. In interactive systems, it is possible to deal with different parts of the software.

light pen
> A device that can be pressed against a display that will inform the computer system of the selected location. See tactile input. Contrast with touch panel and mouse.

linear
> Refers to a CAI program that progresses through a sequence of frames that is not changed by the responses of the learner. Although not necessarily bad, per se, it often is. It offers less potential than a branching program. Contrast with branching.

local area network
> See LAN.

log-in (log-on) (sign-on)
> Process that must be performed in order for a computer system to recognize an authorized user. In CBL this is termed sign-on or log-on. See sign-on.

long shot
> A general view of the subject. Contrast with high-angle and low-angle shot.

low-angle shot
> A view with the camera lower than the subject. Contrast with high-angle and long shot.

M
> Abbreviation for Mega or million (1,048,576, or 2 to the 20th power). Used in the designation of the size of mass storage. For example, hard disk drives may have 100 Mbytes of mass storage.

Macintosh (Mac)
> An operating system used on a popular computer of the same name. Became popular in a short time because of the good user interface that simplified learning. Macintosh was developed by the Apple Corporation.

machine lettering
> A Kroy or Merlin machine that uses pressure on a special film to cut and transfer lettering to paper or film as lettering.

mass storage
> Passe term used to refer to a secondary, on-line repository for data base and application programs. Access is not as rapid as from a computer memory. Typically, mass storage is on diskette or hard-disk drives in microcomputers and on hard-disk drives in larger machines.

mastery learning (system)
A principle of grading based on "mastery" of material according to a predetermined criterion. Also called criterion referenced learning. This stands in contrast to norm referenced learning, where the learner is compared to others instead of against a fixed scale. Criterion referenced learning is well suited for implementation by CBL.

medium (media)
A medium of learning. An instructional medium, such as text, audio, video, film, or computer.

megabyte
See M.

memory
Organized collection of storage elements in a computer into which instructions and data can be deposited and from which information can be retrieved. Compare with mass storage.

menu
A list of choices available for a student, or utilities available for an author or computer user.

microcomputer
Smallest category of computers. See desktop computer, laptop computer, personal computer, or stand-alone.

minicomputer
Original category of computers designed to offer a smaller computer at lower cost (about $25,000). Continued scale and cost reduction created microcomputers. Definitions vary, but minicomputers generally include a range of cost from about $10,000 to $100,000. Definitions based on computing power are meaningless over time.

mockup
A simple form of simulation device. Has the appearance of the object simulated, but not its capabilities.

modeling
Use of the CBL system to represent a system or process, permitting the learner to change values and observe the effects of the change on the system. An example is a model of population. By changing demographic variables such as infant mortality, the results can be observed in changes in the population over time. One of the modes of CAI. The others are drill and practice, instructional games, simulation, and tutorial.

modem
Contraction for modulator-demodulator. Permits computer-to-computer transfer of data over telephone or other data lines. The modem provides the connection between the computer and the communication (telephone) line.

module
A unit of instruction. Usually, a module is constructed to teach one specific thing. Modules can be assembled to form complete courses and curricula.

monitor
See display.

montage
A series of short video scenes to condense time, distance, or action.

motor skills
An area for instruction that falls within the psychomotor domain of learning.

mouse
A device, moved on a desktop or special surface. A cursor moves in a like manner on the monitor. Pushing a button will inform the computer system of the chosen location. See tactile input. Contrast with touch panel and light pen.

MS-DOS
> An operating system. MS-DOS can operate on several different computers. It can support a variety of mass storage devices, can be used with more than one computer language, and therefore, eases the transfer of application programs from one to another. Became popular in a relatively short time because of its widespread use on IBM PC and compatible computers. It is the operating system that supports most CBL on these machines. MS-DOS was developed by the Microsoft Corporation.

multi-image
> Video simultaneously projected by two or more projectors to create a sophisticated presentation.

multi-standard decoder
> Device that converts NTSC, PAL, SECAM, or NTSC 4.43 video to RGB video.

multimedia
> Use of two or more instructional media together. Technically, examples should include tape-slide. In use this term came to represent optical disk technology combined with computer power.

multiscreen
> Two or more screens used with multi-image projection presentations.

near letter quality (printer)
> A category of dot matrix printers capable of producing an output described as "near letter quality" or NLQ. See printer. Contrast with character printer and laser printer.

network
> See LAN and WAN.

NLQ
> See near letter quality.

norm referenced learning
> "Traditional" grading scheme. The principle of grading based on each learner's success compared to other learners. Contrast with mastery learning.

notebook computer
> A term to describe a PC that is portable. The term suggests that it is at the lighter end of the weight range. See laptop computer.

NTSC
> Abbreviation for National Television Standards Committee. The American television standard. The NTSC standard is 525 lines set by the National Television Standards Committee. Not suitable for CBL.

NTSC (video)
> Refers to the video output of video tape or disk players used mainly in North America.

NTSC 4.43 (video)
> Refers to the video output of video tape or disk players used mainly in Middle East countries.

OCR
> Optical character recognition. Technology used in scanners.

off-line
> In computer-based learning, learning that happens away from the learning station. Compare with on-line.

on-line
> Information currently available for direct access. Compare with off-line.

opaque projector
> A device that projects an image from non-transparent originals, such as an open book. A useful technique seen less often in recent years.

operating system
> Category of software that includes utility programs that automatically performs sequences of tasks which would be tedious for a human operator. Compare with computer language and application program.

optical disk
> Any disc using optical storage technology. See CD ROM, optical storage, and videodisc.

optical storage
> A general term for the use of laser disc technology for the storage of data to be accessed and used by a computer. See CD ROM and videodisc.

output
> 1. Computers. Shorthand way of referring to any information, presented on a display or in hard-copy that is the result of the computer following a set of instructions or an application program. Compare with input.
> 2. General. The result of any process. Compare with input.

overhead projector
> A device that projects an image from a specially prepared transparent original called a transparency. Perhaps the most common instructional medium.

overlay
> Refers to placing one transparency over another to increase the information conveyed by the projected image.

PAL (video)
> Refers to the video output of video tape or disk players used mainly in Europe.

page proof
> A trial copy of a document before the final press run.

pan
> Physical movement of video camera from one side to the other. Contrast with dolly and zoom.

part-task simulation
> A technique for the use of computer-based learning in the simulation mode. A CBL terminal may not be able to simulate an entire situation at once. By simulating only one of several parts, effective learning can take place. An example is simulation of a system on an aircraft, instead of the entire aircraft. See simulation.

Pascal
> A computer language designed originally for teaching computing. Increasingly popular for microcomputers since Pascal code is easily read by a human reader. Although no more suitable than Cobol or BASIC, Pascal is used by some advocates to develop CAI courseware.

PC resolution
> Resolutions of various IBM PC compatible computers are: MDA (Monochrome Display Adapter); Hercules, 720 x 348 monochrome; CGA (Color Graphics Adapter) 320 x 200 four color, 640 x 200 monochrome; EGA (Enhanced Graphics Adapter) 640 x 350 16 color. VGA (Video Graphics Adapter) 640 x 480 16 color. Contrast with NTSC.

peripheral device
> Electronic and electromechanical devices that can be attached to the computer. Examples include printers, hard-disk drives, graphics pad, and mouse.

personal computer (PC)
> The preferred term to describe a small computer intended for use by only one person. Personal computers that have an interface to the telephone system may also be used as computer terminals to larger machines. "Personal" sidesteps the processing power issue, permitting us to get on with the learning. Contrast with laptop computer.

pixel
> A picture element. Refers to the basic element of which displays are composed. Display resolution is directly related to the total number of pixels. See resolution.

plasma panel
> Plasma panel refers to the screen technology used in some computer terminals that permits a flat display. Usually has a characteristic orange color. Contrast with LCD and CRT.

plotter
> An output device that draws with one or more pens often on large size paper. Useful for graphics.

plotting capability
> The ability of a display or a hard-copy device to produce graphic output.

portrait
> Orientation of a display that is oriented vertically, as this page. Contrast with landscape.

prescription generation
> The process of matching a learner accurately with the instructional materials actually needed by that individual based on the results of a test. One of the modes of CMI. The others are testing and record keeping.

printer
> Peripheral device that causes hard-copy to be generated by the computer. The principal types, in order of output quality, are dot matrix, character, and laser. See peripheral device.

programmer
> The person that codes computer programs including CBL and expert systems. See programming. Contrast with author.

programmer ready materials
> The term for the output of the scripter during the development process. The programmer can completely program the lesson based on the content of the materials. Sometimes called PRM. See development.

programming
> Total process of developing solutions to the problems in computer applications. Programming involves the following steps: analysis, design, coding, testing, and implementation. See programmer. Contrast with authoring utility.

programming aid (utility) (system)
> See authoring aid.

Prolog
> A language used to develop artificial intelligence programs. See artificial intelligence and expert system.

PROM
> Acronym for Programmable Read Only Memory. As originally developed, ROM could not be altered once it had been created. PROM was the first step in improved flexibility. Subsequently, memory was built in integrated circuits whose contents could be erased (EPROM) with ultraviolet light and then reprogrammed. See RAM and ROM.

psychomotor domain
> Refers to the area of human learning associated with physical movement and skills. Contrast with affective and cognitive.

qwerty keyboard
> The usual keyboard arrangement found on standard typewriters. So called, from the keys in the upper row. The leftmost key is "q." The next is "w," and so on. In advertising, a qwerty keyboard is sometimes made to sound like a feature. A less desirable keyboard would be "Teletype" format, now seldom seen in microcomputers. An alternate keyboard format is Dvorak. Contrast with Dvorak keyboard.

ragged (justification).
> Type with one or both margins uneven. Contrast with centered and flush right or left justification.

RAM
> Acronym for Random Access Memory, computer memory that has electronic units and is capable of having its contents changed. See memory and ROM.

random access
> Refers to the ability to directly reach an information item without accessing other items. This capability is inherent in disc media. It is also a capability of a random access slide projector.

random access memory
> See RAM.

readability
> A measure of at what level text is written. Used to specify the required education level of the reader (learner). May be calculated to produce a Flesch Reading Ease Score (number represents a percentage of American adults who can read the material), Flesch-Kincaid index (Flesch score converted to a grade level), or Gunning-Fog index (also a grade level).

realia
> Term for real objects.

rear screen (projection)
> Projected image travels through the translucent panel of rear screen and forms an image on the front surface.

record keeping
> Computers can capture more data about a learner than can be reasonably used. Typically, the CMI system will record success on pre- and post tests. One of the modes of CMI. The others are testing and prescription generation. See grade book.

registration
> In Computer-based Learning, entering the necessary data about a learner into the CBL system, so that a student will be recognized by the system at "sign-on." See sign-on.

remote computer
> A computer that is not at the site of access. The term implies that such a machine can be accessed through the telephone system and a computer terminal.

resolution
> The degree with which detail can be displayed. Measured in dots (pixel elements) vertically and horizontally. High resolution is necessary to display graphics. Low resolution is adequate for text. The best resolution of which a television screen is capable is low resolution. Overall size of the display does not alter the resolution. See NTSC and PC resolution.

response time
> The time between an entry on a computer terminal keyboard or screen and the resulting change of display. For example, the time it takes to have an answer judged by the computer system. Research shows that a response time of .2 seconds is important.

RGB (video)
> The color video output of computers.

RISC
> Abbreviation for Reduced Instruction Set Computer. An approach to increasing microcomputer processing speed through the use of fewer possible instructions.

role play
> A simulation involving human performers. Often the people are provided with scripts of background from which to participate. It is relatively open-ended..

ROM
> Acronym for Read Only Memory. Describes computer memory whose contents can be read but cannot be altered. Compare with RAM.

roman (type)
> Type with vertical strokes. Contrast with italic.

router
> A facility for directing the student from one place to another within the CBL system. A router may present CAI automatically in a certain sequence, or it may route the learner through the CMI part of the system. See CMI.

sans serif (type)
> Type without serifs.

SECAM (video)
> Refers to the video output of video tape or disk players used mainly in France and USSR.

serif (type)
> Type with additional cross stroke at the end of the stroke, such as this type.

sign-on (log-on)
> 1. The act of entering one's identity into the CBL system to begin work or study.
> 2. The name one uses for recognition by a computer.

simulation
> 1. A representation of an item of equipment, device, system, or subsystem in realistic form. Simulation enables the learner to experience the operation of the target equipment without possibility of destruction of the equipment.
> 2. CBL (usually part-task) simulation contrasts with the very costly, single-purpose special simulators typified by aircraft simulators. Each has a proper role. Simulation is one of the modes of CAI. The others are drill and practice, instructional game, modeling, and tutorial.

simulator
> A special device with the sole purpose of simulating an object, device, equipment, or system. Used to train employees using simulation.

6W
> 1 foot of screen width is required for each 6 feet of viewing distance from the screen. To state this another way, the audience should be no further away than six times the width of the projected image.

slide
> A small photographic image, usually cut from 35mm film. Projected in a specially designed projector. A very common medium.

slot
>A position (on a unitized bus) in a computer where a component board can be installed. The component board is positioned on the bus by inserting the "edge connectors" in the slot. This feature is not shared by all small computers.

SME
>Abbreviation for Subject Matter Expert. The person familiar with the content of instruction to be developed, who works with others on the design of instruction for CBL delivery.

software
>1. In data processing, a category of computer components that is restricted to instructions to the equipment (hardware). Typically, software can be divided into operating systems, computer languages, and application programs.
>2. In computer-based learning it takes on a more specialized meaning. The special software used by the instructors and students is called "courseware." Software simply makes the computer "work." Contrast with hardware and courseware.

sound effects
>Realistic sounds that can be added to audio or videotape.

special effects (generator)
>A device to add various optical effects to video images.

spirit duplicator
>An inexpensive process to duplicate typed images. No longer common in training.

stacks
>General descriptive term for Hypermedia programs.

stand-alone delivery
>Delivery separate from a large computer system or LAN. Achieved by, and synonymous with, microcomputer delivery. Contrast with remote computer and LAN.

storyboard(ing)
>A technique used for film, video, and computer display planning. A series of sketches resembling a cartoon are created to help visualize the sequence of views to be presented.

student-instructor ratio
>A comparison of the number of learners served by one instructor. A typical ratio is 30/1. The ratio in individualized instruction at any one point in time may be 75/1, although it in other circumstances may not differ greatly from traditional, depending on the subject. Over time, the ratio for CBL can be large because of the throughput of learners.

subject matter expert
>See SME.

summative evaluation
>See evaluation.

tactile input
>Interaction with a computer program by use of touch, as compared with keyboard input. May be achieved by use of a light pen, mouse, digitizer, or touch panel screen. Experience shows that categories of users who never use a typewriter strongly prefer tactile input. The learner's status may also be involved. For example: doctors and pilots.

task simulator
>A specially constructed device that resembles the real one after which it is modeled. A simulator of this type offers the opportunity for realistic practice. Contrast with part-task simulation.

telecommuting
> Working at an alternate site, instead of commuting in the traditional site. The alternate site may be the worker's home. Typically involving use of a terminal, communication with the organization, and transmission of work through that means.

teleconferencing
> Conducting a meeting where the participants are at separate locations. A telephone call with three parties would be a very simple teleconference. Some organizations have elaborate facilities for teleconferences. Important as a solution to the high cost of travel.

television resolution
> See NTSC and video

Tencore
> One of several CAI author languages.

terminal
> A peripheral device that enables a user to interact with a computer and use the power of that computer. Although a microcomputer may be used as a terminal, a terminal falls short of the definition of a computer. Contrast with microcomputer.

testing
> 1. CBL sense—testing is used to determine the gaps in a particular learner's knowledge. The information will be used to generate an appropriate instructional prescription. One of the modes of CMI. The others are prescription generation and record keeping.
> 2. Instructional sense—a method of determining a learner's knowledge level in a given area. Testing may be used for a variety of purposes, including certification.

text
> 1. Printed instructional media.
> 2. The computer's alphanumeric visual display. Contrast with graphics.

thermal copier
> Copier that uses heat to make the image. May use thermal film to prepare transparencies. Compare with thermal printer.

thermal film
> A special film for use with a thermal copier to prepare transparencies.

thermal printer
> Printer that uses heat to make the image. Compare with thermal copier.

touch panel
> A special panel fitted in front of the display screen that permits the learner to indicate choices by touching a screen location. The touch panel does not interfere with vision. See tactile input.

transparency
> A specially prepared transparent original containing an image. Used with an overhead projector.

transportability
> Extent to which courseware and other application programs can be transferred from one computer to another without having to rewrite the program.

transportable
> A term to describe a PC that is portable. The term suggests that it is at the heavier end of the weight range.

TTL (video)
> Refers to the video output of certain computers. TTL video cannot be connected to projectors through long wires. TTL video is a type of RGB video.

tutorial

The most typical type of CAI. The program (through the terminal) and the learner interact one-on-one. Ideally, the process advances just as the best tutor might personally conduct the process. One of the modes of CAI. The others are drill and practice, instructional game, modeling, and simulation.

12W

The original artwork or graphic display measures 12 inches wide (including the necessary margins); the evaluators will view the materials from 12 feet.

user-friendly (oriented)

A desirable attribute for any computer system. Implies that the user need not be an expert merely to use the system and that mistakes are easily overcome or avoided by the system. See human factors.

VDT

The preferred term for computer monitors. Preferred, since it can describe a monitor using any of the various display technologies such as CRT, LCD, or plasma panel. See CRT, LCD, or plasma panel.

VHS

The most common $F(1,2)$ inch video tape format. Advent of VHS video equipment made economical video production possible for smaller organizations.

video

1. An instructional medium. Video can be accessed from tape, disk, or semiconductor memory. Compare with text, audiotape, and CAI.

2. Describes the signal that is used by display devices, such as projectors, to generate a picture. This term also refers to the video output of video tape or disk players or computers.

videodisc

Video accessed from a laser disk. The principal form of video combined with CAI to constitute interactive video. The spelling shown is preferred over "videodisk," which is also seen. Contrast with CD-ROM and optical storage.

video monitor

Screen used in computer terminals where the display is based on video technology. A video monitor contains all the components of a television set except those that make it possible to receive broadcast television programs. See display.

video technology

Pertains to hardware devices that make use of the developments created for and by the television industry.

videoteleconfernce

A distance learning technique using video to transmit images of the instructor to distant students. In two-way systems, the image of the students is also transmitted to the instructor.

viewgraph

A synonym for overhead projector transparency. See transparency.

viewing angle

Describes horizontal and vertical viewing angles. Curved screens usually have smaller viewing angles than flat screens.

WAN

Acronym for Wide Area Network. A WAN is a network composed of LANs. In CBL it is typically in several remote locations. Communication and data sharing between locations (LANs) is important, instead of sharing computing power. Compare with LAN.

wide area network

See WAN.

workstation A location for a person to work, typically with a personal computer or computer terminal. Sometimes confused with learning station, when used in the CBL sense. See personal computer. Contrast with learning station.

WORM
Write once, read many. Refers to digital compact disc format. A step toward full read-write capability.

WYSIWYG
Abbreviation for What You See Is What You Get. In software designed to produce an output, sometimes editing shows the editor the exact effect that will eventually be produced. In other software, the software must then be run to see exactly how the outcome will appear. Software that shows the result while in editing mode is called WYSIWYG.

xerographic process
See electrostatic copier.

zoom
Optical (apparent) movement of closer or farther away from the subject Contrast with dolly and pan.

Index